DECK
SCAPING

DECK
SCAPING

Gardening and Landscaping On and Around Your Deck

Barbara W. Ellis

STOREY BOOKS

North Adams
Massachusetts

The mission of Storey Publishing is to serve our customers by publishing practical information that encourages personal independence in harmony with the environment.

Edited by Gwen W. Steege and Karen Levy
Art Direction by Mark Bergin and Meredith Maker
Cover and text design by Rob Johnson
Cover photograph by Frances Litman/www.franceslitman.com
Text production by Erin Lincourt
Indexed by Eileen M. Clawson
Photography and garden design credits given on page 157

The information in this book is true and complete to the best of our knowledge. All recommendations are made without guarantee on the part of the author or Storey Books. The author and publisher disclaim any liability in connection with the use of this information. For additional information, please contact Storey Books, 210 MASS MoCA Way, North Adams, MA 01247.

Storey books are available for special premium and promotional uses and for customized editions. For further information, please call Storey's Custom Publishing Department at (800) 793-9396.

Printed in China by C & C Offset Printing Co., Ltd.
10 9 8 7 6 5 4 3 2 1

Library of Congress Cataloging-in-Publication Data

Ellis, Barbara W.
    Deckscaping : gardening and landscaping on and around your deck / by Barbara W. Ellis.
        p. cm.
        ISBN 1-58017-459-0 (alk. paper) — ISBN 1-58017-408-6 (pbk.)
            1. Landscape gardening. 2. Decks (Architecture, Domestic). I. Title.

SB473 .349 2002
    712.'6—dc21
                                                                200104292

Dedication

To my husband, Peter Evans, who wasn't fazed for even a second when
he realized the main reason I wanted a deck was to expand the garden.

Acknowledgments

Special thanks to my husband, Peter Evans, for designing and
building several of the projects in this book, as well as to Robert
F. Prachar, Sr., who built our deck and also helped with invaluable
suggestions throughout the design and construction phases.

Contents

Introduction:
The Ideal Outdoor Living Space viii

Chapter 1:
Customizing Your Design 4

Chapter 2:
The Surrounding Gardens 24

Chapter 3:
Container Gardening 58

Chapter 4:
Trellises and Arbors 86

Chapter 5:
Decorating with Style 112

Chapter 6:
Favorite Deckside Plants 124

Index 158

The Ideal Outdoor
Living Space

Several years ago, my husband and I added a deck to our old stone farmhouse in Pennsylvania, which dates from the 1780s. Our main objective was to carve out more level living space on a steeply sloping site. From spring to fall, our deck looks and functions like an extension of our living room — albeit an outdoor one that is filled with plants, birds, butterflies, and fresh air — and is an integral part of the timber-frame structure we added to our home in 1990.

Strong design elements link the house and the deck. The deck wraps around the south and west sides of the house and is accessible from the living room and the kitchen, providing ample, comfortable space to pop outdoors with a cup of coffee or a plate of sandwiches for a meal alfresco. Our hot tub bubbles there, inviting us to relax in its warmth after a hard day's work. Deck furniture and flower-packed containers echo the colors and styles used indoors. As a result, the deck beckons us outdoors at all times of day and night — in all types of weather — to watch wildlife, marvel at gathering storm clouds, study the stars, sit and relax, or just wander out to enjoy the garden.

A Deck for Outdoor Living

Practical considerations connect our deck to the house and garden. The deck provides a convenient, level route around the steep south side of our house, something we didn't have before, as well as a place for outdoor cooking. We use a corner near the front door to store wood in winter. And our deck has become a major route to the garden — although I have so many containers on it that it's sometimes hard to tell where the deck ends and the garden begins.

A Reality Check

All too often, decks are simply an afterthought — a no-man's- (or no-woman's) land attached to the back of the house. Neither house nor garden, many decks have little more than level footing to offer, and certainly are not welcoming to human visitors. Take a look at some of the decks in your neighborhood. Are you confronted with too many barren spaces and perhaps a few cheap, premolded plastic chairs stacked up in one corner and maybe a table and a grill? Unfortunately, some decks are nothing more than storage units, cluttered with miscellaneous gardening supplies, tools, barbecue equipment, toys, refuse or recycling cans, and outdoor recreation equipment. Often, the need for storage space prevails — eliminating or at least reducing the usefulness of a deck for other purposes.

Flower beds wrap around the deck to hide its base (it is a full story off the ground at the back of the house) and are chock-full of plants that reflect my gardening and plant-collecting obsessions. They contain a wild, wonderful mix of long-blooming and fragrant perennials, shrubs that offer flowers and ornamental berries, plants to attract hummingbirds and butterflies, vines that provide color and shade, ornamental edibles, culinary herbs, self-sowing annuals, a wide range of bulbs, and much more. In many ways, the deck has become the heart of our garden, and I can't imagine what we did without it.

The most useful — and the most used — decks share one characteristic with ours: They are an appealing place to spend time in their own right, not just a barren (or cluttered!) space that stands between a home's indoor rooms and the lawn or garden and the larger landscape. For this reason, a well-planned deck offers elements of both indoor rooms and outdoor spaces. Functional furniture and decorations can complement your home's indoor decor. Details matter here. You won't be tempted to use your deck if the chairs aren't really comfortable, or if there aren't ample places to set down drinks or to put up your feet.

Containers of plants can bring the garden right up around the doors and windows of your home. Filled with colorful and fragrant flowers, container gardens add appeal to any living space, and a deck is no exception. Plants make the deck feel like it's right in the garden — but with the advantage of many indoor conveniences, such as flat floors, conventional furniture, and access to water and electricity. If you add structures for shade, trellises for privacy, and other comforts, such as lighting and convenient storage, you'll have a deck you'll want to use whenever the weather is nice — and sometimes even when it isn't.

Finding Design Inspiration in Colors and Materials

Creating a deck that is comfortable, safe, and appealing involves elements of home decoration and garden design. Looking to both sources for design inspiration helps unify, or strengthen, the link between these living spaces. Extending your indoor color scheme onto the deck, and even into the garden, gives the clear message that the deck is a room of your home that just happens to be outdoors.

The view onto a deck should be inviting and compatible with a home's interior. Fill containers on the deck with flowers that echo the color scheme of the adjacent indoor rooms, and use some of the same colors farther out in the garden as well. If your house features modern, angular furniture constructed of metal and glass in an earth-tone color scheme, use those elements when choosing furnishings for your deck. The repetition of colors, materials, textures, and designs helps produce a comfortable atmosphere and creates a unified space that is pleasing to the eye.

Duplicating the use of building materials and styles also helps forge the link from house to deck to garden. For example, on our deck, the timbers of an arbor make an architectural connection to the house. They continue the lines of the rafters in our timber-frame living room and strengthen the visual connection between the house and the deck. A comfy, cottage-style home may be best served by country-style furniture. For a house with a modern design, both matching and contrasting styles are very effective.

In some cases, the natural environment that surrounds your house may play a vital role in determining the visual connections that will most closely link house, deck, and garden. If you live on a lake or at the seashore, in the Southwest, or in the mountains, for example, use the views that surround your home for inspiration.

It's important to consider functional links between the deck and the house as well; they are vital to the success of a deck's design. It should be about as easy to walk out from the house onto the deck as it is to go from room to room indoors. Access to the garden should be nearly as smooth, unless you have a second-story deck that serves primarily as a promontory from which to view the garden and surrounding landscape. If possible, provide safe steps and a broad, comfortable, well-marked path so it's easy to wander out into the garden. Safe, level transitions to the deck and unblocked doors are especially important if you're going to be carrying food or beverages outdoors. Adequate lighting and unobstructed walkways on the deck also are essential.

Throughout this book, you'll find a host of ideas for transforming your deck into a compelling and comfortable outdoor living space that fulfills a wide variety of needs, whether you'd like a spot to sit outdoors and enjoy the garden with a cup of coffee and a newspaper, a comfortable place to sit with your laptop and surf the Internet, an attractive space to visit with friends — or all of the above.

▲ A deck that functions as an extension of your house is like an added-on room — and one that features all the charm of a garden.

CHAPTER ONE

Customizing
Your Design

Whether you have an existing deck that could use a face-lift or want to add one to your home for the first time, the design process starts at the same place: with a careful evaluation of your needs and desires. To develop a deck design that really fits your lifestyle, analyze how you want to use it, how you want it to connect to your house, and what sort of links it will have to the rest of your lanscape.

Use the photos of outstanding decks on the following pages to get your ideas flowing, then follow the design process suggested in this chapter to evaluate your own needs and develop a unique plan for building, renovating, or adding on to your deck. The rest of the book builds on the ideas gleaned from this process, because the design you develop will affect everything from landscaping around the deck to lighting it.

At this point, it really pays to experiment with design ideas you haven't considered before. It won't cost you anything to dream, and you just may come up with the perfect idea that makes all the difference for your deck. If your final plan exceeds your budget, consider phasing in the construction over several years.

Gathering Ideas

A deck design that suits your lifestyle and your house starts with some basic planning homework. Sure, you can ask a contractor to design a deck or pick one from a book of landscape and house design plans. Those routes have their pitfalls, however. You are likely to end up with a cookie-cutter design that only partially fulfills what you want — and what this all-important outdoor living space could be.

Start the design process by gathering ideas about how you want to use your deck and what you want it to look like. Analyze how it should function with your house, garden, and family. Our deck started out as a notebook of ideas. In addition to sketches of the house and the site, my husband and I included drawings of designs we liked, pictures clipped from magazines, and notes about features we wanted to incorporate into the final design. By the time we had worked through the design process, we had also collected a small stack of books and magazines (ones I didn't want to rip up!) with notes marking pictures of decks we liked.

Start your own deck design notebook by photocopying the checklist on pages 16 and 17 and filling it out. It will help you identify some basic features you'd like to include and undoubtedly identify problems you need to deal with in the design. Then start making lists of features or questions you want to consider. Don't worry if you end up with a jumble of sketches and notes — at this point, too many ideas are better than too few.

Go with the Flow

Start your planning from indoors. Right from the beginning, it is important to consider how the design will flow from the house to the deck to the garden.

There's no better place to start this process than inside looking out at where you envision the deck will be. You'll need a pencil and your design notebook or a few pages of drawing paper for this step.

Begin in a room that will be (or is) adjacent to the deck. In our case, we started from the living room. We had a very small deck and a hot tub on the west side of the house and originally thought the new deck would be adjacent to it. After careful consideration, we decided to make the deck wrap around the west and south sides of the house. If you already have a deck, think about the features that you like about it, as well as things that you could change to make it more comfortable to use. Remember: It's inexpensive to dream about what you want to do, so use your imagination!

A Room with a View

Spend some time looking out each window and door of your home that will be, or could be, affected by the deck. Jot down notes or scribble pictures of what you see — or could see. Keep in mind that your design can take advantage of nice views or help obstruct unattractive ones. Spend some time outdoors on the proposed site and take notes about what you see or will be able to see if the deck is well above ground level. You may want to use your camera to record your views. (See Using a Camera for Design on page 8 for ideas on how to use photography to aid the design process.)

Obviously, the final design should make the most of views of the garden and surrounding landscape. Scenery or vistas of the garden may help determine the best positions for sitting or dining areas. Think in terms of creating a view to enjoy. What about a path flanked with flowers that leads into the yard, or a water garden you can see from the deck?

Make notes about views you'd like to hide, too. Think about tentative solutions: A mixed planting of evergreen and flowering trees toward the back of your yard, or close around one side of the deck, may hide the neighbor's garage or backyard. Link these ideas to ones you gathered while inside. A planting may look nice from the living room windows and make your deck more private. Strategically placed trellises, arbors, and other structures are also worth considering, as they can hide unattractive views and add privacy (see chapter 4 for more information).

▼ "Borrowed views" can be very effective if you make the effort to highlight them. A glimpse of a distant mountain or a lake is an obvious example of scenery worth doing some selective pruning or design reorientation to capture.

Using a Camera for Design

Whether you have an ordinary "point-and-shoot," a fancy single-lens reflex, or a digital camera, you have at your fingertips an invaluable design tool. Here are some ways you can use your camera to develop the perfect deck design for your home.

Record the views. Take snapshots of views from the house out to where the deck will be, as well as shots from the house out to the larger landscape. Stand indoors and shoot outdoors, or position yourself just outside windows and doors. Not only will these pictures help you develop an idea for what the deck will look like from indoors, but you can also use them to record views of the garden or surrounding countryside that are worth highlighting. Be sure to take snapshots of views that you'd prefer to be hidden, such as utility areas and the back of the neighbor's garage.

Photograph the house. Views of your house taken from several angles in the yard are also useful for the design process. Use them to envision how the deck will look when attached to the back of the house, as well as the best options for creating transitions between the deck and the garden.

Take a panorama. A series of snapshots taken methodically from a single vantage point can be taped together to form a panorama. Not only will a panorama be an invaluable tool for planning landscaping and other features around your deck, but it also will become a fun and interesting "before" record of your yard. To take a panorama, select a central spot with your back to the house and shoot a series of pictures to record the entire site. Keep the camera level, and carefully note a feature on the far left of the frame, then pivot enough to move that feature to the far right of the frame for the next shot. You can also buy a disposable panorama camera and use that instead.

Photograph the details. Record special features of your house and garden that you want to preserve or highlight with the deck design. This includes trees and tree roots that need to be protected during the construction process — or incorporated into the deck's design — architectural features, walls or paths, and garden beds. Also take shots of features you don't want to forget to accommodate, such as water spigots, cable connections, septic fields, and electrical hookups.

Use Your Pictures

"Before" pictures are a great record of where you've started — you'll want to refer to them to see how trees have grown or how your landscape has improved over the years. They also offer a practical way to experiment with designs, because you can develop and record ideas by drawing directly on the photos. For this purpose, enlargements are best. If you decide to use enlargements from a photo lab, tape tracing paper over them to experiment and chronicle ideas. Making copies with a conventional photocopy machine is less expensive and certainly suitable, too.

Another option is to print photos from your computer, using either a digital camera or a digital copy of pictures from a photo lab. It's also easy to use a scanner to capture snapshots in your computer. For computer images, draw your design ideas using one of the photo or drawing programs, or print out copies and sketch your designs by hand.

▲ "Before" shots of the author's house (above) made it easy to draw designs and visualize the final deck plan (top right). Both the deck and the surrounding garden transform a tough-to-mow site into an appealing outdoor living space (bottom right).

Creating Privacy and Shade

If creating a quiet outdoor living space with an "away from it all" feeling is your dream, evaluate your options for blocking the outside world. The most secluded outdoor rooms have a floor, walls, and a ceiling, just as indoor rooms do. Obviously, the surface of the deck is your floor, but what are your options for walls and a ceiling that will create a sense of refuge and security?

Write down ideas and sketch drawings of ways to create a feeling of privacy. Keep in mind that the "walls" of any outdoor room can be made of a mix of elements, such as shrubs, trees, fences, trellises, and large container plantings. Annual vines trained to grow on strings can provide a seasonal visual screen that will make your deck feel cozier.

The screening that best suits your needs will depend on the site, too. You may need a trellis with a thick vine cover on one side, where the neighbors are close by, and a mixed planting of dense shrubs and trees toward the lot line on another side. An earth mound or berm planted with shrubs and low-maintenance perennials is another option. Avoid enclosing the deck with tall plantings, because you'll end up with a claustrophobic feeling. Instead, use different screening elements and vary their distance from the deck to create a sense of seclusion that is at the same time open and airy.

▼ A small fountain, like the one on this shady deck, adds "white noise," which helps cover up sounds from neighbors or nearby streets.

Outdoor rooms that have a "ceiling" feel especially sheltered and secluded. They also are shaded, making them comfortable to use on hot, sunny days. Outdoor ceilings can consist of a vine-covered arbor or the overhanging branches of a tree. For an appealing outdoor dining area with a roomlike feeling, erect trellises to screen the deck with walls and shelter it with an arbor or other "ceiling."

If noise from the outside world — such as cars on a busy street — affects the ambience of your deck, consider a small fountain or water feature. The water will provide "white noise" that helps block out the outside world.

Plan for Shade

If there is one single problem that makes most decks uncomfortable to use, it is lack of shade. Consider incorporating a beautiful vine-covered arbor over at least a portion of your deck. Eight feet is the minimum height, so that people will feel comfortable standing and walking under it; however, a taller structure creates a more open feeling. (See page 89 for ideas and information on awnings.) Another option is to incorporate into the deck's design a gazebo with a conventional shingle roof. Keep in mind that you will need to support heavy configurations, such as gazebos, in that section of the deck's structure.

Planting trees offers a longer-range solution that has decided appeal. Ideally, you should fence off any sites where you plan to plant trees and shrubs before deck construction begins. Soil compaction caused by parked vehicles and stored materials (such as wood and masonry) not only will make it more difficult to plant but will also reduce soil aeration and drainage and therefore make growing conditions less than ideal without a great deal of soil improvement afterward.

Decks on Shady Sites

If you are lucky enough to have a shaded site, take steps to preserve existing trees from the outset. A deck is the best option for creating an outdoor space with a level floor beneath trees. That's because, unlike terraces and paved areas, a deck can be constructed with minimal disturbance to tree roots. If you have trees that you would like to incorporate into the deck, it is essential that you consult a skilled contractor or landscape architect experienced in dealing with such sites. With a little planning, the spans between the posts and the size of the joists can be adjusted to minimize root damage.

For trees that are near the site but will not be incorporated into the actual design, erect snow fencing or another barrier around the outside of the drip line (where the tips of the branches end) to prevent soil compaction and other damage. Before the deck is finished, be prepared to remove lower limbs from trees or to erect barriers (such as railings around a trunk) so that guests will not hit their heads on low-hanging branches or a trunk that leans at an odd angle.

Traffic and Usage Considerations

Especially during the summer, a deck can become the hub of family life, and that means traffic. Do you have children running from the yard into the house? In that case, an entrance straight into the living room may not be the best idea. Designing another door from the deck to the kitchen — or, better yet, the entryway — may be in order.

You can design your deck to function as a traffic route. For instance, for a house that is on a steep site, you may want to design a deck that offers a route over hilly terrain. If you have a high deck with no convenient way to get down into the yard, consider a series of steps and landings to complete the connection from the house to the garden. You also may want to look at your house and deck site from neighboring yards, so you can be considerate of what neighbors see and plan accordingly.

Take special note of doors, and spend time thinking about walking from your indoor rooms onto your new deck/outdoor room. Once you imagine carrying trays of food to the deck — and opening and closing doors in the process — you'll realize the value of smooth, safe transitions that are easy to negotiate. Ideally, you will want the

▼ This deck provides a viewing platform from which to enjoy the surrounding garden and is also a great spot for bird-watching. Once the plants along the lot line leaf out in late spring, they screen out the house next door.

deck to be level with the floor of adjacent rooms. If that isn't possible, plan for wide landings to make it safe and simple to get from one place to another, even with your hands full. It is especially important to have ample space so you can step aside to open the door. You'll also want to think about traffic in relation to any entertaining space or furniture you have in mind. Don't plan on locating sitting areas or the dining table in the path of the main route used to walk between the house and the yard, for example. An area off to one side will ensure fewer interruptions, and probably less wear and tear on furniture. In addition, guests should have ample room to pass around all sides of a table, even when the chairs have been pushed out during a meal.

◄ Make sure a landing extends far enough to open the door without having to step backward, as shown here. This can be an especially treacherous situation when you are juggling trays of food or beverages.

How Much Space?

When planning an area for entertaining — or just for family use — keep in mind that you want a space that is large enough to accommodate furniture and other equipment (such as a grill), plus guests. One way to figure out how large your deck should be is to think about the various areas and furniture it needs to contain. Use the following dimension guidelines to help determine the size of various portions of your deck.

In general, try to plan a deck or areas within a deck that have equal proportions (length and width). Relatively square spaces are more desirable than long, narrow ones, because they make it easier to arrange furniture into comfortable conversational groupings. If you're designing a large deck, plan on breaking down the space into several smaller areas, such as a dining area, sitting area, and cooking or sunning area.

Areas for Tables and Chairs

Square, for 2: 6' x 8'
Square, for 4: Minimum area, 6' x 6'; ideal area, 8'–9' x 8'–9'
Round, for 6: 10' in diameter
Rectangular, for 8: 8' x 12'

Picnic Tables

Small, for 6: Minimum, 5' x 6'; ideal, 7' x 8'
Large, for 8: Minimum, 5' x 7½'; ideal, 7' x 9½'

Sitting Areas

For comfortable conversation, arrange chairs roughly in a circle or square that is no more than 8 to 10 feet across (larger areas make conversation difficult). For a U-shaped area with benches on three sides:

Small, for 5 or 6: 7½' x 7½'
Large, for 9–12: 10'–12' x 10'–12'

Sunning Areas

Deck chairs, for 4: 7½' x 7½'
Lounge chairs, for 2: 7½' x 7½'

Grilling Areas

Locate a grilling area where prevailing winds don't blow smoke toward dining or sitting areas or into the house.

Make sure there's plenty of room around grills and other cooking areas, too, so guests and family members don't crowd the cook and the grill isn't pushed up against railings or other wooden structures.

2' x 2' grill and 2' x 4' counter area: Minimum, 4½' x 4½', (20 sq. ft.)

Walkways

2 people walking side by side: Minimum, 4½'; wider is better

Lighting

Effective lighting is a vital part of a well-designed deck. Not only does lighting make it possible to enjoy your deck at night, but it also makes a deck safer to use after dark. When planning lighting, be sure to illuminate walkways, steps, landings, and any other changes in level. You can also install lights that illuminate special architectural features, sculptures, and plants. In addition, consider your neighbors when planning and installing lights. Spotlights and general glare from neighboring properties isn't pleasant, so try to keep light on your own property by directing it down and keeping it at low levels.

Storage

Make a list of all the items you routinely store on the deck — hose, garden tools, seat cushions, barbecue equipment. As your design develops, you'll want to incorporate storage facilities for all of these items, and possibly more. Keep in mind that you also can use space under the deck for storage.

Deck boxes come in various sizes and are practical alternatives for storing everything from chair cushions to grilling tools right on the deck. They can also double as seating. A good deck box should be weather resistant but also provide ventilation so items stored inside it will not mildew. Look for boxes made from rot-resistant woods, such as cedar and teak, as well as painted pine. For hardware, brass or stainless steel — neither of which rusts — is best. Depending on what you intend to store, you may want to customize the interior with partitions, to keep hoses away from chair cushions, for example. Specially designed benches with tops that flip up also add valuable storage space.

◄ This effective lighting design spotlights a specimen tree to provide visual interest after dark. The low-level lighting also allows for viewing the night sky.

As for under-deck storage, your site plays a major role in determining the possibilities. While there may be room to construct a full-size toolshed under a deck that's a full story off the ground, don't give up on decks with less space. With a little creative thinking, you may be able to figure out how to store all manner of bulky items, from ladders and hoses to garden carts, under a lower deck. Keep in mind that you'll have to install a "roof" under the decking to keep rain off stored items. In addition, be sure to leave space below the decking so it can dry out between rainstorms.

▲ Careful planning is important if you want to incorporate a hot tub in your deck design. Think about overall weight, where you'll store the top when the tub is in use, and how you'll access the pumps and filters for routine maintenance.

Special Structures

If you plan to incorporate really heavy items on your deck, you'll need to make sure the structural design accommodates the extra weight. Hot tubs top the list, but masses of container plants, a gazebo, and a large water garden also qualify. If you remember the old saying, "A pint's a pound the world around," you'll understand why it takes special planning to accommodate a hot tub on a deck. With 8 pints to a gallon of water, a single gallon weighs 8 pounds. That means the water in an 800-gallon hot tub weighs 6,400 pounds. To accommodate the extra weight, the section of deck under a hot tub should have double posts and twice as many beams that are of double thickness.

How tub users will get in and out is another important planning consideration. It's crucial to provide a well-lighted, sizable landing area so users can either step safely into the tub or sit on the edge and swing both legs over. (*Note:* The steps in the water can be slippery, so footing outside the tub must be especially secure.) You'll also need to determine how you'll get the lid off and then leave enough room to set it down when the tub is in use. Finally, you must have enough room to access the pump and other equipment that run the tub.

Evaluating Deck Structure and Safety

If you plan to renovate or add on to an existing deck, be sure to evaluate carefully its structural condition. Look at some of the features listed below to assess the stability and safety of your present deck.

Building Materials

☐ Are the materials used for the existing deck still in good condition? If boards are cracked or dried out, it may be difficult to blend them with the materials used on a new deck.

☐ Are the boards made of pressure-treated lumber or raw wood?

☐ Has the structure begun to dry- or wet-rot after several years? Closely examine the places where moisture gathers, such as at the bottom of posts.

☐ Do portions of the deck need to be replaced because of deterioration?

☐ Are there splintered or gouged boards on decking, railings, or other places that could scrape skin?

Construction

☐ Was the existing deck constructed well?

☐ How is it fastened to the building?

☐ How is the deck supported?

☐ How far apart are the joists to which the floor is fastened?

☐ Are the railings secured?

☐ Are the vertical pilasters spaced properly?

☐ Are the decking boards loose or warped? Are nails popping up?

☐ Is the old structure so worn or impractical that it needs to go?

Compatibility

☐ Will the existing structure blend well with additions to the deck?

☐ Will joining the existing structure to a new structure be complicated?

☐ Will the new deck overpower the existing deck or the house?

☐ Will the style of deck additions clash with the existing structure?

What Do I Want My Deck to Be?

Undoubtedly, you already have a partial list of how you'd like to use your deck — for dining, cooking, reading outdoors, visiting with friends, and gardening, to name a few popular activities. While you are planning, take time to think about these and other activities that the deck will need to accommodate.

Imagine how you and your family and friends will spend time on the deck. Do you want to be able to host large parties? Will children need a play area incorporated into the final design? If small children (or pets, for that matter) will be playing on a high deck, in addition to railings you may need a gate to keep them safely off the steps. Also think about the amenities you would like. If you enjoy lying down to read or sunbathe, for example, you may want to install benches along the railings.

Filling out the following checklist will help you identify how you want to use your deck and what features you want to include in its design. Use your answers to guide you through the entire process, from basic deck design to lighting and landscaping.

When do I want to use the deck?
Months of the year: _____ to _____
Times of day: _____

Which activities do I want the deck to accommodate?
☐ Outdoor dining
☐ Cooking
☐ Sitting and visiting with one or two friends
☐ Sitting and visiting with large groups of friends and family. How many people? ____
☐ Hot tub
☐ Sunbathing
☐ Container gardening
☐ Water gardening
☐ Outdoor shower
☐ Plant collections
☐ Bird-watching
☐ Butterfly-watching
☐ Viewing the garden
☐ Reading and relaxing
☐ Sandbox for kids
☐ Other play area for kids _____

What size seating areas do I need?
CASUAL DINING
☐ Dining table that seats ____
☐ Barbecue area
☐ Extra table(s) for serving trays, etc.

RECREATIONAL SEATING
☐ Benches
☐ Hammock
☐ Lounge chairs
☐ Other chairs

PARTIES
☐ Small: How many people? ____ How often? _____
☐ Large: How many people? ____ How often? _____

How much storage do I need?

☐ Charcoal and cooking utensils
☐ Grill and counter space for cooking
☐ Hoses
☐ Garden tools
☐ Potting soil, fertilizer, peat moss, etc.
☐ Toys
☐ Wood (in winter)

What problems could a new deck solve?

☐ Awkward transition between house and garden
☐ Step or steps too large
☐ Landing too small
☐ Need way to get from house to yard
☐ No flat area for grill or table
☐ Steep slope in backyard/side yard where it is difficult/impossible to walk/garden
☐ Area with damp, soggy soil
☐ Need easy access to water for container plants
☐ Need easy access to water for garden plants
☐ Lumpy, uneven area caused by tree roots

What utilities do I need?

ELECTRICITY

☐ On house walls
☐ On the deck. Location(s) _____

WATER

☐ Convenient spigot(s)
☐ Space for hanging/storing hoses
☐ Hoses and spigots for watering containers

LIGHTING

☐ Overhead floodlights
☐ Illumination for cooking area
☐ Low-level lighting for walking after dark/getting into and out of hot tub

What makes my existing deck unpleasant/uncomfortable to use?

☐ Too hot and sunny
☐ Too small
☐ Not enough room for adequate furniture
☐ Not enough room to walk from one place to another
☐ Too cluttered with stored items
☐ Too large; chairs are set around the edges, without comfortable areas for conversation
☐ No privacy; overlooks neighbor's deck/back windows
☐ Need to add screening (plantings, trellises, fences, hedges)
　☐ Along side yard
　☐ To hide backyard neighbors
　☐ To hide utility areas (garage, compost)
　☐ Other _____
☐ Too much noise from neighbors and/or street
☐ Ugly view
☐ Potentially nice view but blocked by _____
☐ Just grass to look at
☐ No way to get from the house — or deck — to the yard
☐ Wood is slippery and dangerous, even when it hasn't rained
☐ Cracked wood and nails that protrude are unsafe
☐ Other _____
_____

Are there problem spots to deal with during design/construction?

☐ Steep slope
☐ Damp or swampy area
☐ Children's playing field
☐ Large rocks/bedrock
☐ Septic field
☐ Buried electric cable
☐ Tree roots/trees to be protected during construction

Create a Working Drawing

An accurate working map of your site is an invaluable tool both for designing your deck and for planning the landscaping around it. You'll use a working drawing to determine how much space you have for a deck and the various configurations that are possible. Once your final design is in place, a working drawing will also help you plan landscaping and other amenities.

Although creating an accurate working drawing takes time, you don't need to produce anything fancy. It should be drawn to scale and include the details about your site that will affect the design of the deck. Once you have the necessary information on paper, you never have to draw it again. You'll use overlays, or sheets of tracing paper, on top of the master drawing to sketch out ideas and make notes. When an overlay becomes too messy, add another on top of it, transfer any ideas you'd like to save, and start over.

Record the Basic Features

The first step is to draw the relevant parts of your house to scale (the walls where the deck may be attached). If you already have blueprints of your house, use them as the basis for your drawing. If not, make a rough sketch of the area on scrap paper, then measure the house in detail.

Because you'll want to include all the parts of your property that will be affected by the design, put the house at the top or side of the drawing. This leaves room for other landscape features, such as views you'd like to highlight and sites where you plan to install shrubs. The farther these elements are from the construction area, the less accurate you have to be. Mark *North* on the drawing; you'll need this to help track sun and shade patterns.

Geometry in Real Life

It's easy to get stumped on how to locate accurately a feature on your drawing that isn't directly attached to the house. If you think back to high school geometry class, you may remember a process called triangulation. This real-life application of geometry makes it easy to position any feature on your map.

For this process, you'll need a piece of graph paper, two colored pencils (different colors), a drawing compass, and a 100-foot measuring tape. For longer distances, a homemade stakes-and-string measurer is handy. To make one, measure and mark 10-foot intervals on a long, fairly heavy string with masking tape or a black waterproof marker. To use it without a helper, stretch the string between posts pounded into the ground. Here's how to locate a specific feature by triangulation:

Step 1. Choose a structure, such as your house, to which all others features will be related. Draw this structure on your graph paper and then mark on it two fixed points, such as two corners. Circle each reference point with pencils of different colors. (If using two colors seems fussy or silly, be patient, because there's method to this madness!)

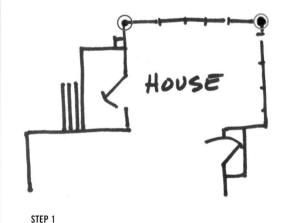

STEP 1

Step 2. Measure the distance from one of the fixed points to the feature you want to position on the map, and note the measurement on your sketch in the same color you used to circle the related reference point.

Step 3. Measure the distance from the other fixed point to the feature and record the measurement in the other color.

Step 4. To transfer the measurements to your working drawing, set the compass at the first measurement using the scale you selected for the drawing. Put the point of the compass on the first reference point and with the pencil draw a faint arc on the graph paper.

Step 5. Reset the compass to correspond to the second measurement and draw a second arc. The point where the two arcs intersect indicates the exact location of the feature you are recording.

Continue gathering measurements and recording them until you've added all the necessary features to your map. Just be sure to record each measurement with a pencil of the correct color.

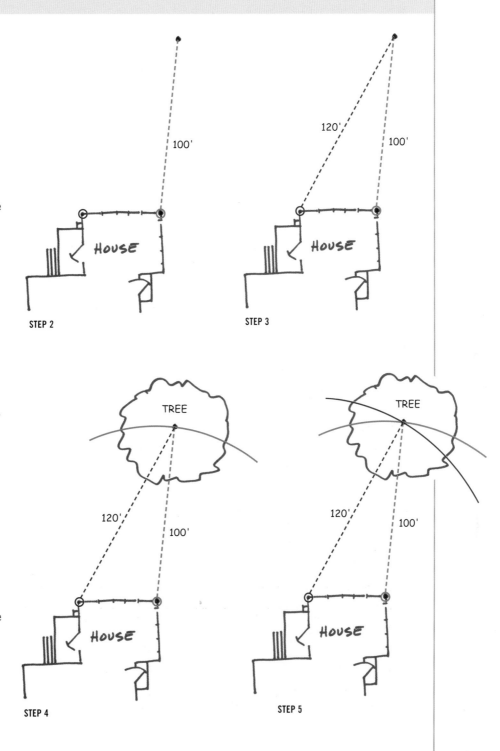

Fill In the Details

Once you have a basic sketch of your house and the prominent landscape features, the next step is to add any other elements that will affect your design. The following are valuable to have on a working drawing.

Doors and windows. These are essential! Identify the location of all doors and windows that may be affected by your design. Don't forget any doors that are below the surface of the deck. For instance, our rear basement door comes out under the deck, and we needed a design that allowed us to get in and out of it easily.

Other house features. Consider carefully what other features of your house may affect the design, such as a chimney and downspouts. Make sure you measure accurately and record the loca-

tions of utilities such as water spigots and electrical outlets.

Hardscaping. Cement or brick walks, driveways, walls, terraces, and fences are commonly referred to as *hardscaping.* Because these features are difficult to alter, they should be included on your working drawing.

Trees, shrubs, and other plantings. For each tree, draw in the trunk and mark the drip line (the full extent of the branches). Use rough circles to mark the location of shrubs and larger free-form shapes to record other established plantings. This is especially important for plants that will be near the construction site or that you plan to build around. You'll want to erect snow fencing or other barriers out to the drip line to keep equipment away from the trunks and off the roots.

▼ The design for this deck came together beautifully. A stunning arbor shelters a table that can be used for dining, visiting, or reading; vines and loads of container plantings give the whole space a gardenlike feel.

Views. Note attractive and unsightly views.

Utilities. Locate underground cables, water mains, wellheads, septic fields or tanks, and any other utilities.

Surface water. Adjacent streams and ponds are obvious features to record. Also mark areas where storm runoff may affect your design.

Traffic patterns. Note formal walkways (hardscaping), informal paths, and unofficial routes family and friends take to get around the site.

Sun and shade patterns. It is helpful to observe a site at different times of day so you can determine where pergolas, trellises, or awnings should go. Keep in mind that sun and shade patterns vary according to the time of year and are dependent on the angle of the sun. Ideally, you'll want to note where the sunny and shady areas are in the spring, summer, fall, and winter.

Problem spots. Slopes are obvious features to record. Other things to watch out for include wet spots and rock outcrops. One reason you want to map problem spots is that you can use a deck to eliminate some of them.

Organize Your Ideas

By now you should have a working drawing and a design notebook chock-full of notes, pictures, and scribbled drawings. Depending on how you approach such tasks, you may be ready to start drawing designs. Or you may want to organize your ideas a bit more. One option is to sort and copy your ideas into organized lists. Another is to copy them onto index cards, which you can then sort into piles that correspond to certain features or areas of the deck. For example, cards for "dining area," "table for using computer," and "table for playing bridge" would all fall into the same pile — and indicate you need an area that accommodates a comfortable table and chairs for all of these activities.

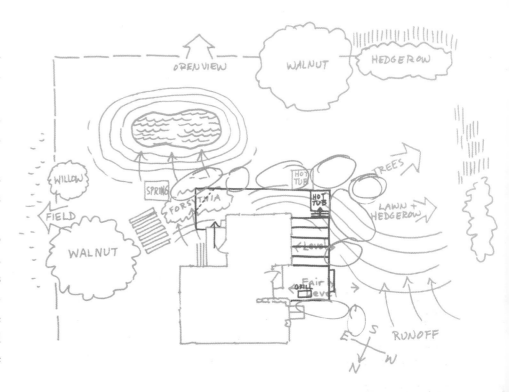

▲ A working drawing, like this one of the author's house and yard (shown in gray), illustrates all the features that should be taken into account during the design process. Use tracing paper overlays on top of the drawing to experiment with the shapes and dimensions for your deck and flower beds (shown in brown and green).

Gather your notebook, working drawing, and tracing paper for overlays. Spread out your notes, sketches, lists, and snapshots. All you absolutely need for this process is a pencil and a pencil sharpener, but if you want to get fancy, have colored pens, pencils, or markers on hand as well. Place a sheet of tracing paper over your drawing and mark a prominent feature so that you can line up the overlays easily. Use the same feature on all the overlays you create.

Now the checklist of What Do I Want My Deck to Be? comes in handy. Draw squares and rectangles to indicate areas of the deck — a dining area and a sitting area, for example. Firm up the ultimate size and shape you'd like to have. Add specific built-in features, such as benches and storage areas. As necessary, start a new overlay by transferring the essential details from the previous copy, and start again. Keep all the overlays until you've settled on a final design.

The Final Touches

Once you've come up with a design that you and your family like, try to poke holes in your ideas. This helps identify potential problems or design modifications. Here are some ideas to consider:

• Measure the space you've allotted for a large dining table, remembering that you need room to pass on both sides, *plus* room for diners to sit comfortably with their chairs pushed back. (See How Much Space? on page 13 for recommended dimensions of tables and other features.)

• Measure and remeasure the space allocated for storage, hot tubs, and play areas. After going through this process with our design, we pushed out the west side of our deck several feet in order to make sure we could have a table and plenty of room to walk around it.

• Think about moving from place to place on your deck, and analyze whether you'll really have enough space to walk to various areas once the deck is finished and the furniture is in place. For example, allocate space for a walkway if you want guests to be able to walk past a table while others are seated.

Professional Advice

To help you take your plans to the next level, find a good contractor. Selecting a contractor is vitally important in any home construction project. Someone with extensive experience building decks will have valuable design suggestions, plus ideas for handling problem spots and standardizing measurements to use materials efficiently. In addition to handling necessary building permits, a contractor should

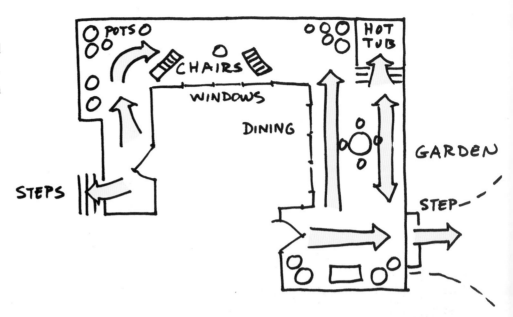

◄ A cozy sitting area was created to capture the afternoon breeze but provide welcome shade during the hottest part of the day. Evergreen shrubbery offers a sense of enclosure and privacy.

be able to help you phase in a design over time if the deck you want is bigger than your budget allows.

In addition, find a contractor who has lots of examples of completed projects to show you — along with satisfied customers you can call. Ask for references and check them. Better yet, go to see the projects, if possible. Keep in mind that a builder who has to put your project into a queue is not always a bad thing — good contractors don't lack for customers, while poor ones often have some time on their hands.

Getting estimates from contractors means you can zero in on the real price of the job. When comparing bids, be sure to look closely at the details, such as the specifics on hardware and on the construction techniques that will be used. The lowest price is not always the best price, and shoddy workmanship and/or cheaper materials aren't a bargain. (Our builder took a whole day just to pick out the lumber he used so that he would be happy with the quality of each board and timber that went into our deck.) Finally, always read the contract very carefully and insist that the builder carry proper insurance for the carpenters and other workers.

▲ Use a tape measure to help analyze traffic patterns and furniture placement. Put it on the floor and imagine it is a passageway on the deck. In general, 3 feet is a good minimum width for single-file walkways (a bit more for high-traffic areas); 4½ feet is recommended if you want people to be able to walk side by side.

CHAPTER TWO

The Surrounding Gardens

Basic deck design is only the beginning. The next step is to develop a plan that will make your deck a real part of your garden as well as a key link between your home and the rest of your landscape. Imagine your deck surrounded by shrubs, small trees, ornamental grasses, perennials, annuals, and vines rather than a boring stretch of lawn. With a bit of planning and good plant selection, you can create an outdoor living space amid the special color and fragrance only a garden can bring.

Mixed plantings provide something beautiful to look at while you are sitting on your deck. With good planning, you can have something blooming throughout the entire season of deck use, as well as some visual interest during colder months to lure you outside. In addition, fragrant flowers included in your plantings will scent the air as their perfume wafts on breezes across the deck. Redolent night-blooming flowers can provide an extra touch of magic for moonlit nights outside. Incorporate plants that attract butterflies, hummingbirds, and other wildlife in your design, and you have a ready-made show to enjoy from the deck. And what better way to forge a strong link between the garden and the kitchen than by including some ornamental edibles in your design?

Getting Started with Garden Design

Pure pleasure is always an important incentive for gardening, but there are other, supremely practical reasons for planting around your deck. Mixed plantings hide the deck's undercarriage and the empty, often weed-filled space underneath. Plantings enhance the look of a deck whether it is at ground level or high off the ground. Our deck happens to be at ground level on one end and a full story off the ground on the other, but this doesn't pose any landscaping problem to speak of. I've adjusted the height of plants around it accordingly. In beds along the sides where the deck is at ground level, the tallest plants reach to just above the top of the railing — 4 or 5 feet. Toward the high south side, larger shrubs and small trees that mature anywhere from 10 to 20 feet form the backbone of the planting. In both cases, the tallest plants are next to the base of the deck, with shorter ones — a mix of perennials, ground covers, bulbs, annuals, herbs, and roses — out toward the edge of the bed, where they can be enjoyed.

Replacing grass around the deck's base has the added advantage of lower maintenance. Getting rid of grass eliminates (or at least greatly reduces) the aggravating, time-consuming chores of mowing and trimming grass and weeds around deck supports. Plantings also block the base of a deck and cut down on the amount of light underneath it, thus hiding and reducing the vigor of weeds that might grow there. In addition, installing edging strips along the perimeter of the beds along the deck keeps grass separate from ground covers. This technique helps reduce weeding and cuts down on trimming chores, because these strips leave a single clean edge to mow. Some people also prefer the more formal, tidy appearance of edging strips, but that is a matter of personal taste.

The process of creating flower beds to surround your deck isn't really much different from designing plantings for other parts of your landscape. You may have a clear idea already in mind, so all you have to do is select the right plants to make it a reality. Sometimes the conditions of the site impose their own restrictions. For instance, in our rocky soils, I generally prepare the soil first (and see how many rocks I have to deal with), then decide how to arrange the plantings.

▼ A small water garden stocked with brightly colored goldfish gives this ground-level deck decided style and appeal, bringing water, plants, and nature "up close and personal."

Although you'll find a popular approach to garden design in the pages that follow, keep in mind that there's no one way to accomplish this task, so use the parts of this system that seem to work for you and ignore the rest. You can design the plantings on paper, select the plants, and install them yourself. Or you can hire a garden designer to do the entire job for you. Another option is to hire a designer or a nursery to select and install some of the garden — perhaps the woody plants, shrubs, and some perennials — but leave plenty of room in the bed for you to add more perennials, annuals, bulbs, and other plants. In my own garden, I prefer to bypass the paper planning process altogether. (See Paperless Design on page 35 for my favorite system.)

Get to Know Your Site

When you are designing a garden, it's important first to get to know your site — its soil, exposure, and shade or sun patterns. Then use the golden rule for choosing plants: Match the plant to the site. Plants that are selected because they thrive in the conditions you have inevitably grow better, require less maintenance, and have fewer problems with pests and diseases.

Study shade and sun patterns. Note on your garden plan which sites never get direct sun and which ones get sun or shade for only half a day and at what times.

Consider how the prevailing winds affect your site. On a wind-whipped site, a windbreak may make your planting easier to manage (and also make your deck more comfortable to use). For wind protection, a mixed planting of both evergreen and deciduous trees and shrubs is most effective. A fence offers a quick solution but provides less wind protection.

Stepping-Stone Paths

If you plant very wide beds, it is best to install informal stepping-stone paths within the planting, so you can get in to weed, mulch, harvest edibles, and do other maintenance. Stepping-stones are especially useful in densely planted beds, as there isn't any other way to get into them without trampling the plants.

Because these informal paths aren't major landscape elements (they're almost covered by plants by midsummer, in fact), you can use a mix of materials. Chipped stepping-stones are quite inexpensive and plants usu-ally cover them up. You can also use odd-sized pieces of bluestone and hand-cast cement pavers. Small sizes about a foot square are usually fine; for utility areas (such as the path to the basement door), larger stones or a narrow mulched path is best.

To install the stones, simply level the area with a trowel or other tool and set them in place. However, they'll last longer if you set them on a 1- or 2-inch layer of packed, crushed stone, because they'll remain drier and will be protected from freezing and thawing cycles in winter.

Note the direction the site faces. Sites that face south are usually warmer and more exposed, especially in winter, than are north-facing ones. Because east-facing sites receive morning sun and afternoon shade, they are usually cooler than west-facing sites, which are sunny in the afternoon, when temperatures are higher.

Look at the soil. Dig a few test holes to examine the soil. Do you have heavy, wet clay? Rich loam? Sandy conditions? Although any soil can be improved by mulching, adding organic matter, and double digging, it's always best to start a garden with plants that thrive in the soil you already have. Later you can improve the soil to accommodate a wider range of plants. If you have rocky soil, you can build stone walls, install raised beds, or plant shallow-rooted ground covers. If the soil is clogged with roots from a shallow-rooted tree, such as a maple, see Deck Plantings in Shady Spots on page 41 for suggestions on how to plant effectively in this space.

Develop the Shape of a Bed

There are a variety of techniques for visualizing the shape of a bed. You can use your working drawing with an overlay of tracing paper to experiment with the best size and shape of the beds around the deck, as shown in the illustration at right, or you can use a hose or a long rope to outline the shape on the ground. A sprinkling of flour around the perimeter of the bed also works well. Stakes and string are another option.

Examine the shape from up on the deck as well as out in the yard. Imagine the bed filled with plants, and consider whether the shape you have accomplishes what you want it to.

◀ When planning your garden beds, consider those at a distance from the deck as well as those immediately surrounding it. The entire landscape should work as an integrated whole.

Ask yourself the following questions:

• Will the plants in the bed hide what you want them to hide?

• Will the plants be more visible from the deck if the bed is wider?

• Will you need taller plants than you had originally thought?

• Can you eliminate an awkward mowing area if you move or expand the bed's outline?

Create Wide Beds for Viewing

Wide beds allow you to enjoy some of the plants while seated and create the feeling that the deck is surrounded by vegetation. For me, wide beds helped solve the problem of what used to be a tough-to-mow slope. I used stone pulled out of the soil to create terraces that gradually taper the bed to a fairly level area of lawn around the outside of the bed.

Note that If you want to be able to enjoy plantings from up on the deck, they'll have to be fairly wide. Conventional 3-foot-wide plantings along the base of the railings may be visible only if you look straight down over the railing.

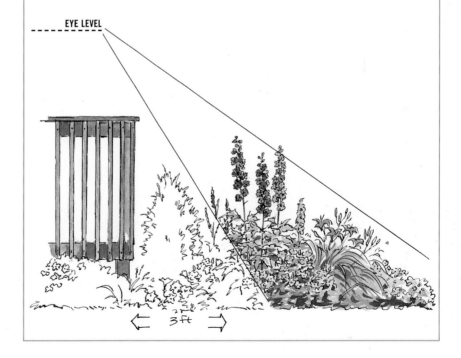

Pick the Perfect Plants

Deciding which plants to grow can be a challenge, especially if you're a collector and want to grow one of everything. As much as I'm sometimes tempted to do otherwise, I stick to plants that have the same cultural requirements. That's because I want them both to look good and to grow well together with a minimum of effort on my part. And I take care not to pair really vigorous plants with companions that may be overwhelmed by them.

Because these plants will grow where you'll see them up close and often, be sure to consider the following criteria:

Choose for the long term. Select plants that offer a long season of interest. Perennials and annuals should bloom for a long time and have foliage that stays attractive throughout the season. Trees shrubs should offer at least two seasons of interest — spring flowers and colorful fall foliage, for example.

Look for low maintenance. Choose plants that require a minimum of attention for pinching, staking, or other maintenance chores.

Limit size. Stick to shrubs and small trees that won't grow too big for your site and thus require extensive pruning.

Seek fragrances. Choose plants with appealing fragrance, either from flowers or from foliage.

Enjoy nature. Select plants that attract butterflies, hummingbirds, and other wildlife to your deck and garden.

Look for clues. Study your setting for inspiration and pick plants that echo the colors and textures of the landscape. Another option is to repeat plants you like from other parts of your garden.

Know your site. As you evaluate plants, always consider the growing conditions they require. For example, if your deck is in a shady site, eliminate from your list shrubs and perennials that demand full sun. Not only does this winnow down the plants you'd like to grow, but it also removes the frustration of trying to grow plants that won't ever do well in that site.

Select your seasons. Choose plants that will be at their best during the seasons when you use your deck most often. In most cases, you'll want to concentrate on plants that provide a progression of color from early summer through early fall. Gardeners in warmer zones may want to concentrate on spring and fall bloom, because summers are often too hot to enjoy spending time outside.

▼ Low-maintenance lavender softens the edges of the steps leading from this deck down into the yard, and it also complements the shape and texture of the rocks that abut the steps.

Another option for warm-climate gardeners is to select some plants for spring and fall bloom, and then concentrate on night-blooming plants for the summer months, because the deck may be comfortable to use after the heat of the day has waned. Adding shrubs and perennials that feature evergreen foliage or small trees that have ornamental bark is always a good idea, because it ensures that the bed isn't barren and empty over the winter.

Select colors that appeal. Choose plants that feature your favorite colors — ones that appear in the house, that turn up again and again in your closet, or that you tend to buy at flower shops. Another great way to develop a color scheme is to look for a pattern that appeals to you in a rug, quilt, or piece of fabric, and then select colors that echo it. Play off the colors of your house as well.

Don't forget foliage. Getting caught up in flower color is an easy trap to fall in to, but blossoms usually last only a short time, while foliage is the backbone of any garden and essential for keeping it attractive all season long. Be sure to include plants with a mix of leaf shapes, sizes, and colors. Contrast dark green with chartreuse and burgundy, mix in plants with patterns of variegated leaves, and combine a range of textures and shapes.

Create combinations. If you select two or three plants you are really excited about, use them to build the rest of the planting. Allow the colors, textures, and habits of this core group to inspire you, and select other plants to complement their characteristics. Or use a good combination as the basis of a planting that features a few carefully chosen plants en masse in large, free-form drifts.

▲ An abundance of flowers gives this deck a romantic appeal. The pots of tulips that decorate the space in spring can give way to containers of annuals and tender perennials come summer.

Make a Plant Chart

One of the best ways to select plants is to make a list and assess each plant as you go along. A chart like the one shown below is an invaluable design tool. Use graph paper and colored pens or pencils, or create a spreadsheet on your computer, then use the plants described in chapter 6 or a plant encyclopedia to identify the species you want to consider. Each time you see a plant that's appealing, check the growing conditions it requires, and don't add it to your list unless those conditions match the ones your site has to offer.

Next, winnow your list. To get a good start on a bed, you probably need only 15 to 20 plants on your final list, so try to identify the best ones and the best mix. You can always add plants later. Balancing bloom times is a good place to begin. For example, you may have many shrubs and perennials that flower in early spring, but not much to speak of in late summer. If so, remove some of the spring bloomers and look for plants that will add late-summer color. Also check to make sure you have a good mix of plant shapes and sizes, as well as plants that feature attractive foliage all season long.

Draw a Planting Plan

The final step in the design process is to make a rough planting plan. Use tracing paper overlays on top of your working drawing for this or on an outline of the bed drawn to scale. Start with the plants located along the deck foundation at the back of the bed. Don't forget vines against the deck, too,

PLANT NAME	BLOOM TIME				Foliage	Height	Special Features	Notes
Perennials	Spring	Early Summer	Summer	Fall				
Coreopsis 'Moonbeam'			yellow		Lacy	1'high 3'wide	long bloom	Reblooms best if sheared
Platycodon grandiflora			lavender blue			2'high 3'wide	good fall color	Rebloom if dead headed; self-sow
P. grandiflora 'Shell Pink'			pale pink			2'high	good in evening garden	
Perovskia atriplicifolia				violet blue	Gray-green Lacy	3'-5' high	aromatic leaves	Great with ornamental grasses
Hemerocallis			all colors		Grassy strap-shaped	2'-3' high	some fragrant	Mix early, midseason & late cultivars

▲ A chart is a good tool to aid in plant selection. Write the plant name in the first column, then fill in the columns for bloom seasons in color, so that you can see the range of colors chosen. Also note the plant type and its shape, height, spread at maturity, and other features, such as berries and bark. Jot down suggested companion plants from catalogs or demonstration beds at a garden center or make notes about cultural techniques that prolong bloom.

especially if you want plants to climb a pergola or trellis. Place the best shrubs on your list first, then gradually add other plants around them.

You probably will run out of room before you run out of plants on your list. That's okay. Check to see if any of the leftover plants are more suitable to use than the ones you've already drawn in, and make substitutions as necessary. Then keep the list of "leftovers" for future reference.

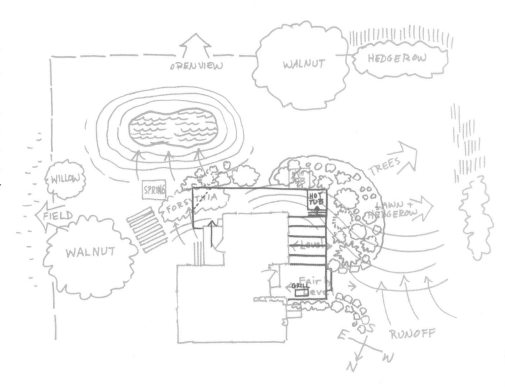

▶ Draw circles or ovals to represent individual trees and shrubs, as well as free-form shapes to indicate clumps of perennials. Label each oval as you go or use a key of some sort to keep track of the plants. Try to draw the ovals to scale and make sure they represent the size of the plants at maturity, so the drawing will provide a true picture of how many plants you'll need.

◀ To create a balanced, pleasing design, arrange the plantings so the colors and textures appear throughout the planting. Otherwise, you can end up with a lopsided look.

▲ Arrange perennials in groups of three or more, to create an established, dramatic effect.

Creating a Balanced Design

As you work with your planting plan, use these basic principles to help you achieve an attractive, balanced design:

Use repetition to unify. Repeating colors and textures throughout the planting helps create rhythm in the design and pulls it together visually. For example, you could use several clumps of the same yellow daylily down the center of the bed, and perhaps mirror the color with marigolds of the same shade. Concentrate on repeating plants that offer especially long bloom times, good foliage, and other appealing features.

Vary plant heights. Although you'll generally put taller perennials and shrubs at the back and shorter ones in front, you don't want a design that resembles a police lineup. Bring some taller plants out a bit, mixed with medium-sized ones, and move some mid-size plants to the front to give the planting depth and variety. Mix plant forms, too, interspersing upright clumps with mounding plants.

Add interest with contrast. A garden with plants that are all the same shape is boring. Mix rounded, vertical, and prostrate plants throughout the garden for visual contrast. Combining plants that have very large leaves with those with small, fine-textured ones also adds interest. Repeating these contrasting combinations both unifies and creates rhythm in your design.

Echo shapes and textures. Add visual symmetry by echoing the shapes and textures of certain plants. For example, plant clumps of perennials with a rounded habit (such as 'Autumn Joy' sedum) along the front of a bed. Think of large ornamental grasses (such as *Miscanthus* 'Gracillimus') as exclamation points and use them at intervals along the back of the bed. Then repeat those shapes with smaller grasses or clumps of yuccas toward the front of the bed.

Paperless Design

In spite of all the preceding advice, I have to admit that I've designed most plantings in my garden without first drawing them out, simply because I enjoy experimenting with plants right in the garden more than planning gardens on paper.

After I prepare the soil at the site, I select a few outstanding specimens or combinations I want to work around and then choose companions that will complement them. I most often select plant combinations right at the nursery by grouping the containers on the spot, to get an idea of how they'll look.

For the bed around our deck, I started with two viburnums *(Viburnum rhytidophyllum* and *V. x rhytidophylloides)* as the basis for the planting, then added a few other shrubs that offer interesting foliage contrast. I also selected vines to be planted right next to the deck so they could be trained onto the arbor.

Finally, I added perennials and other plants, mixing them in cottage-garden style. Our deck bed now features shrubs that offer spring flowers for early color and fall berries for birds, plants that attract hummingbirds and butterflies, fragrant flowers to enjoy from the deck, self-sowing annuals, ornamental edibles, herbs, and shrubs and small trees with four-season interest. (The more plants the better, as far as I'm concerned!)

If I don't like a particular combination, I use one of the most valuable tools a gardener has for redesign: a shovel. Although I don't usually move woody plants (trees, shrubs, roses, and perennial vines) around too much, perennials and many ground covers are easy to rearrange. Seedlings of self-sown annuals are especially simple to move, particularly when they are still small. If they're in the wrong place, I simply dig them up with a trowel and tuck them in somewhere else.

▼ Annuals are a perfect choice if you need to fill in a gap, whether it's left by bulbs that have died back for the year or by clumps of perennials that haven't yet filled the space available.

Phase In a Project

Installing a large planting around a deck can be an intimidating project — especially if you are planning to do all the work yourself. Although it's possible to prepare the soil over the entire site before planting anything, I like to spread things out by preparing and planting in sections over several weekends, or over a season or two. Fall is my favorite time for digging new beds, as the weather is cool and the soil is usually moist. Then I mulch heavily for the winter and plant in spring. I plant trees, shrubs, and vines first, followed by perennials and other plants.

Consider hiring someone to help remove lawn grass and weeds and prepare the soil. Don't till weeds and grass into the soil; the chopped-up weeds will quickly resprout, creating a weeding nightmare for years to come. Instead, cut off the lawn in strips with a sharp spade or rent a sod cutter to remove it. Then, to discourage any weeds that remain, add a thick layer of newspaper (eight sheets or so) before spreading a layer of bark mulch on top.

Layered Plantings

I'm always adding more plants to my gardens, creating a layered effect. Densely planted beds crowd out most weeds and cover and protect the soil, so they need less weeding and mulching than do sparsely planted gardens. This also results in a season-long show that's full of surprises. I never know quite what these areas are going to look like from one season to the next, but that's part of the appeal. Here's how it works:

Instead of trying to maintain a mulched, weed-free area under shrubs, I've filled the space with perennials and ground covers. Viburnum is underplanted with vigorous ground covers such as a

◀ **This deck provides a perfect viewing platform for a charming mix of plants, such as dianthus, hardy geraniums, and peonies, which have been tucked in among the rocks.**

No-Dig Soil Improvement

Can't bear the thought of digging up an entire site, or is the soil really poor? Try scalping off the weeds, then cover the site with a thick layer of newspaper; 8 to 10 sheets will suffice. (Use sheets of corrugated cardboard if you're dealing with really tenacious weeds.) Top the newspaper with 5 inches of straw, an inch or so of compost, then about 2 inches of bark mulch. Leave the site unplanted for a year, or make holes in the mulch, fill them with bagged topsoil, and plant annuals. Weed regularly and renew the mulch for a year, then install permanent plantings.

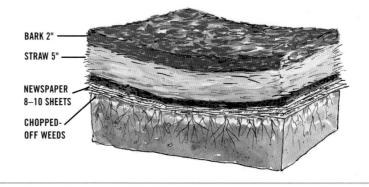

BARK 2"
STRAW 5"
NEWSPAPER 8–10 SHEETS
CHOPPED-OFF WEEDS

purple-leaved common bugleweed (*Ajuga reptans*) and plumbago (*Ceratostigma plumbaginoides*). I've also added seedlings of hellebore (*Helleborus* x *hybridus*) dug from other parts of the garden. Ground-covering shrubs, such as cotoneaster and 'Max Graf' rose, have found their way here, as have self-sowing annuals, such as love-in-a-mist (*Nigella damascena*) and larkspur (*Consolida ajacis*).

A layer of hardy bulbs beneath all the other plants — crocuses and daffodils for spring, along with autumn crocuses (*Colchicum* spp.) — add color at the beginning and end of the year. I also plant annual vines, such as scarlet runner beans (*Phaseolus coccineus*) and moonflower (*Ipomoea alba*), at the back, so they can clamber up the arbor and share space with the permanent Dutchman's pipe (*Aristolochia durior*) intended to shade the deck. If any "holes" are apparent in spring (it's hard to imagine, but I manage to find them), I tuck in annuals.

Perennials

Achilleas, Yarrows, *Achillea* spp.

Artemisias, *Artemisia* spp.

Red valerian, *Centranthus ruber*

Coreopsis, *Coreopsis* spp.

Purple coneflowers, *Echinacea* spp.

Cranesbills, *Geranium* spp.

Daylilies, *Hemerocallis* spp.

Rose mallow, *Hibiscus moscheutos*

Lavender, *Lavandula angustifolia*

Linaria, *Linaria purpurea*

Mallow, *Malva alcea* 'Fastigiata'

Catmints, *Nepeta* spp.

Russian sage, *Perovskia atriplicifolia*

Balloon flower, *Platycodon grandiflorus*

Orange coneflowers, *Rudbeckia* spp.

Sedums, *Sedum* spp.

Adam's needle, *Yucca filamentosa*

Large Ornamental Grasses

Feather reed grass, *Calamagrostis* x *acutiflora* 'Stricta'*

Miscanthus, *Miscanthus sinensis*[+]

Purple moor grass, *Molinia caerulea*[+]

Switch grass, *Panicum virgatum*[+]

Medium to Small Grasses

Blue fescue, *Festuca glauca**

Blue oat grass, *Helictotrichon sempervirens**

Blood grass, *Imperata cylindrica* 'Red Baron'[+]

Fountain grass, *Pennisetum alopecuroides*[+]

* Cool-season grass
[+] Warm-season grass

Enduring Perennials for Deck Gardens

For beds close to the deck — or, for that matter, any gardens close to the house — choose perennials that have long blooming seasons, handsome foliage, and tough constitutions that tolerate changes in weather. It's also vital that they be matched to the site: It doesn't pay to fool yourself into thinking your soil and sun exposure are something they're not — the plants certainly won't be fooled. Better by far to start with species that thrive in the conditions you have for them.

A deck garden isn't the place for plants with spectacular but fleeting flowers that then look unsightly for weeks on end. However, if the flowers are accompanied by nice foliage, I do include them. Peonies, for example, don't bloom for long, but their foliage remains attractive all summer. I also have daffodils and other bulbs in my deck garden to start off the season in early spring. In exchange for their early color, I choose to overlook their dying foliage. I simply overplant clumps of daffodils with annuals such as marigolds, zinnias, or ornamental peppers to help hide the foliage while it dies back. Unless otherwise noted, the perennials and ornamental grasses listed at left thrive in full sun and average, well-drained soil (see chapter 6 for detailed information on many of these plants).

Ornamental Grasses for Deck Gardens

Ornamental grasses are sturdy plants that provide four seasons of interest to landscapes and for this reason are ideal plants for a deck garden. They bring texture to the garden, as well as movement and sound as clumps rustle in the breeze. Clumps left to stand over the winter also add color, interest, and structure to the landscape. Several grasses exhibit spectacular fall color, too, before the leaves ripen to tawny shades of brown.

Give ornamental grasses a spot in full sun with average-to-rich, well-drained, evenly moist soil; however, most also tolerate dry soil. Warm-season and cool-season grasses have slightly different growth cycles. Warm-season species grow actively from spring through summer, like most perennials. They are dormant and brown from fall through winter. Leave warm-season grasses standing through winter and cut them to a few inches above the ground in late winter or very early spring before growth resumes.

As their name suggests, cool-season grasses grow during cool weather (60 to 75°F), primarily from late summer to fall and then again in spring. Many cool-season grasses are evergreen. Cut back cool-season grasses in fall or early spring, to about two-thirds of their height.

When selecting grasses, keep in mind that they can be clump-forming or running. Clump-formers develop into large mounds; running or rhizomatous grasses spread — some slowly, others very quickly. Clump-forming grasses usually are the best choices for

the garden, but most will form clumps at least as wide as their height, so give them plenty of room at planting time. Plan on dividing the clumps every few years; otherwise, most species tend to die out toward the center of the clump.

Large ornamental grasses. Use these shrub-sized grasses toward the back of deck plantings. While established clumps of large grasses, such as miscanthus, are dense enough to hide the deck's undercarriage like a full-fledged shrub, the other large species listed on page 38 are less imposing. Site them slightly in front of substantial shrubs, which will then act as backdrops for the airy grass flowers. Large grasses also add attractive textural contrast when combined with broad-leaved shrubs. All of the large grasses listed are clump-forming, warm-season grasses, with the exception of feather reed grass, which is a cool-season clumper.

Medium to small grasses. Use smaller grasses among perennials, annuals, and low shrubs in beds around the deck. Like their larger cousins, they add effective foliage contrast when combined with broad-leaved perennials. Unless otherwise noted, all of the medium to small grasses listed on page 38 are clump-forming species (see chapter 6 for detailed information on many of these plants).

▲ A lush mix of perennials, ornamental grasses, and shrubs decorate this porch-style deck. The low container filled with a handsome clump of variegated hakone grass (*Hakonechloa macra* 'Aureola') makes a handsome specimen that marks the step and edge of the deck.

Broad-Leaved Evergreens

Glossy abelia, *Abelia* x *grandiflora*

Boxwoods, *Buxus* spp.

Hollies, *Ilex* spp.

Mountain laurel, *Kalmia latifolia*

Drooping leucothoe, *Leucothoe fontanesiana*

Mahonias, *Mahonia* spp.

Japanese pieris, *Pieris japonica*

Scarlet firethorn, *Pyracantha coccinea*

Rhododendrons, Azaleas, *Rhododendron* spp.

Viburnums, *Viburnum* spp.

Deciduous Shrubs and Small Trees

Cotoneasters, *Cotoneaster* spp.

Fothergillas, *Fothergilla* spp.

Hollies, *Ilex* spp.

Magnolias, *Magnolia* spp.

Crabapples, *Malus* spp.

Roses, *Rosa* spp.

Viburnums, *Viburnum* spp.

▼ Mass plantings of dwarf evergreens — a low-growing blue spruce and yews — frame the edges of this deck and provide year-round color.

Shrubs and Small Trees for Deck Plantings

Flowers, showy fruit, handsome foliage, good fall color, and interesting bark or branching patterns are all qualities that shrubs and small trees can bring to deck plantings. The plants listed at left offer multiple seasons of interest to keep a border looking attractive for months on end. (See chapter 6 for detailed information on many of these plants.) For more ideas, visit a local arboretum or botanical garden, talk to local gardeners, or stop in at a nearby nursery.

Broad-leaved evergreens. These contribute green foliage in winter, giving substance to a border year-round. They are especially effective when contrasted with the fine-textured foliage of conifers. Many rhododendrons (*Rhododendron* spp.) feature showy flowers and evergreen foliage. In areas with acidic soil, rhododendrons and related plants make wonderful additions to deck borders. Hundreds of cultivars are available, so visit your local nursery and choose colors and sizes that appeal to you. For a progression of bloom, plant early- to late-spring-blooming selections, as well as summer-blooming species. Some even provide fragrance (see the list on page 56).

Conifers. Although full-size pines and spruces are too large for most situations around a deck (unless you need privacy), there are hundreds of dwarf conifers that make handsome additions to deck plantings. Some have golden or variegated needles and others have distinct textures, shapes, and growth habits. Be sure to read labels to determine the height at maturity, because it varies widely. Weeping and/or prostrate conifers can add an exotic touch. For example, white pine *(Pinus strobus)* has cultivars with both habits: 'Pendula' features a weeping habit; 'Prostrata' remains under 8 feet and can spread about as far.

Deck Plantings in Shady Spots

A deck on a wooded spot, or on a site shaded by a large tree or two, offers both benefits and challenges. It can become an inviting outdoor living space with a built-in ceiling of tree limbs and leaves that is comfortable on hot summer afternoons and delightful once evening arrives. Depending on the trees providing the shade, such sites can pose a planting challenge, however. If you are blessed with oaks and other deep-rooted trees, a lush shade garden is in order. On the other hand, if shallow-rooted trees, such as maples and beeches, are the predominant species, planting may be nearly impossible.

If you haven't done so already, take a spade to the site and dig a few test holes (dig carefully to avoid damaging tree roots). The root-clogged soil under many species of maples simply won't accommodate any perennials. In this case, your best bet is to pull weeds and mulch the soil to discourage their return. Don't consider adding soil on top of the roots and planting into that. Not only will the tree roots invade the new soil, but you can kill or damage trees in the process. Plant out beyond the drip line. If you need spots of color on such sites, set large tubs (half whiskey barrels work well) on top of the mulch and plant them with annuals or shade-loving perennials, such as hostas. Another option is to design an extension of the deck built around the trunks and with wide spans that bridge the roots.

▲ Decking paths are an ideal solution for traversing areas that have wet soil. This wooden pathway winds through just such an area, so visitors can get a good look at the viburnum and ferns at the edge of the garden.

Planting Beneath Deep-Rooted Trees

On a site where roots allow planting, plan a mix of shrubs, perennials, annuals, and perhaps even small trees. You can prepare pockets of soil between roots that are perfect for accommodating small perennials and woodland flowers. Use a small trowel to gently dig up the soil between roots, amend it with compost, and plant. Avoid damaging the tree roots as much as possible when you dig. Once the garden is planted, keep it mulched with chopped leaves to discourage weeds, to keep the soil moist and rich in organic matter, and to give the planting a woodsy look.

Annuals, Biennials, and Tender Perennials for Partial Shade

Begonias, *Begonia* spp.

Bush violets, *Browallia americana* and *B. speciosa*

Periwinkle, *Catharanthus roseus*

Sweet rocket, *Hesperis matronalis*

Polka-dot plant, *Hypoestes phyllostachya*

Impatiens, *Impatiens wallerana*

Lobelia, *Lobelia erinus*

Money plant, *Lunaria annua*

Flowering tobaccos, *Nicotiana* spp.

Plectranthus, *Plectranthus* spp.

Common mignonette, *Reseda odorata*

Coleus, *Solenostemon scutellarioides*

Persian shield, *Strobilanthes dyeranus*

Wishbone flower, *Torenia fournieri*

Tradescantias, *Tradescantia* spp.

Pansies and Violets, *Viola* spp. and hybrids

Ferns for Shade

Lady ferns, Wood ferns, *Athyrium* spp.

European lady fern, *A. filix-femina*

Japanese painted fern, *A. niponicum* var. *pictum*

Wood ferns, *Dryopteris* spp.

Autumn fern, *D. erythrosora*

Male fern, *D. filix-mas*

Ostrich fern, *Matteuccia struthiopteris*

Osmunda spp.

Cinnamon fern, *O. cinnamomea*

Royal fern, *O. regalis*

Christmas fern, *Polystichum acrostichoides*

Ground Covers for Shade

Bugleweeds, *Ajuga* spp.

Wild gingers, *Asarum* spp.

Liriopes, Lilyturfs, *Liriope* spp.

Pachysandras, *Pachysandra* spp.

Vinca, Lesser periwinkle, *Vinca minor*

Shade-Tolerant Annuals

Wax begonia *(Begonia semperflorens)* and common impatiens *(Impatiens wallerana)* are the most popular annuals for shady sites. Both bloom reliably from early summer to frost and although they'll tolerate full shade, plants in light, dappled shade or morning sun produce the best blooms. However, instead of filling the garden with a sea of one or two kinds of plants, experiment with a mix of annuals as well as perennials. This lets you determine which plants grow best on your site and also creates a richer, more interesting tapestry.

If your deck is in full shade all day long, your choices of shade-tolerant annuals are somewhat limited, because most do best in partial shade. Common impatiens and coleus will grow in full shade but provide more color with better light. Here's where observing your site carefully over the course of a few days can help. Look for bright spots that receive good light for much of the day, or sites that are in sun in the morning but shaded in the afternoon. Then plant these pockets with drifts of colorful annuals to make the most of the light available. You may also want to consider removing a tree limb here and there to let more light into the garden. (See chapter 6 for detailed information on the plants in the list at left.)

Grasses and Sedges for Shade

Variegated hakone grass, *Hakonechloa macra* 'Aureola', perhaps the most spectacular and sought-after shade grass, produces rounded mounds of arching, bamboolike green leaves striped with yellow; it is hardy to Zone 5.

Northern sea oats (*Chasmanthium latifolium,* once listed as *Uniola latifolia*) is a native grass producing 2- to 3-foot-tall clumps of bamboolike leaves topped by clusters of attractive, drooping seed heads that ripen from green to warm brown. Plants self-sow with enthusiasm; pull seedlings or cut back the seed heads in mid-fall to curtail this tendency.

Sedges (*Carex* spp.) are grasslike perennials that are often overlooked by gardeners. Most commonly grown plants feature variegated or chartreuse foliage and are ideal for adding textures and colors to the shade garden. Sedges can be deciduous, semi-evergreen, or evergreen. The following species are easy to grow in rich, moist, well-drained soil:

C. conica bears arching, evergreen to semi-evergreen leaves; variegated cultivars, such as white-edged 'Marginata', are most commonly grown.

C. morrowii is a 20-inch-tall evergreen species forming foot-wide clumps of stiff, shiny leaves.

C. oshimensis is a deciduous species forming clumps of glossy leaves. Its cultivar, 'Evergold', which has leaves with dark green edges and creamy white centers, is very popular.

C. siderosticha produces broad clumps of deciduous, strap-shaped leaves. 'Variegata', with white-margined leaves, is more often grown than the species.

Shade-Loving Perennials

To create a shade garden that's interesting to look at all summer long, plant a variety of perennials that have the winning combination of handsome foliage and long blooming seasons. Ferns also add a nice touch to a woodland garden and provide interesting texture and great foliage. You will also want to include ground covers for filling in and around other perennials, annuals, and shrubs in the shade garden. There's more to shade-tolerant ground covers than English ivy — consider any one of the ground covers listed on page 42 (see chapter 6 for detailed information on these plants).

In some cases — such as if your deck is on the north side of the house — you will be confronted with a site that is shaded by a building rather than by trees. In general, you can treat such sites just like wooded ones by filling them with shade-loving plants. Keep in mind, however, that buildings can block rain, creating dry, shady conditions, especially if overhanging eaves protect the site. In that case, deep soil preparation is a good idea, to encourage deep roots and increased drought tolerance. Use mulch to retain soil moisture. It's also wise to install soaker hoses at planting time (they can be left in place year-round) and use them to water regularly. Be sure to check for dryness and then water the area, even if the rest of the garden has received enough rainfall.

Perennials for Shade

Columbines, *Aquilegia* spp.

Bleeding hearts, *Dicentra* spp.

Epimediums, *Epimedium* spp.

Hardy geraniums, *Geranium* spp.

Hellebores, *Helleborus* spp.

Heucheras, *Heuchera* spp.

Hostas, *Hosta* spp.

Lamiums, *Lamium* spp.

Solomon's seals, *Polygonatum* spp.

Pulmonarias, Lungworts, *Pulmonaria* spp.

Tradescantias, Spiderworts, *Tradescantia* spp.

▼ A lush planting of shade-loving hostas, heucheras, and other perennials fills the beds around this ground-level deck. Hardy lilies· (*Lilium* spp.) also thrive here, since the surrounding trees cast only high, bright shade.

▲ Mass plantings of a single species of shrub help visually unify the various areas of this large deck. For a more colorful effect, use a mix of shrubs, repeating some key specimens for visual unity.

Shade-Loving Shrubs and Small Trees

Pawpaw, *Asimina triloba*

Sweetshrub, *Calycanthys floridus*

Plum yew, *Cephalotaxus harringtonia*

Dogwoods, *Cornus* spp.

Euonymus, *Euonymus* spp.

Witch hazels, *Hamamelis* spp.

Hydrangeas, *Hydrangea* spp.

Virginia sweetspire, *Itea virginica*

Rhododendrons and Azaleas, *Rhododendron* spp.

Yews, *Taxus* spp.

Hemlocks, *Tsuga* spp.

Blueberries, *Vaccinium* spp.

Viburnums, *Viburnum* spp.

Shrubs for Shade

A variety of shrubs are suitable for planting in the shade. As in a sunny yard, consider grouping shrubs around the base of the deck to hide the undercarriage or using them for privacy. If developers have cleared away the underbrush on a wooded lot (which generally means they have replaced shade plants with sun-loving lawn grass that never will grow well), you may not have many plantings to shield views of the neighbor's yard. Re-create a woodland effect and add valuable privacy by using the shade-loving shrubs listed at left (see chapter 6 for detailed information on many of these plants). Space shrubs randomly among the trees, create borders of mixed shrubs along lot lines, or plant strategic clumps designed to block a neighbor's yard.

Just as if you were planting a sunny site, be sure to pay attention to the mature height and spread of specimens you choose, and stick to plants that won't outgrow your site or need drastic annual pruning to keep them in bounds. Give plants enough space that they will not crowd the deck or one another once they are full size, or nearly so. Keep in mind that selective pruning is useful for shaping plants designed to screen your deck and yard. To encourage bushy growth, trim back branches to a node (just above where another branch or leaf emerges from the stem). To create an open, airy screen, remove branches by cutting them to the ground or back to where they are attached to the trunk or another large branch.

Deckside Theme Gardens

Whether you have a passion for a special type or species of plant or for a particular style of garden — or simply don't know where to start your design — a theme planting may be just the ticket to inspire a deckside garden. Kitchen gardens full of herbs and other edibles and plantings designed to attract butterflies or hummingbirds are popular choices, but a theme garden can be anything you want it to be. Create one that celebrates your passion for roses, hostas, dwarf conifers, or rock garden plants, for example, by displaying all your best plants in a single bed.

Other options include a garden devoted to native prairie or woodland plants, a color theme garden (all white flowers, for example), or one specially designed for your children to enjoy, perhaps with sunflowers and a bean-covered house constructed of bamboo covered with poultry wire. If your passion is water lilies, aquatic plants, and fish, a large water garden adjoining the deck may be the best choice. If you have a house that dates to a particular period, consider a garden devoted to plants of that era — Colonial or Victorian, for example. Or consider a period-style design.

▼ This small deck overlooks *Euphorbia characias* ssp. *wulenii* and a rock garden. The evergreens and rock-garden plants ensure that there's always something interesting to look at.

Kitchen Garden Favorites

Peppers, *Capsicum* spp.

Basil, *Ocimum basilicum*

Parsleys, *Petroselinum crispum*

Perennial herbs, such as chives, mints, oregano, sage, and thyme

Edible flowers, such as marigolds and nasturtiums

Ornamental salad greens, such as leaf lettuce, Swiss chard, bok choy, kale, and mustards

Vegetables, such as beans, squash, and zucchini (choose bush, not climbing, types), and compact tomato cultivars

▼ Because your deckside kitchen garden will be highly visible from both the house and the deck, include ornamental edibles, such as brightly colored lettuces, purple basil, and tasty flowers.

Kitchen Gardens

A bed filled with salad fixings, herbs, and other edibles is a natural choice for a garden close to a deck — especially one that's a convenient step or two from the kitchen. Depending on your site, you may have room for teepees covered with beans, caged cherry tomatoes, and other larger plants as well. You'll probably need a fence to keep rabbits and other animals at bay, even this close to the house. Look for an ornamental style, and if it has holes big enough to allow small animals access to your precious plants, line it with poultry wire.

The vegetables, herbs, and edible flowers described here are ideal for a deckside kitchen garden. Unless otherwise noted, all these plants need full sun. In addition, page through a seed catalog or two and you'll find many more plants to try. Leaf crops, such as mustards, spinach, red-leaved orache, bok choy, endive, escarole, and cabbages, are very attractive, as are eggplants, bush-type squashes or zucchini, beans (both bush and climbing types), peppers, and tomatoes, especially the smaller, determinate types. And don't overlook annual herbs — dill bears ferny blue-green leaves and yellow flowers; cilantro features tiny white flowers and ferny green leaves.

Basil. Green-leaved basils, such as 'Lettuce Leaf', 'Mammoth', and 'Genovese,' all bear extra-large leaves with the typical basil flavor. Also include some purple-leaved forms, such as 'Purple Ruffles' and 'Red Rubin', to bring rich, deep color to plantings. Thai basils, including 'Siam Queen', feature spicy, anise-flavored leaves plus handsome purple flowers. For a twist, consider planting lime- or lemon-flavored basils. Another good choice is 'Spicy Globe', a rounded, compact, 6- to 8-inch-tall plant with tiny, delicious leaves. 'Spicy Globe' plants remain compact without pinching and are especially attractive when used as low edging or hedge plants.

Swiss chard. A heat-tolerant leaf crop for summer, Swiss chard produces erect clumps of leaves handsome enough to mix into flower beds. 'Rhubarb' has deep green leaves accented by scarlet stalks and veins, while 'Bright Lights' produces stunning clumps of leaves with yellow, red, rose, gold, or white stems and veins.

Lettuces. Mixed plantings of lettuces — with flat and ruffled leaves and a range of colors from green to red — are really quite beautiful. Most are strictly spring or fall crops; they abhor hot weather. Look for slow-bolting cultivars, such as 'Red Sails', to grow in warmer weather.

Kales. Most kales feature attractive (and nutritious) foliage. They usually have ruffled, blue-green leaves, but consider growing magenta-leaved 'Redbor'. 'Red Russian' bears gray-green, oak-leaf-shaped foliage with red to purple leaves and stems. Heat-tolerant 'Toscano' produces clumps of dramatic-looking dark green, strap-shaped leaves that are savoyed or blistered.

Peppers. A number of pepper cultivars, both sweet and hot, have been developed strictly as ornamentals. The red, purple, chocolate brown, yellow, orange, or green fruits may point up or hang down. They usually ripen through several colors, thus creating a really nice show on a single plant. If you like hot peppers, plant the degree of "heat" you prefer. Most ornamental cultivars are very hot, but 'Sweet Pickle' is an ornamental selection that features sweet fruit. For pretty leaves, plant 'Tri-Fetti', also sold as 'Variegata', with purple fruits and green leaves blotched with cream and purple or 'Pretty in Purple', with purple leaves and fruits that ripen from purple to pale orange to scarlet.

Parsleys. Both flat- and curly-leaved parsleys have dark green leaves that are especially nice when contrasted with fine-textured basils or edible-flowered marigolds such as 'Lemon Gem'. Curly-leaved types form low mounds; flat-leaved ones grow in taller clumps.

Perennial herbs. Don't forget a convenient spot near the deck for perennial culinary herbs, such as oreganos, thymes, chives, and sages. All are decidedly ornamental.

Edible flowers. Edible flowers add color to salads and other dishes and make a pretty garnish. For great flavor as well, plant nasturtium *(Tropaeolum majus),* with spicy-tasting flowers, foliage, and stems; marigolds *(Tagetes* spp.); and herbs, including basils, lavenders, chives, and thymes.

Kitchen Garden Care

A sunny site with deeply prepared, well-drained soil is best for a kitchen garden. Work in plenty of organic matter, as you would for any vegetable garden. Unlike a conventional vegetable garden, though, where it doesn't really matter if plants look a bit ragged toward the end of their cycles, you'll want those in a kitchen garden near the deck to look their best. Here are some tips to give these plants some extra TLC:

- Pinch basils and other bushy herbs frequently to keep them compact and attractive — regular harvesting has the same effect.
- Remove damaged leaves as soon as they appear.
- Water and feed regularly.
- Remove crops that are nearing the end of their cycles and replace them with new plants. For instance, as temperatures warm in early summer, harvest lettuce plants and fill the space with more heat-tolerant edibles.

Note: If you have a larger vegetable garden elsewhere, you may want to keep extra plants coming along in a corner of the main plot that you can pop into the kitchen garden whenever there's enough space. Either keep them in pots sunk into the soil or grow them in rows and then transplant. Think in terms of crop rotation and companion planting when deciding what to add. A good reference book on vegetable or herb gardening will offer lots of suggestions.

Perennials, Biennials, and Bulbs for Hummingbirds

Columbines, *Aquilegia* spp.

Montbretias, *Crocosmia* spp.

Pinks, Carnations, *Dianthus* spp.

Foxgloves, *Digitalis* spp.

Daylilies, *Hemerocallis* spp.

Coralbells, *Heuchera* spp.

Hibiscus, *Hibiscus* spp.

Hostas, Plantain lilies, *Hosta* spp.

Red-hot pokers, *Kniphofia* spp.

Gayfeathers, Blazing stars, *Liatris* spp.

Lilies, *Lilium* spp.

Cardinal flower, *Lobelia cardinalis*

Spider lilies, Magic lilies, *Lycoris* spp.

Bee balm, *Monarda didyma*

Beardtongues, *Penstemon* spp.

Phlox, *Phlox* spp.

Sages, *Salvia* spp.

Bouncing bet, *Saponaria officinalis*

Pincushion flower, *Scabiosa caucasica*

Catchflies, Campions, *Silene virginica* and *S. regia*

Annuals for Hummingbirds

Snapdragons, *Antirrhinum majus*

Wax begonias, *Begonia* x *semperflorens* hybrids

Spider flower, *Cleome hasslerana*

Larkspurs, *Consolida* spp.

Dahlias, *Dahlia* hybrids

Sweet William, *Dianthus barbatus*

Four-o'clock, *Mirabilis jalapa*

Flowering tobaccos, *Nicotiana* spp.

Zonal geraniums, *Pelargonium* spp.

Egyptian star cluster, *Pentas lanceolata*

Petunias, *Petunia* x *hybrida*

Marigolds, *Tagetes* spp.

Mexican sunflower, *Tithonia rotundifolia*

Garden verbenas, *Verbena* spp.

Zinnias, *Zinnia* spp.

Hummingbird Gardens

There's no doubt that hummingbirds add a magical touch to the garden as they zip from flower to flower. These spectacular fliers hover miraculously in midair as they sip nectar, are able to back up in mid-flight as they move among flowers, and can speed away at up to 60 miles per hour.

Bright red and orange flowers that have a tubular shape attract hummers like magnets. I like to think of them as "hummingbird billboards." Fortunately, although red and orange flowers are a good place to start, don't despair if your garden color scheme leans toward other hues. Watch carefully and you'll see hummingbirds visiting pink columbines, lavender lilacs, white hostas, and many other flowers as well.

Plant the colors that you like, either in a specially designed hummingbird patch or mixed throughout the garden. In fact, scattering hummingbird plants probably attracts more individual birds, as they guard feeding and nesting territories during the summer. In addition to nectar, which makes up a large part of their diet, hummingbirds eat a variety of insects, including aphids, mosquitoes, flying ants, leafhoppers, and flies.

Having lots of flowers is one key to success — hummers need to feed almost constantly during the daytime. (They store food overnight in their crops, and in cool weather actually enter a state of dormancy, called torpor, to conserve food.) For best results, try to plan a progression of blooms starting in late spring or early summer and continuing through late summer or early fall. Gardeners in the warmest part of the country may have hummingbirds all year long, but in most areas the birds migrate and arrive in spring or

Attracting Birds and Other Wildlife

With just a little effort, you can encourage all kinds of birds and other wildlife to visit your deck. Among our favorite summer visitors are dragonflies, which cruise up from the spring pond, and a toad that hops up the steps in the evening to hunt under the low-level lights that illuminate the walkway on the deck.

From spring to fall, we hang bird feeders from the porch and arbor so we can enjoy these visitors close at hand. When positioning feeders, keep in mind that tracked-in seed hulls can be a problem if they fall on the deck proper. Suet feeders attract woodpeckers and a variety of other birds. Mount them on the posts of an arbor or on a nearby tree.

A birdbath set among container plantings will satisfy a variety of species. Be prepared to wash it out and provide fresh water daily. A slowly dripping "fountain" makes water especially appealing, and you can buy fixtures that spray or drip water. (Hummingbirds actually bathe on the wing by flying through a spray of water.) Low-voltage heaters are available, making it possible to provide fresh water for birds all winter long.

early summer. Ask a local wild-bird center or birding club when they will be in your area. In the eastern United States, gardeners see only ruby-throated hummingbirds, but eight or more species visit gardens in the western part of the country.

Other garden features hummingbirds enjoy include a mix of sun and shade: The flowers they feed on grow in full sun, but shady sites are best for nesting. They stick their tiny, cup-shaped nests together with spiderwebs, so an organic garden with a rich population of spiders is ideal. Hummers are also attracted to birdbaths and other water features. They especially appreciate fountains that offer a fine mist or spray.

To attract hummingbirds to your deckside beds, find room for some or all of the plants listed on page 48 and at right. Unless otherwise noted, select a site in full sun or light shade and average-to-rich, well-drained soil. In addition to the annuals listed here, several popular vines also attract hummingbirds. (See Annual and Tender Perennial Vines on page 102 and chapter 6 for information on those plants.)

Woody Trees, Shrubs, and Vines for Hummingbirds

Red buckeye, *Aesculus pavia*

Butterfly bushes, *Buddleia* spp.

Trumpet vines, *Campsis radicans* spp.

Honeysuckles, *Lonicera* spp.

Crabapples, Apples, *Malus* spp.

Rhododendrons, Azaleas, *Rhododendron* spp.

Lilacs, *Syringa* spp.

Old-fashioned weigela, *Weigela florida*

▼ A collection of lilies (*Lilium* spp.) adjoining this deck is guaranteed to draw in hummingbirds, which also visit the pots of zonal geraniums on the deck steps.

Butterfly Garden Favorites

**Aster Family
(Asteraceae)**

New England aster, *Aster novae-angliae*

New York aster, *A. novae-beglii*

Coreopsis, *Coreopsis* spp.

Cosmos, *Cosmos* spp.

Purple coneflowers, *Echinacea* spp.

Fleabanes, *Erigeron* spp.

Blanket flowers, *Gaillardia* spp.

Sneezeweed, *Helenium autumnale*

Sunflowers, *Helianthus* spp.

Oxeye, *Heliopsis helianthoides*

Ox-eye daisy, *Leucanthemum vulgare*

Shasta daisy, *Leucanthemum x superbum*

Rudbeckias, *Rudbeckia* spp.

Marigolds, *Tagetes* spp.

Mexican sunflower, *Tithonia rotundifolia*

Zinnias, *Zinnia* spp.

**Buddleia Family
(Loganiaceae)**

Butterfly bush, *Buddleia davidii*

**Milkweed Family
(Asclepiadaceae)**

Bloodflower, *Asclepias curassavica*

Swamp milkweed, *A. incarnata*

Butterfly weed, *A. tuberosa*

**Mint Family
(Lamiaceae)**

Hyssops, *Agastache* spp.

Lavenders, *Lavandula* spp.

Mints, *Mentha* spp.

Bee balms, *Monarda* spp.

Catnips and Catmints, *Nepeta* spp.

Rosemary, *Rosmarinus officinalis*

Sages, *Salvia* spp.

Thymes, *Thymus* spp.

Butterfly Gardens

Hanging over the deck railing to watch butterflies as they flit over the garden is one of our favorite summertime activities. Butterflies are endlessly fascinating, like flowers in flight, and we never tire of watching them. By surrounding our deck with perennials and annuals that attract them, we can enjoy them up close.

Butterflies visit thousands of different plants, and you don't have to include one of each to attract them to your garden. In fact, when planning a butterfly garden, it's easiest to think about a few plant families that are of prime importance instead of individual species of perennials or annuals. The major plant families that attract butterflies are discussed on these two pages, and you'll also find lists of some specific species to consider in the margins. Most of these plants thrive in full sun with average-to-rich, well-drained soil (see chapter 6 for detailed information on many of these plants).

Parsley Family (Apiaceae). The larvae of several species of swallowtails feed on the foliage of Apiaceae plants, including parsley, carrots, dill, and fennel. When planning your herb or vegetable garden, plant enough of these crops to share. Use floating row covers to protect the plants you want for harvesting. Another option is to gently move larvae from "your" plants to those in the butterfly planting.

Milkweed Family (Asclepiadaceae). Of the nearly 350 genera in the milkweed family, one stands out as a must for the butterfly garden: *Asclepias*. Butterfly weed *(A. tuberosa)*, the best known of the milkweeds, is vital for the larvae of monarch butterflies. Adults of other species that visit milkweed flowers for nectar include swallowtails, sulfurs, fritillaries, painted ladies, viceroys, skippers, and question marks. Another good choice is swamp milkweed *(A. incarnata)*, which, despite its common name, grows in average, evenly moist soil but survives in dry conditions. The annual bloodflower *(A. currassavica)* is another butterfly favorite.

Aster Family (Asteraceae). Aster family plants attract many species of adult butterflies, including sulfurs, question marks, painted ladies, skippers, buckeyes, and fritillaries. Asters aren't particularly important to butterfly larvae, although painted ladies and pearly crescentspots lay their eggs on aster-family plants. As a bonus, hummingbirds also visit many asters looking for nectar, and these plants provide seeds for songbirds in winter, too.

Mustard Family (Brassicaceae). Mustard family plants, such as basket-of-gold, sea kale, wallflowers, dame's rocket, and sweet alyssum, lure several species of whites and long-tailed skippers. However, this also includes the cabbage white butterfly, a pest of cabbages, broccoli, cauliflower, and kale. Keep the adults off your vegetable crops with floating row covers, but enjoy them in the butterfly garden.

Pea Family (Fabaceae). Peas, clovers, and other legumes are important plants for attracting adult butterflies, as well as for feeding their larvae.

Mint Family (Lamiaceae). In addition to attracting a wide range of butterflies, mints are very popular with beneficial insects.

Buddleia Family (Loganiaceae). One of the plants in this little-known family is a prime choice for butterflies — butterfly bush, or summer lilac *(Buddleia davidii)*. As its name suggests, it produces trusses of small trumpet-shaped flowers that resemble lilacs. Plants bloom from midsummer to fall, especially if they are deadheaded.

Violet Family (Violaceae). These dainty garden flowers attract several species of fritillaries, which use them to feed their larvae, as well as adult spring azures, which visit the flowers for nectar.

◀ This informal, cottage-style planting is guaranteed to attract a wide range of butterflies.

Mustard Family (Brassicaceae)

Basket-of-gold, *Aurinia saxatilis*

Wallflowers, *Cherianthus* spp.

Sea kale, *Crambe maritima*

Dame's rocket, *Hesperis matronalis*

Sweet alyssum, *Lobularia maritima*

Parsley Family (Apiaceae)

Dill, *Anethum graveolens*

Queen Anne's lace, *Daucus carota*

Carrot, *Daucus carota* var. *sativus*

Fennel, *Foeniculum vulgare*

Wild parsnip, *Pastinaca sativa*

Parsley, *Petroselinum crispum*

Pea Family (Fabaceae)

False indigos, *Amorpha* spp.

Sennas, *Cassia* spp.

Redbuds, *Cercis* spp.

Crown vetch, *Coronilla varia*

Indigos, *Indigofera* spp.

Bush clovers, *Lespedeza* spp.

Lupines, *Lupinus* spp.

Alfalfa, *Medicago sativa* (for nectar)

Clovers, *Melilotus* spp. and *Trifolium* spp. (for nectar)

Scarlet runner beans, *Phaseolus coccineus*

Mesquites, *Prosopis* spp.

Locusts, *Robinia* spp.

Broad beans, *Vicia faba*

Wisterias, *Wisteria* spp.

Violet Family (Violaceae)

Canada violet, *Viola canadensis*

Horned violet, *V. cornuta*

Sweet violet, *V. odorata*

Johnny-jump-ups, *V. tricolor*

Other Annuals and Tender Perennials for Butterflies

Snapdragons, *Antirrhinum* spp.*

Spider flower, *Cleome hasslerana**

Sweet William, *Dianthus barbatus**

Cherry pie, *Heliotropium arborescens*

Lantanas, *Lantana* spp.

Four-o'clock, *Mirabilis jalapa**

Flowering tobacco, *Nicotiana alata**

Petunias, *Petunia* spp.*

Other Perennials for Butterflies

Yarrows, *Achillea* spp.

Hardy ageratum, *Ageratum houstonianum*

Hollyhock, *Alcea rosea**

Onions, Garlics, *Allium* spp.

Astilbes, *Astilbe* spp.

Bellflowers, *Campanula* spp.

Cornflowers, *Centaurea* spp.

Red valerian, *Centranthus ruber*

Pinks, *Dianthus* spp.*

Joe-pye weeds, *Eupatorium* spp.

Queen-of-the-prairies, *Filipendula* spp.

Hardy geraniums, *Geranium* spp.

Daylilies, *Hemerocallis* spp.*

Hibiscus, *Hibiscus* spp.*

Gayfeathers, *Liatris* spp.

Sea lavenders, *Limonium* spp.

Cardinal flowers, Lobelias, *Lobelia* spp.*

Penstemons, *Penstemon* spp.*

Phlox, *Phlox* spp.*

Sweet scabious, *Scabiosa* spp.

Sedums, *Sedum* spp., especially *S. spectabile*

Goldenrods, *Solidago* spp.

Meadow rues, *Thalictrum* spp.

Ironweeds, *Vernonia* spp.

Yuccas, Adam's needles, *Yucca* spp.

*Also attract hummingbirds

Food for Butterfly Babies

To make butterflies really happy in your yard, you have to provide food for their babies, or caterpillars, as well as nectar for the adults. Here are some tips on what will attract them:

• Leave a weedy patch in your yard or create a meadow garden. Painted lady larvae feed on burdock (*Arctium lappa*) as well as asters, for example, and several species of butterflies visit plantains (*Plantago* spp.). Other plants that attract butterflies are nettles (*Urtica* spp.), milkweeds (*Asclepias* spp.), thistles (*Cirsium* spp.), docks (*Rumex* spp.), Queen Anne's lace (*Daucus carota*), and beggar-ticks (*Bidens* spp.).

• Skippers visit many species of grasses and sedges, and grasses offer protected hideouts for many species.

• Larvae of some swallowtails prefer the foliage of carrots, dill, parsley, and other members of the parsley family (Apiaceae). Other swallowtails are more finicky: Pipevine swallowtails require Dutchman's pipes (*Aristolochia* spp.) for their larvae, while zebra swallowtails need pawpaws (*Asimina* spp.).

• Other good plants for butterfly larvae are passionflowers (*Passiflora* spp.), willows (*Salix* spp.), poplars (*Populus* spp.), cherries and plums (*Prunus* spp.), lilacs (*Syringa* spp.), dogwoods (*Cornus* spp.), and sycamores (*Platanus* spp.).

More Butterfly Plants

Butterflies don't have degrees in botany, of course, and they'll visit a wide range of flowers in search of nectar — not just ones in the families listed on pages 50 and 51. At left are more flowers to consider for your butterfly garden. Many also attract hummingbirds; those that do are marked with an asterisk (*).

Up Close and Personal

If you're serious about learning to recognize the different species, buy a butterfly field guide and keep it handy. For really "up close and personal" observation, invest in a pair of binoculars that have as short a minimum focal length as possible. Butterfly enthusiasts commonly prefer "pocket" binoculars, and models are available that focus on objects as close as 6 feet. When buying, ask about and test for this feature, as models vary. My best birding binoculars focus on objects no closer than 18 feet away, but I also have a pair of zoom binoculars, which are still fine for birding, that focus on objects as close as 9 feet. Still, closer would be better!

Fragrance Gardens

Plants that feature aromatic foliage and/or flowers add another dimension to deckside plantings. Fragrant flowers are especially enjoyable early in the evening, when their perfume is carried on cooling, slightly humid air. Because scent lingers longest in still air, you may want to install trellises or other windbreaks if your deck is located in a breezy site. To get the most from fragrant plants, plant them along the steps leading from the deck to your garden. Most foliage releases its fragrance when brushed against or crushed, and keeping such plants where you pass by makes it easier to enjoy their scent.

Summer and fall are best for spending time out on the deck, so the suggestions on pages 54 and 55 emphasize plants that bloom during those seasons (see chapter 6 for detailed information on many of these plants). You'll want to include fragrant plants in containers on the deck (see page 80 in chapter 3) as well as vines with scented flowers.

▼ A rustic arbor festooned with roses and *Clematis montana* lends a romantic touch to this deck. In addition to providing welcome shade, the arbor reduces the flow of air and thus encourages scents to linger.

Fragrant Lilies

Candidum Hybrid lilies, particularly
  Madonna lily, *Lilium candidum*

Longiflorum Hybrid lilies, including Easter
  lilies, *Lilium longiflorum*

Oriental Hybrid lilies

Species lilies, such as Goldband lily,
  L. auratum; Regal lily, *L. regale;*
  and Japanese lily, *L. speciosum*

Trumpet and Aurelian Hybrid lilies

Fragrant Roses

Rugosa

'Apart'

'Blanc Double de Coubert'

'Carefree Beauty'

'Country Dancer'

'Dart's Dash'

Explorer series: 'Charles Albanel',
  'David Thompson', 'Henry Hudson'

'Foxi Pavement'

'Hawkeye Belle'

'Prairie Flower'

Others

Rosa alba

Apothecary's rose, *Rosa gallica* var. *officinalis*

'Quatre Saisons'

Fragrant Perennials and Herbs

Hyssops, *Agastache* spp.

Lavender, *Lavandula angustifolia*

Catmints, *Nepeta* spp.

Oregano, *Oreganum vulgare*

Russian sage, *Perovskia atriplicifolia*

Thymes, *Thymus* spp.

Fragrant Summer-Blooming Shrubs

Sweetshrub, Carolina allspice,
  Calycanthys floridus

Summersweet, Sweet pepperbush
  Clethra alnifolia

Lilacs, especially *Syringa pubescens* ssp.
  patula 'Miss Kim'

Lilies. When it comes to fragrance, true lilies (*Lilium* spp.) have few rivals. I tuck them toward the back of the deck bed, near the railings, so I can enjoy their scent to its fullest. Siting these bulbs toward the back has another advantage: Lilies aren't too attractive after they've finished flowering, and planting them among perennials and low shrubs will hide their yellowing foliage as they go dormant. (Be sure to leave plants standing until their leaves turn completely yellow, because they are manufacturing food to fuel next year's flowers. Then cut the plants to the ground.) Give lilies full sun and rich, well-drained soil that is deeply prepared. When selecting lilies, choose cultivars from more than one of the hybrid groups, and look for plants that bloom at different times. The plants in the list at left are the most fragrant.

Roses. Don't overlook the legendary fragrance of roses when selecting aromatic plants for a deck garden. It's important to choose carefully, however, as not all roses are scented. In addition, by midsummer disease-prone roses, such as most hybrid teas, are rendered quite unappealing by blackspot and other problems unless they are sprayed regularly. It's best to select plants with foliage that remains relatively attractive all summer. All of the fragrant roses listed at left are disease resistant and almost disease-free with just a minimum of attention.

Can't be without high-maintenance hybrid tea and grandiflora roses? By all means, include them. Many are not fragrant, so read their descriptions and, if possible, sniff before you buy. Disease resistance varies, too. Because roses tend to lose their lower leaves, underplant them with fragrant-leaved perennials, such as catmints (*Nepeta* spp.) and lavender (*Lavandula angustifolia*), to cover up their bare "ankles." (For more information on growing and using roses, see Deckside Roses on pages 106 to 111.)

Perennials and herbs. Peonies (*Paeonia* spp.) and pinks (*Dianthus* spp.) come to mind first when I think of fragrant perennials, but many other popular plants also fit the bill. Although most daylilies grown today have unscented flowers, the classic yellow-flowered cultivar 'Hyperion' is an exception. Fragrant species of daylilies include citron daylily (*Hemerocallis citrina*) and lemon lily (*H. lilioasphodelus*). For spots in light shade, look to August lily (*Hosta plantaginea*) for summer fragrance. It bears lemony-scented white blooms that are especially fragrant in the evening. See Shade-Loving Perennials on page 43 for other fragrant perennials.

Fragrant-flowered shrubs. Summertime is the main season to enjoy the deck, so when planning your deckscape, it's worth looking beyond popular spring-blooming shrubs. That said, if you spend a good deal of time on your deck in late winter or early spring, you may want to add fragrant, early-blooming plants to the mix, including winter hazel (*Corylopsis pauciflora*), winter honeysuckle (*Lonicera fragrantissima*), and winter jasmine (*Jasminum nudiflorum*). Witch hazels (*Hamamelis* spp.) feature fragrant late-winter to early-spring flowers and spectacular fall foliage.

Hardy spring bulbs. Although you may not be spending much time outdoors on your deck in early spring, that's no reason not to plant fragrant spring bulbs alongside it. Hyacinths *(Hyacinthus orientalis)* are the most highly scented of the hardy bulbs, but many daffodils and tulips are fragrant as well. Catalog descriptions and signs accompanying bulb displays will call attention to this characteristic.

Annuals. Several annuals bear flowers worth planting for their fragrance alone. Mignonette *(Reseda odorata)* tops the list. Its insignificant greenish and brownish flowers aren't much to look at, but their sweet scent is quite addictive. If you're choosing mignonette for its aroma, avoid newer hybrids with showier blooms; they aren't as fragrant as the species. See Evening Gardens on pages 56 and 57 for more suggestions.

All of the plants listed at right will add scent and color to summer plantings. (You'll find information on many of them in chapter 6.)

Fragrant Bulbs
Spring
Scotch crocus, *Crocus chrysanthus*
Snowdrops, *Galanthus* spp.
Hyacinth, *Hyacinthus orientalis*
Snowflake, *Leucojum vernum*
Grape hyacinth, *Muscari armeniacum*

Summer
Belladonna lily, *Amaryllis belladonna*
Crinums, *Crinum* spp.
Summer hyacinth, *Galtonia candicans*
Peruvian daffodils, *Hymenocallis* spp.
Tuberose, *Polianthes tuberosa*

Fragrant Annuals
Heliotrope, *Heliotropium arborescens*
Moonflower, *Ipomoea alba*
Stocks, *Matthiola incana* spp.
Four-o'clock, *Mirabilis jalapa*
Flowering tobaccos, *Nicotiana* spp.
Mignonette, *Reseda odorata*

◄ Plant roses and other fragrant shrubs close to sitting areas where they'll scent the air.

Aromatic Annuals and Tender Perennials

Brugmansias, Angel's trumpets, *Brugmansia* spp.

Jessamines, *Cestrum* spp.

Datura, Angel's trumpet, *Datura metel,* especially 'Evening Fragrance'

Heliotrope, *Heliotropium arborescens,* especially 'Alba'

Sweet rocket, *Hesperis matronalis, H. matronalis* var. *albiflora*

Stocks, *Matthiola incana,* especially night-scented stock, *M. longipetala*

Four-o'clock, *Mirabilis jalapa*

Flowering tobaccos, *Nicotiana alata,* sometimes called Jasmine tobacco; *N.* x *sanderae* 'Fragrant Cloud'; and *N. sylvestris*

Aromatic Bulbs

Gladiolas, *Gladiolus callianthus* 'Murieliae' and *G. tristis*

Lilies, *Lilium* spp., such as Madonna lily, *Lilium candidum*; White-flowered hybrids 'Bright Star' and 'Casa Blanca'; White regal lily, *Lilium regale* 'Album'; and White Japanese lily, *L. speciosum* 'Album'

Aromatic Shrubs

Mock oranges, *Philadelphus* spp.

Sweet azalea, *Rhododendron arborescens*

Pontic azalea, *R. luteum*

Pinxterbloom azalea, *R. periclymenoides*

Roseshell azalea, *R. prinophyllum*

Royal azalea, *R. schlippenbachii*

Northern Lights series rhododendrons (including 'Golden Lights', 'Rosy Lights', and Spicy Lights')

Evening Gardens

Enjoyment of your deck and garden shouldn't end at sundowns as the early evening and twilight hours of a summer's day are among the loveliest times to sit outside. Especially if you are able to enjoy the garden only after hours on weekdays, consider planting an evening garden. In any case, be sure to include plants alongside your deck that offer features to enjoy during the early evening. The suggestions here emphasize plants that bloom during summer and fall, as decks are used the most during those seasons. Surround your deck with some of them, and you may be tempted to throw a party to celebrate flowers in moonlight.

As surprising as it may seem, there are lots of plants that are at their best when the sun goes down. In fact, many of the annuals, perennials, and shrubs listed on these two pages become aromatic only in the late afternoon and evening. Under the hot sun, they may not be as noticeable to the nose, but step out onto your deck as the day begins to cool, and their fragrance suddenly fills the air. (For plants that are fragrant regardless of the time of day, see Fragrance Gardens on page 53.)

Your first impulse may be to buy one of each plant mentioned here, but let me assure you that moderation is in order. That's because a bed filled with every night-scented plant you can lay your hands on may end up smelling more like a hodgepodge than a carefully chosen bouquet. Instead, consider good-sized clumps of a few plants so you can enjoy their individual scents.

Although flowers that are fragrant at night top the list for evening gardens, plants with white and other pale-colored blossoms are striking under moonlight even if they have no scent. By making the right selections beginning with those listed on page 57, it's possible to create a garden that glistens in the evening, especially under a full moon. To create an effective moonlight planting, select flowers for their fragrance and plant in clumps or drifts. While white flowers will show up regardless of where you plant them, arranging them in drifts or clumps is most effective. You can repeat clumps down the length of the flower bed to create a sinuous drift that winds through the garden.

◀ This natural planting of perennials and wildflowers includes daisies and *Coreopisis* 'Sunray' that continue to stand out well into the evening.

White Perennials for Evening

White-flowered purple coneflowers, *Echinacea purpurea* 'White Swan' and 'White Lustre'

August lily, *Hosta plantaginea*

White-flowered Oriental poppies, *Papaver orientale* 'Black and White' and 'Perry's White'

Phlox, *Phlox divaricata* 'Fuller's White', *P. maculata* 'Omega' and 'Miss Lingard', and *P. paniculata* 'David'

Balloon flowers, *Platycodon grandiflorus* f. *albus* and 'Shell Pink'

White Annuals for Evening

Spider flower, *Cleome hasslerana* 'Helen Campbell'

Cosmos, *Cosmos* 'Purity' and 'Sonata White'

Sunflower, *Helianthus annuus* 'Italian White'

Impatiens, *Impatiens* spp. (any white-flowered cultivars)

Lavatera, tree mallow, *Lavatera trimestris* 'Mont Blanc'

Nigella, fennel flower, *Nigella damascena* 'Miss Jekyll Alba'

Petunias, *Petunia* spp. (any white-flowered cultivars)

CHAPTER THREE

Container
Gardening

A deck filled to overflowing with plant-packed containers has a special feeling of abundance — a warm and welcoming allure that is sure to draw you outdoors. Container gardens also strengthen the link between the house and the garden, helping transform a deck into a gardenlike outdoor living space.

Container gardens offer a wonderful way to express yourself, whether you decide to go rustic with wooden tubs and chipped pots or formal with terra-cotta urns. When choosing containers as well as the plants to fill them, think in terms of expressing your personal style by using colors, textures, plants, and containers that appeal to you. Look at your interior decorating style for clues, but don't be afraid to experiment. After all, it's easy to change a container garden if you aren't happy with it. Either replace a plant or two and try something else or move everything to the garden and start over completely. You can keep notes in a garden diary about what worked and what didn't, or just have fun and try something new each year.

Container gardens offer an especially great opportunity for learning about color and developing your design sense. Use them to try out new combinations of foliage and flowers and see what works for you and what doesn't.

Choosing Containers

These days, gardeners can choose from a wide range of container materials and styles. Cost, weight, availability, size, and winter care are factors to consider when selecting containers for your deck. Whatever you decide to use, make sure every container has an adequate drainage hole in the bottom.

While a formal design features matching containers, for a more casual and informal look, choose a mix of containers in various sizes and styles that you find appealing. For example, to complement my cottage-style garden, I settled on a look that's halfway between. I invested in several very large matching containers made of polyurethane foam that look like terra-cotta but weigh much less — a bonus because of their size. These set the overall style on the deck. Because the plant combinations are different in all the containers, the large matching pots create a unifying element in the overall design. In addition, I've grouped the large containers with other pots in many shapes and sizes. Most of those are terra-cotta; the others are harmonious natural shades, such as browns and tans. As a result, the containers complement and highlight the plants inside them.

Sizes, Styles, and Materials

As far as I'm concerned, when it comes to containers, the larger the better. Group several large ones and you instantly have a gardenlike feel because of the masses of plants they can accommodate. From a design standpoint, large containers are also in scale with most decks, especially when you cluster them. In spots where a few small pots of plants would seem lost, large, plant-packed containers make a statement that can't be overlooked.

There is another, purely practical reason I concentrate on using large pots: They're easier to care for than groups of many small ones, simply because they need watering less often. Although this may not be a factor in areas with cool, rainy summers, it is an important consideration in regions where heat and humidity are facts of life. Even here in eastern Pennsylvania (Zone 6), in the hottest months of summer, smaller pots need at least daily watering; during hot summers and in hotter areas, they often need watering twice a day. On the other hand, plants in tubs and large containers usually grow just fine when soaked thoroughly every other day or so, even in very hot weather. That's a much easier schedule to accommodate, especially if you work away from home and can't just pop outdoors to

▼ For a gardenlike feel, cluster several large containers. This showy group, which features maiden grass, Hawaiian hibiscus, licorice plant, verbena, and scaevola, also serves to mark the main path to the deck — a good use of containers.

revive a plant that's flagging. (See Keeping Pots Watered on pages 68 and 69 for more suggestions on how to manage watering needs.)

Terra-cotta. Made of fired clay, terra-cotta containers are a warm, orangy brown color that is very effective for setting off plant foliage. Terra-cotta containers are porous — they both absorb and release moisture through their sides. For this reason, they dry out more quickly than do nonporous containers, but they "breathe," and many gardeners wouldn't plant in anything else. Large terra-cotta containers are quite heavy, even without soil, so decide where you want to display them before you fill and plant them. If they will be home to very tall plants, avoid placing them in windy spots, because they can blow over and break. If you need to, tie the trunk of a standard or the top of the pot itself to a deck railing.

Caring for Terra-Cotta Pots over Winter

Because terra-cotta pots absorb water, they crack when they freeze. Therefore, it's best to store them indoors over winter. Here are some options for their care:

- After the first hard frost, dump the soil and remaining plants onto the compost pile and store the pots indoors. They don't need to be in a heated room (I store mine in an unheated garage); they just need to be protected from absorbing moisture, which will create cracks.
- To store them outdoors, empty the soil out of terra-cotta pots and turn them upside down on wooden slats, so that rain drains away immediately. Or wrap the emptied pots in burlap, then cover them with black plastic.
- Move the pots to a frost-free spot and leave them filled with soil. As long as they don't freeze, and the soil is dry, they'll be just fine.

Glazed clay. Containers made of glazed clay have long been available for indoor use. Now garden centers offer some marked frost or weather resistant. These reportedly can be left outdoors year-round. Although I've seen some really tempting ones, I tend not to be too experimental when it comes to risking a container outdoors, so I take glazed clay pots indoors over winter. If you want to try leaving them out, set them up off the ground so they don't sit in water, and use a fairly fast-draining soil mix to minimize water retention.

▲ These low containers overflowing with a mix of nasturtiums, verbena, and creeping zinnias (*Sanvitalia procumbens*) are a perfect accent for the steps of a deck.

Plastic and polyethylene. Stylish, high-quality polyethylene containers come in all the shapes, sizes, and styles once offered only in stone. Many types of plastic urns and pots also have decorative sculpted exteriors. Furthermore, while plastic once meant pots in shades of green, black, brown, or white — or an occasional garish selection of colors that could overwhelm any plant combination — today, polyethylene containers come in realistic-looking shades that imitate terra-cotta, stone, and other earth tones. Polyethylene containers are also lightweight, durable, and weather resistant. Because you can leave them outdoors over winter without danger of cracking, they're

---

Quick-and-Easy Pot Covers

Here's an inexpensive way to make large black polyethylene pots attractive enough to use on a deck. These pot covers can be slipped over pots that are about 19 inches in diameter. If you want to cover larger or smaller pots, adjust the dimensions. This project makes two sleeves from a single section of fence.

Materials
- 1 section 4' x 8' privacy fence
- 2 sawhorses
- Ruler
- Chalk line
- 2 8' pieces 1x3 or 2x3 wooden fence rails
- Box of 1" construction screws
- Drill
- Electric screwdriver
- Circular saw
- Miter saw (optional)
- Hammer and nails (optional)
- Stain or paint (optional)

1. Place the fence on sawhorses, with the pickets facing down and the two fence rails in view.

2. Use a ruler to decide the height of the pot sleeves. They should be about 4 inches taller than the pot. Measure up from the bottom of the fence for a sleeve with a flat top, from the top of the fence down for a cover with decorative pickets. Strike two chalk lines across the back of the pickets to mark these measurements.

3. Each fence section has one rail that runs across the pickets. Attach a second rail at a proportional distance from the original one, using construction screws long enough to go through the rail and solidly into the pickets. Drill pilot holes for each screw, then use an electric screwdriver to insert one screw per picket. Be very careful not to drive the screws in so far that they come out the front of the picket.

4. Decide how wide the pot sleeves should be. You need to use a width that will yield four equal sections of fence (each side of the sleeve must have the same number of pickets). For instance, my 8-foot fence had 27 pickets and the sleeve width required six on each side, which came to 24 pickets in all.

5. Mark the width on the fence rails between pickets, making four equal sections out of the fence. Set the circular saw to the depth of the fence rails, and trim four full-length sections of pickets, cutting only the rails.

6. Cut along the chalk lines that you made in step 2, and you have created eight sides for pot sleeves (plus some bonus kindling wood).

7. Cut off 1½ inches of the rail on each end of the pot sleeve sides, or miter-cut the rail ends. Match the corners and screw or nail the sides together through the end pickets.

8. Stain or paint the pot covers, or leave them natural if you prefer.

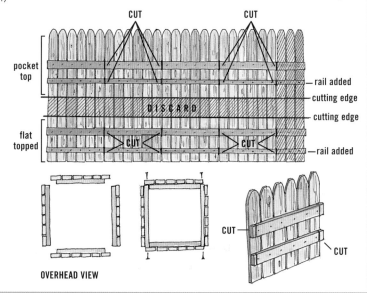

OVERHEAD VIEW

---

useful for adding interest to the deck in the colder months, not just during the growing season.

Cast stone. Containers made of cast stone and/or cement are dense, durable, and much more difficult to break than those made of terra-cotta. They come in an array of shapes and sizes, from troughs for alpine plants to huge urns for specimen shrubs. Those with sculpted exteriors can be handsome and imposing landscape elements. However, cast-stone pots are heavy, so consider the weight on your deck if you're planning a collection of them. Also, pick a fairly permanent site before you fill and plant — the larger ones can be very hard to move.

Although cast-stone containers can be left outdoors year-round, they may crack, especially if filled with soil. Unless you are using ones designed for year-round outdoor use, such as troughs for growing alpine plants, for absolute safety empty them and store them indoors as you would terra-cotta containers. If you decide to leave them outdoors, either remove or dry out the soil, then wrap them in burlap and black plastic to keep them dry. Containers that are not filled with soil can be set up off the ground and turned upside down for outdoor storage. Set troughs designed for outdoor use on "pot feet" or other low supports to keep them from sitting in water over winter.

Wood. Square planters, half whiskey barrels, and window boxes are three commonly available options for this popular type of container. You can leave wood containers outdoors year-round, and actually build them right into the structure of a

▶ Top right: *Solenostemon scutellaroides* 'Gold Bound' and *Pelargonium hortorum* 'Stadt Bern' form a brilliant mound of color in this cast-stone container. A vertical tuft of New Zealand flax (*Phormium cookianum hookeri* 'Tricolor') adds height and dramatic contrast to the combination.

Bottom right: A large wooden built-in planter offers the convenience of a raised bed on this deck. A variety of plants thrive here, including giant horsetail and nasturtium.

deck, such as planters on both ends of a flight of stairs or a landing. Wooden planters can also be designed with a bench seat that fits between them.

Keep in mind that all wooden planters are next to impossible to move once they are filled with soil, so figure out exactly where you want them before planting. Either fill them with soil and plant in them directly or use them as "sleeves" by first setting polyethylene containers inside them.

Found objects. The sky's the limit when it comes to found objects that make interesting and unique planters. For instance, I've used cracked iron pots, chipped terra-cotta containers found in the "scratch and dent" section of the local nursery, and leaky watering cans. Stop in at tag sales and

thrift shops and see what fun objects you can find. Some ideas include a used wagon, galvanized buckets that have been dented or punctured, an old wheelbarrow, bushel baskets (these are best lined with plastic), even an old sink or bathtub. For a nearly instant cushion of flowers, you can actually plant directly in a bag of potting mix — just wet the mix thoroughly, poke holes in the bag, and plant annuals in the holes. As with other containers, make sure your found treasures have adequate drainage.

Polyurethane foam. Containers made of this material resemble terra-cotta or cast stone and come in many sizes and styles. The major difference is that containers created from polyurethane foam (Thermo-lite is one brand) weigh 90 percent less than similar-sized terra-cotta ones. They resist cracking and chipping, even when left outdoors filled with soil in freezing weather. This means that overwintering them indoors is unnecessary. Because they insulate against both heat and cold, they keep roots cool during hot weather and warm in cold weather.

Hayracks and wire baskets. A variety of hayracks, baskets, and other heavy-duty metal planting containers are available. Many are replicas of antiques once used for feeding hay to farm animals. They're handsome when used on deck railings, suspended as window boxes, hung from arbors, and mounted on walls. Use freestanding styles alone as accents or incorporate them into other groups of containers.

The best-quality wire containers are made of hand-welded steel and are thickly covered in black plastic or rust-resistant paint. They drain very quickly, making them ideal in areas with rainy summers, but they may be difficult to keep moist in hot, dry weather. You can leave them outdoors

▼ A bathtub makes a fabulous found container that's actually more like a raised bed. To reduce the weight of such a large, heavy object, consider filling it with mulch (don't leave a stopper in the drain!), and then set pots in the mulch. This also makes it easy to change the display anytime you want.

year-round, and they are attractive filled with evergreen branches over winter for extra color on the deck.

In order to plant a wire basket or hayrack, you need a liner to hold the soil in place; preformed coco-fiber liners are easy to use. Mount or position hayracks before filling them. Put the liner in place, and fill it with moistened potting medium (dry mix can be hard to wet, especially in such a fast-draining container). For added insurance against the soil's draining out, you may want to incorporate water-retaining polymers into the potting mix (see Keeping Pots Watered on pages 68 and 69 for information on polymers).

Weighty Matters

On a well-made deck that's in good repair, a few containers won't pose a problem from a weight standpoint. However, a large group of terra-cotta or cast-stone containers filled with soil can be very heavy, especially when the soil is wet. One way to lighten the load on the deck is to stick to lighter-weight pots (plastic or polyurethane foam), at least for the largest containers. This not only will be less of a threat to the deck structure but will also make it easier for you to move your containers around.

To reduce the overall weight of terra-cotta, stone, and wooden containers, replace the planting mix in the bottom third of large containers with a lightweight material that does not retain water, such as foam packing "peanuts." This technique also reduces the amount of planting mix you need to buy, saving you a bit of money as well as the work of hauling as many bags of it. (Make sure you don't use water-soluble "peanuts"; they'll turn to mush as soon as you water the planting mix and the whole thing will collapse into a horrible mess.)

▲ A mix of annuals, including 'Million Bells', vinca, and lamium, cascade out of this handsome hayrack. Note the preformed liner that holds the soil in place.

False-Bottom Containers

Make a false bottom for square or rectangular containers by folding a piece of hardware cloth to fit inside. Be sure to raise the bottom enough to leave 8 to 12 inches for the planting area. Cover the cloth with a black-plastic trash bag or other piece of heavy plastic so the soil won't fall through, then poke lots of holes in the plastic for drainage. Fill with potting soil and then plant.

Designing with Containers

When deciding how many containers to have on your deck and where to place them, take some time to think about purely practical considerations, such as available space, traffic flow, and sun exposure. Although I always end the season with more containers on the deck than I had intended, I *try* not to clog the entire deck. After all, you want to leave a bit of room to sit down and enjoy the flowers. Here are some basic things to keep in mind when deciding where to place containers.

▼ Pairs of large, boldly planted containers help ensure that important transitions on the deck are clearly defined, such as dividing a passageway from a dining area.

Location and Placement

Containers set around the deck at random create a hodgepodge effect. Instead, group them or use pairs of pots planted with similar combinations to mark the location of stairways and doors and the transitions between areas on the deck. This formal touch is an effective way to call attention to the entrance to the deck, the doorway between the house and the deck, or the top of a stairway to the garden. It also serves to define areas within the deck and create a sense of order.

Don't crowd doorways. Containers positioned too close to hinged doors are a recipe for aggravation. Even if you won't smack the container itself each time the door opens, the plants in them will certainly be damaged. With sliding doors, place containers far enough away on both sides so they don't interfere with people coming and going, and so the plants won't be crushed or torn by traffic or get caught in the doors.

Leave reasonable walkways. To be a comfortable outdoor living space, your deck shouldn't be so crowded with plants that visitors are afraid to move for fear they'll knock over something or damage plants hanging above walkways. For two people to walk comfortably side by side, walkways should be at least 4½ feet wide.

Plan for plant growth. Don't forget to account for the mature spread of plants. My container plantings generally spread a bit farther than the height of the pots. Plants in a 2-foot-tall pot will spread to about 3 feet, for example.

Consider utility areas. Before you fill your containers, think carefully about where you will need open space come summer, such as around a grill, a hot tub, an electrical outlet, a water spigot, a trapdoor leading to the basement, or a chimney-cleaning outlet. Make sure plants don't crowd those areas, or using them will become a chore.

Make Your Plants Comfortable

The sites you choose for your containers affect the cultural needs of the plants. If your deck faces south and you have pots along the railing, you'll need to routinely turn containers, as you would houseplants, so the flowers and foliage don't all face away from the deck. If you place pots *against* the south wall, so that you'll walk between them and the sun, turning is unnecessary. Here are some other suggestions for keeping plants happy and healthy.

Look for afternoon shade. If you work away from home or can't water later in the day, a spot with afternoon shade is best. Deck areas that receive morning sun and afternoon shade are cooler than those exposed to all-day sun or morning shade and afternoon sun. Plants in afternoon shade won't suffer from the heat as much, and will be less likely to need watering in midafternoon.

Also, by late spring, sites with afternoon shade are generally better choices for cool-weather annuals, such as pansies, because they're protected from heat, which prolongs the display. On the other hand, if you live in an area where summers are generally cool and rainy, you'll probably want to search out a site *with* afternoon sun to give summer annuals the heat they crave.

Protect plants from wind. Plants grown in a windy spot dry out more quickly, because they transpire more — that is, they lose more water through their leaves. Brown, dried-out leaf margins and tattered leaves are signs of wind damage. Wind disperses fragrance as well, so use sheltered pockets or upright trellises to help block wind and keep scents lingering around the deck.

Avoid hot spots. Microclimates are evident on a deck. Two spots may receive roughly the same sun exposure, but the area protected from the prevailing breeze will be much hotter. Reflected heat from a sidewalk or wall can also make one spot hotter than

another. If you garden where summers are hot and humid, it pays to know where your hot spots are. Either avoid them altogether or decorate them with heat-tolerant plants, such as ornamental peppers. Also, be prepared to water regularly.

Plan to enjoy fragrant plants. Set pots near sitting areas and along walkways, then fill them with aromatic plants. Select plants with fragrant flowers or ones with foliage that releases its scent when you brush against it. Flowers that feature subtle fragrances are best next to benches or low seats, so that they are close to nose level and won't be missed.

▲ Protect plants by grouping containers. The plants and containers create microclimates of their own, cutting down on wind and reducing transpiration. As a result, grouping containers cuts down on the need to water.

Keeping Pots Watered

Watering container plants will be easier and more effective when you follow some simple, practical procedures.

Larger is better. Hanging baskets and other small containers may require watering as often as twice a day in hot weather, making them impractical for the average homeowner who works away from home or may be too busy to take on this responsibility. Larger containers need water less frequently.

Go for the shade. Positioning containers so they are shaded during the hottest part of the day reduces the need to water. For gardeners who work full time, it also provides some breathing space at the end of the day; plants aren't languishing in the hot sun waiting for a lifesaving drink.

Water thoroughly. When you water, be sure to soak the soil ball thoroughly. Flood the soil surface, let it drain, and repeat until water comes out the hole in the bottom of the container.

Keep hoses handy. A spigot and hose right on the deck makes it easy to deliver enough water to saturate each container. You may want to buy a watering wand, which produces a gentle spray, makes it easy to reach any container, and can be turned on and off as you move from place to place on the deck.

Consider saucers. Many plants don't appreciate sitting in standing water, especially in cool weather, when they're not growing actively. During the hot summer months, however, a saucer can act as a temporary lifesaving water reservoir. I don't bother with saucers for really large containers, but nearly all of the smaller pots on my deck sit in them all summer long. I fill the saucers when I water and leave the water to seep up into the soil as needed. Even cacti and succulents summering on the deck often sit in saucers, albeit shallower ones. Especially during hot, dry weather, they seem to thrive with the extra water. During spells of cool, rainy weather, however, I empty or turn over the saucers of cacti and succulents (and some other plants as well, depending on how rainy it has been) to prevent root rot.

Add water-retaining polymers. Sometimes called superabsorbents, polymer crystals resemble coarse salt when dry, but they absorb and hold up to 200 times their weight in water. When mixed with a potting medium, they hold water and release it to plants as needed. Adding polymers to your potting medium can greatly reduce the frequency of your watering. Don't add more polymer than the recommended amount (follow the package directions), because the crystals expand amaz-

---

Self-Watering Containers

Made of polyethylene, self-watering pots and window boxes have a reservoir at the bottom that is kept filled with water, which is dispensed from an easily refillable cylinder. Water wicks up into the soil, which is kept above the reservoir by a platform. With time, plant roots extend down into the water. To keep plants watered, just keep the reservoir filled via a hole in the side of the container near the bottom.

ingly when you add water, and once they're wet, you're likely to have a volcano of gelatin-like polymer and potting mix erupt in your containers if you overdo it. Terra-Sorb is one brand to look for. The company makes a potassium-based polymer that breaks down into fertilizer (not organic) instead of salts, the way some other brands do.

Emergency treatment. If plants dry out and start to droop in hot weather, give them a good deep drink as soon as you notice a problem. If they're in small enough containers, move them to the shade until they recover. I've revived even drastically wilted plants in this manner, and they seem to perk up not much the worse for wear.

▶ A watering wand delivers a gentle spray of water that is ideal for soaking container gardens. When watering, be sure to soak the root ball thoroughly — ideally until water comes out the bottom of the container. This encourages plants to send their roots deep into the pot, making them more drought tolerant.

Drip Emitting System

Watering tops the list as far as cultural demands are concerned. Keep the soil evenly moist. It's likely you'll have to water daily — or at least every other day — in hot, dry weather, or if you have plants in small pots. I enjoy watering my containers and find it relaxing. I use a watering wand that delivers a gentle spray. It takes a while to drench each container, but I spend the time grooming plants or simply daydreaming. If this method doesn't appeal to you, consider installing a drip irrigation system. Depending on the layout of your containers and the deck, you may be able to install a spigot and a delivery pipe around the perimeter with emitters in each pot, creating a drip emitting system, as illustrated at right.

Planting and Caring for Container Gardens

Bagged commercial potting mixes are the best choice for filling containers. These mixes contain a variety of ingredients, including composted bark, vermiculite, perlite, peat, sand, and sometimes real soil, which is usually pasteurized. Some commercial mixes also contain fertilizer, so if you garden organically, you'll want to avoid those. Although perfect loamy soil can be used as an ingredient for homemade potting mixes, most ordinary garden soil isn't suitable, because it's too heavy, compacts easily in pots, and doesn't drain freely enough. In addition, garden soil may contain pathogens that cause plant diseases.

Initially, you'll need to buy enough mix to fill all your containers, but in subsequent years, there are some ways to cheat a bit and save some money on soil. I usually try to replace about half the soil in each pot annually. I add the spent soil to the compost pile or use it to pot up donations to a spring plant sale. Then I loosen the remaining soil in each pot and amend it with perlite or vermiculite before replanting.

Large terra-cotta or cast-stone containers and wooden tubs are cumbersome to move, so set them in position before filling them with potting mix. Even with lighter pots, it's often easiest to fill them at the spot where they'll reside.

Working with potting mix. Always moisten potting mix before filling the containers. Premoistening is important, because potting mix can be very difficult to wet — especially if it contains composted bark. Sometimes it seems like the water just runs through it without getting the mix wet at all, and unless you premoisten, it's possible to end up with pockets of mix that stay dry. Dry mix pulls water right out of plant roots and damages them. Here are two techniques for premoistening a bag of potting mix. Either way, it's a messy process, so dress accordingly!

Designing a Planting

When you're ready to plant, fill the containers within an inch or two of the top, and gently firm down the soil. Set the plants in place and step back to try to picture how they'll fill in and work together. For containers against walls, position the tall plants at the back and surround them with other plants. For large hanging baskets and containers viewed from all sides, set the tallest plants in the center and arrange the others around them.

Once you're happy with the arrangement, dig out holes with your hands or a trowel, set the plants in place, and gently firm the soil around each plant. Water containers thoroughly by flooding the soil surface with water and letting it drain. Repeat the process until water comes out the bottom of the containers. Sometimes the soil settles at this point, so check and add more, if necessary. Mulching the soil surface with well-rotted compost adds some nutrients and also helps hold in moisture.

• **Garden-cart method.** Dump the potting mix into a garden cart or a wheelbarrow, add plenty of water, and stir it with a long-handled trowel or a hoe. When the mix is evenly moist — you'll know it's in good shape when it's uniformly damp and a rich, dark brown color — transport it to the containers. I've also used a variation of this method to premoisten. If you prefer, fill large containers with dry mix, run water into the mix (take care that the containers don't fill up and slosh dry mix out the top), then let it stand. Examine the mix in a few hours and moisten again before planting, if necessary.

• **In-the-bag method.** Carry the bag of mix to the containers. Poke a hole in the top of the bag for the hose and one or two smaller holes toward the bottom to let excess water drain away. Then stick the hose into the bag and let the water run into it. Leave the bag for a few hours or overnight so the mix can absorb the water before you fill the pots. Then open the top of the bag, gently stir the mix, and wet it again, if necessary.

Fertilizing. Regular feeding is a must, especially in plant-packed containers where there's lots of competition for nutrients. Ideally, feed containers weekly — or at least every other week — with a balanced fertilizer according to the package directions. Or use a dilute solution, mixed according to package directions, every time you water.

Pruning and grooming. At the beginning of the season, pinch plants that have branching habits — salvias, cupheas, and basils — to encourage bushy growth. After that, pinch or prune the plants as necessary to keep them compact, encourage branching, and direct growth in the direction you want.

Removing flowers as they fade keeps plants looking their best, directs energy away from seed production, and encourages new buds to form. Use sharp shears to cut off flowers just above a node. When plants are on the leggy side, feel free to cut them back a bit harder to encourage branching and more compact growth. Tugging at plants with your fingers can break stems and roots; at the least, it will cause additional plant stress. Take time to groom plants, too. Remove yellowed, damaged, or imperfect leaves and reposition branches or leaves to display them to best effect.

Pruning and Grooming

To keep plants looking their best and encourage new flowers to form, remove faded flowers regularly. Use sharp shears to cut them off; tugging at the plants can damage the roots and slow the growth.

Regular pinching keeps plants bushy and compact. Pinch stem tips between your thumb and forefinger. Use sharp shears if you need to cut plants back a bit harder; otherwise, it's easy to damage stems and do more harm than good. Remove faded flowers and check for pest problems while you groom.

Continuous Color in Containers

The main show from container gardens comes from plants that are at their peak from early summer to fall. This means that in most cases, you'll want to select heat-loving annuals and tender perennials that bloom over a long season or have great foliage throughout the entire period. Regular deadheading, pruning, and feeding will keep plants at their peak performance. In addition, consider the following options for adding color and variety to container gardens early in the season, as well as after frost.

Hardy spring bulbs. Plant hardy spring bulbs, such as daffodils, crocuses, hyacinths, and tulips, in containers in the fall. Set the containers in a cool, protected spot, such as an unheated garage, for the winter, then move them to the deck in very early spring. If you plant in large containers, such as half whiskey barrels, use a dolly to move them around.

After the plants are on the deck, make sure you keep the soil evenly moist, as it will dry out fairly quickly on an exposed site, even in spring. If there's room in the containers, fill in around the bulbs with cold-tolerant annuals, such as pansies and Johnny-jump-ups. You can also add trailing plants, such as variegated ivy, for contrast and visual interest, then move those plants to the garden or to other containers once the bulbs have finished blooming. Move forced bulbs to the garden as the flowers fade; they generally will take a season or two to recover and bloom again in the ground.

◀ For a burst of spring color — either for a special occasion or for everyday enjoyment — set barrels of hardy spring bulbs, such as hyacinths, out on the deck. To lighten the load of such heavy containers on a deck, see Weighty Matters on page 65.

Filling In the Gaps

In most cases, containers packed with heat-tolerant annuals and tender perennials will stay full and at their peak all summer long. Occasionally, however, a "hole" may develop if a particular plant doesn't do well. This may also happen if you combine cool-season plants with warm-season ones; once hot weather arrives, the cool-season plants will begin to die back. If you can't fix the problem by pinching, pruning, or retraining the container's remaining inhabitants, you'll need to make space for another plant.

Deal with the plant that needs to be replaced by cutting it to the level of the planting mix, pulling it up, or digging it up and moving it to the garden. Then loosen the soil in the spot that's left (it probably will be filled with roots) to make room for the new plant. Amend the soil with a few handfuls of compost. If the rest of the plants in the container are already well established, you may want to cut them back to make room for the newcomer. Then water thoroughly. Once the plants are again growing actively, feed them about once a week.

Cold-tolerant annuals. In mild climates, plant containers in fall for winter bloom. In all areas, fill containers with cold-tolerant annuals and biennials, such as pansies, for extra-early spring color. When the weather is still quite cool at the beginning of the season, keep pots in a spot protected from wind and weather extremes, then move them out of sheltered areas as the weather permits.

Keep in mind that you can sow seeds of cool-weather annuals right into pots. Try this with mignonette *(Reseda odorata),* pot marigolds *(Calendula officinalis),* and love-in-a-mist *(Nigella damascena).* Move the plants to the garden or discard them when warm weather arrives, then plant the containers with heat-tolerant selections.

Cool-weather vegetables. In spring or early fall, plant containers with ornamental leaf lettuces, bush peas, and other greens. Protect the plants if very cold weather threatens. When warm weather arrives, harvest and replant. For fall containers, ornamental kales and cabbages provide welcome, dramatic spots of color. You'll need to start them from seeds in midsummer or buy plants in late summer. In mild climates, these plants will remain attractive all winter long.

Greens for winter. If the containers on your deck won't crack in harsh weather, use cut live evergreen branches to keep them looking good. (If you garden where winters are cold, use insulated containers for this purpose.) Stick branches into the soil (first pour some boiling water onto the ground if it is already frozen hard). Display the branches as you would a flower arrangement or create an upright, treelike effect.

Branches of berries and ornamental grass plumes add additional color and texture. Depending on the look you wish to achieve, add a bow, pinecones, or ornaments designed to attract birds, such as popcorn strings, pinecones spread with suet and covered with seeds, and millet sprays. If you have trellises in your containers, consider wrapping them with swags of pine or other holiday greens and adding ornaments. In the spring, move the plants to the garden, or keep them in containers year-round.

▶ This exuberant basket celebrates summer with a mix of edible flowers and cold-tolerant vegetables. Nasturtiums, with spicy edible flowers and foliage, share space with red-leaved lettuces and kale. Spikes of fragrant lavender erupt from the top.

Plants to Use as Flags

Red-hot-cat's tail, *Acalypha* spp.

Copperleaf, Jacob's-coat, *A. wilkesiana*

Giant hyssops, *Agastache* hybrids

Angelonia, *Angelonia angustifolia*

Rose mallow, *Anisodontea* × *hypomandarum*

Swiss chard, *Beta vulgaris*

Dwarf cannas, *Canna* × *generalis* hybrids

Lion's ear, *Leonotis leonurus*

Purple fountain grass, *Pennisetum setaceum* 'Purpureum'

New Zealand flax, *Phormium tenax*

Cape fuchsias, *Phygelius* spp.

Salvias, Sages, *Salvia* spp.

Coleus, *Solenostemon scutellarioides*

Designing Container Combinations

Spectacular containers overflowing with plants are all the rage these days. Although in books and magazines you can find step-by-step plans for exact combinations to copy, it's much more fun — and satisfying — to experiment on your own. Fortunately, creating great container combinations is easy, and if you plant one that doesn't do well or isn't to your liking, it's not a disaster. Either replant with another mix next year or dump out the container right away, move plants to the garden (or discard them), and try again. It's a fun, creative way to learn about designing combinations, using color, and growing plants. With experience, you'll learn what you like.

The Mix-and-Match System

I use a simple mix-and-match system to design combinations. It roughly divides container plants into four general categories: "flags," "fillers," "contrast and accent plants," and "trailers and weavers" (see pages 77 and 78 for a definition of these terms). When I design my containers, every pot includes plants from each category — the exact number depends on the size of the container. In the largest ones, I usually include one or two flags, two or three fillers, one or two contrast and accent plants, and two or three trailers and weavers. (Yes, my favorite combinations really pack in the plants!) For a small container, I often plant just one from each category or eliminate one of the categories.

To design container combinations, I look for plants that fit into each category as I wander through a garden center. At the same time, I try to keep in mind seeds I've started at home, plants I've overwintered, and ones I've ordered by mail, so I can include them come planting time. While shopping, I pick up plants I've used (or seen) before and want to try again, and I'm likely to end up with one or two plants in hand as I continue looking for likely companions. Gradually, I gather together candidates for a particular container, striving for an interesting mix of flowers and foliage. My final choices are guided by many of the same design principles that I use to create an effective bed or border. Once you understand the basic design functions that each category fills in container

◄ The best container combinations include a carefully chosen mix of plants that exhibit a variety of leaf and flower shapes and colors, together with varying plant forms. Here, geraniums function as bold contrast and accent plants, while edging lobelia and sweet alyssum trail over the container's rim.

gardens, you can use the lists of great container plants here and on the following pages to get started (see chapter 6 for detailed information on many of them). Unless otherwise noted, all these plants require full sun.

Flags. These have an upright, vertical habit and add height to plant combinations. They also add a bannerlike flair to any design. Flags can contribute foliage and/or flowers. Ornamental grasses primarily provide foliage; dwarf cannas add both bold foliage and flowers.

Fillers. The best plants to use as fillers have handsome, fine-textured foliage and/or small flowers. As their name suggests, these plants fill in the combination, but more important, they add texture and set off the foliage and flowers of bolder participants in the combination.

Contrast and accent plants. Essential for adding surprise and color to your combinations, contrast and accent plants often feature bold foliage. Leaves that are variegated or exhibit unusual color, such as burgundy or chartreuse, are especially effective. Large flowers can also be the main accents in a container garden.

Vines as Flags

Vines trained on a handsome trellis at the back or center of a container function as flags, because they add height and flair to a combination. For this reason, they can be used like cannas, ornamental grasses, and other flags. Keep in mind that all the branches of a vine don't have to be trained onto the trellis. Let them wander among the other plants, acting as fillers or trailers. Pinch the stem tips, if you like, to increase branching on these wanderers. (See chapter 4 for more information on vines to use in containers.)

Plants to Use as Fillers

Joseph's coat, Parrot leaf, *Alternanthera ficoidea*

Cushionbush, *Calocephalus brownii*

Dusty millers, *Centaurea cineraria* and *Senecio cineraria*

Cupheas, *Cuphea* spp.

Persian violet, *Exacum affine*

Blue daisy, *Felicia amelloides*

Gomphrenas, *Gomphrena* spp.

Curry plants, *Helichrysum italicum* spp. *serotinum*

Polka-dot plant, *Hypoestes phyllostachya*

Beefsteak plant, Painted blood leaf, *Iresine herbstii*

Flowering tobacco, *Nicotiana alata*

Scented geraniums, *Pelargonium* spp.

Plectranthus, *Plectranthus* spp.

Persian shield, *Strobilanthes dyeranus*

Contrast and Accent Plants

Begonias, *Begonia* spp.

Caladium, *Caladium bicolor*

Ornamental peppers, *Capsicum annuum*

Madagascar periwinkle, *Catharanthus roseus*

Coreopsis, *Coreopsis grandiflora*

Cosmos, *Cosmos* spp.

Dwarf dahlias, *Dahlia* spp.

Fuchsias, *Fuchsia* spp.

Transvaal or Barberton daisy, *Gerbera jamesonii*

Heliotrope, *Heliotropium arborescens*

Garden impatiens, *Impatiens wallerana*

Zonal geraniums, *Pelargonium* spp.

Egyptian star-cluster, *Pentas lanceolata*

Coleus, *Solenostemon scotellarioides*

Black-eyed Susan, *Rudbeckia hirta*

Marigolds, *Tagetes* spp.

Plants to Use as Trailers and Weavers

Bacopas, *Bacopa* spp.

Licorice plant, *Helichrysum petiolare*

Ornamental sweet potato, *Ipomea batatas*

Weeping lantana, *Lantana montevidensis*

Edging lobelia, *Lobelia erinus*

Parrot's beak, Lotus vine, *Lotus berthelotii*

Petunias, *Petunia* spp.

Creeping zinnia, *Sanvitalia procumbens*

Fan flower, *Scaevola aemula*

Purple heart, *Tradescantia pallida* 'Purpurea'

Common nasturtium, *Tropaeolum majus*

Verbenas, *Verbena* spp.

Greater periwinkle, *Vinca major* 'Variegata'

▼ In this stunning combination, boldly colored coleus are used as contrast and accent plants while ornamental sweet potato 'Blackie', a trailer and weaver with deeply cut burgundy-black leaves, spills over the container's edge.

Trailers and weavers. These plants, which provide much of the charm to a plant combination, are at their best trailing over the edges of containers, spilling out of hanging baskets, or mingling among other container inhabitants. They can feature ornamental foliage or handsome flowers, as well.

Designing with Foliage and Flowers

Many people think of flowers as the central feature of container gardens, but foliage is usually the most important element in many of the best combinations. Instead of starting your selection with flower color, look at foliage first. Plants with attractive leaves all season long can echo or complement the color scheme you want. Foliage in a planting combination should set off the flowers, but it should also be interesting and handsome in its own right. In fact, it's not hard to create fabulous combinations based entirely on foliage, with no flowers at all. Try it sometime as a design exercise!

Using a variety of leaf and flower sizes adds excitement and interest to a planting combination. A container filled with plants that all have small, fine-textured leaves and flowers will look bland and uninteresting. On the other hand, a planting that combines large, tropical-looking leaves with fine-textured, ferny foliage will have pizzazz. Combining bold flowers with tiny, lacy-looking ones creates a similar effect. When it comes to contrast, don't stop with size. Look for contrasting shapes, textures, and other characteristics you can use to bring life to your designs.

The use of repeating elements in a container, just as in a garden, helps integrate a design visually, making it look like a well-defined entity. Mirror colors by combining a plant with purple-flushed leaves with another that picks up the same shade of purple in its flowers. Or include two different purple-foliage plants with one as a flag and one as a contrast or accent plant. (This is where wandering around a garden center with pots in hand comes into play. I like to hold plants against one another.) Also, select other plants for the container that repeat or echo leaf or flower shapes and textures.

Combinations with exceptionally tall or bold flags that are not balanced by an adequate number of lower-growing plants tend to seem top-heavy and are unsettling to look at. Be sure to include enough plants in the combination to balance out the tallest specimens, then pinch and train the plants to encourage bushy growth. On the other hand, a combination that contains lots of low-growing plants without a bold upright specimen toward the center may look just fine, especially if you are trying to achieve a rounded mound of flowers and foliage.

▶ Cannas and purple fountain grass form the flags in the large container in this grouping on the author's deck. Flowering maple (*Abutilon pictum* 'Aureo-maculatum') is one of the accents; bacopa and ornamental sweet potato spill over the container's edge.

Herbs and Vegetables for Culinary Containers

Chives, *Allium schoenoprasum*

Swiss chard, *Beta vulgaris*

Peppers (hot or sweet), *Capsicum annuum*

Lemongrass, *Cymbopogon citratus*

Leaf lettuces, *Lactuca sativa*

Tomatoes, *Lycopersicon lycopersicum* ('Micro-Tom', 'Patio f. Hybrid', 'Red Robin', 'Tiny Tim')

Lemon balm, *Melissa officinalis*

Basil, *Ocimum basilicum*

Marjoram, *Origanum majorana*

Oregano, *Origanum vulgare* ssp. *hirtum*

Parsley, *Petroselinum crispum*

Rosemary, *Rosmarinus officinalis*

Variegated sages, *Salvia officinalis* 'Icterina', 'Purpurascens', 'Tricolor'

▼ Basil, arugula, and golden thyme are easy to harvest from this container set near the kitchen door.

Theme in a Pot

Theme gardens are just as much fun up on the deck as they are out in the garden. Consider decorating your deck with a tiny kitchen garden or two, or create containers designed to welcome butterflies or hummingbirds.

Culinary Containers

For an extra-handy source of herbs, leafy crops, and edible flowers, perhaps you'll want to plant a container devoted to edibles — a kitchen garden in miniature. (What I tend to do, however, is to combine edibles with the ornamentals in all my containers.) For foliage color, use green- and purple-leaved basils, leaf lettuces, and Swiss chard. Parsley, especially the curly-leaved type, adds attractive texture and rich green color to any combination. Pop in other herbs, too, such as chives, lemon balm, marjoram, oregano, rosemary, and sage. A clump of lemongrass adds a nice vertical accent; however, don't plant this tender perennial until the weather warms in early summer.

For fruit color, experiment with some of the hot peppers or try growing 'Sweet Pickle', which bears sweet, colorful ornamental fruits carried upright on the top of the plant. Some dwarf cherry tomatoes also are quite pretty in containers, or, for bigger harvests, grow patio tomatoes.

Container-Grown Fragrance

There's simply no better place to use fragrant plants than in pots on the deck. Mix plants with scented foliage or flowers into your container gardens, or grow them alone. For example, fill containers with tuberoses *(Polianthes tuberosa)*, fragrant lilies (low-growing Oriental hybrids are ideal), or heliotrope *(Heliotropium arborescens)*. You can keep them in an out-of-the-way spot until the plants begin to bloom, then move them to center stage to enjoy the fragrance. Set them among other containers or next to a chair or table.

Some plants, such as heliotrope, bloom all summer long (provided they are deadheaded), but others are best moved out of sight once the flowers fade. Move lilies that have been forced in pots to the garden after they bloom. For tender perennials, including tuberoses, discard them after they have bloomed or save them for another year. To carry over tuberoses, continue feeding and watering them until the foliage turns yellow (you may have to move them indoors before frost), then overwinter the roots in their pots or in a plastic grocery bag left open at the top. Store them in a cool, dry place and check the roots every few weeks for signs of rot. Sparingly moisten the soil or the bare roots if they begin to shrivel, and discard any that turn soft or begin to rot, an indication that they probably have been stored too wet.

Hummingbird Container Gardens

With a little encouragement, hummingbirds will come right up to the deck to visit flowers and sip nectar. Among the best container plants to attract them are the annual sages, including *Salvia coccinea* and scarlet sage *(S. splendens)*. Although brilliant red cultivars of this long-blooming annual are the best known, it also comes in nice shades of mauve-purple, creamy white, and pink.

To keep sages blooming all summer, deadhead regularly. When plants become too leggy, cut them back hard in midsummer, then water and feed them: They will produce new flowers and foliage within a few weeks. See Hummingbird Gardens on page 48 for more plant suggestions and chapter 6 for detailed information on each plant.

Plants for Hummingbird Containers

Dwarf dahlias, *Dahlia* hybrids

Flowering tobaccos, *Nicotiana* spp.

Egyptian star cluster, *Pentas lanceolata*

Petunias, *Petunia* x *hybrida*

Annual sages *Salvia* spp.

▼ Hummingbirds are a delightful addition to a deck, and they are sure to visit the pot-grown dahlias featured here. Butterflies and moths also visit container plants, including geraniums.

Plants for Large Specimens

Flowering maple, *Abutilon* × *hybridum*

Angel's trumpets, *Brugmansia* spp.

Lantana, *Lantana camara*

Sweet bay, *Laurus nobilis*

Large Specimen Plants

Not every container must be designed with a combination of plants. To add interest to your overall deck display, consider including some specimen plants — individual plants grown in a single pot. A number of shrub-sized plants — most are tender perennials — are effective when displayed alone or surrounded by mixed containers. Like all good container plants, the best choices feature long bloom seasons or foliage that remains attractive throughout the summer. Some good choices are angel's trumpets (*Brugmansia* spp.) and lantana (*Lantana camara*). A few ornamental grasses can be used this way as well, such as purple fountain grass (*Pennisetum setaceum* 'Rubrum'), with burgundy leaves, and even pampas grass (*Cortaderia selloana*), especially dwarf forms such as 'Pumila'. Both of these grasses are tender, so treat them as annuals or take them indoors over winter where they are not hardy.

I also like the look of specimen pots planted with a single, good-sized clump of a lower-growing species. Agapanthus (*Agapanthus* spp.), variegated society garlic (*Tulbaghia violacea* 'Variegata'), and variegated-leaved geraniums (*Pelargonium* spp.) are effective when displayed in this manner. Although these can't match the sheer size of shrubby specimens, well-grown, smaller specimens are handsome in their own right. They act as nice accents when combined with other containers.

For shade or partial shade, consider a solo planting of caladiums (*Caladium* spp.) or begonias; tuberous begonias (*Begonia* × *tuberhybrida*) and orange-flowered sutherland begonias (*B. sutherlandii*) are good options. Unless otherwise noted, all plants are tender perennials that thrive in full sun (see chapter 6 for detailed information on many of these plants).

Variations on a theme. Specimen plants typically are grown one to a container; however, I often plant groups of low-growing annuals or tender perennials around large shrublike specimens. "Ground covers" like these are especially effective when used around plants such as angel's trumpets, which tend to lose their leaves toward the base.

◄ This hibiscus is a stunning specimen plant that actually consists of three plants braided together to form a single trunk. Trailing variegated ivy and pink geraniums add extra color, soften the edge of the pot, and help visually balance the composition.

◄ Cacti and succulents, outdoors for their summer vacation, make a charming centerpiece for the dining table on the author's deck. Even sun-loving houseplants such as these plants need to be moved outdoors gradually. They'll also require much more water outdoors than they do when growing indoors.

A low-growing layer of trailing plants also injects an extra bit of color into the container. Fantasy series petunias (sometimes called Milliflora petunias) are my favorites for this purpose. I've also used bacopas (*Bacopa* spp.) and licorice plant *(Helichrysum petiolare)*.

Summer Digs for Houseplants

A deck can be a great spot for giving houseplants a much-needed summer vacation. Nearly all of my houseplants spend the summer outdoors, and they make handsome additions to my groups of containers. All respond to the warmth, fresh air, rainfall, and sunshine with vigorous growth spurts that leave them looking glorious by fall.

To successfully summer houseplants outdoors, it's essential to move them outside gradually. They need to be hardened off much like seedlings. Begin the process only after temperatures have warmed up and the weather has settled. At first set plants — even sun-loving ones, such as cacti and succulents — in a very protected, shady spot. Full sun will scorch plants, including those that have been in a south-facing window all winter. Gradually expose them to more sun over the course of a week or two. Check daily to make sure the soil stays evenly moist, because dry soil leads to scorching.

By early summer, many of my houseplants are displayed among containers of sun-loving annuals and tender perennials, although I keep most of them in spots that receive morning sun and afternoon shade throughout summer. Ferns and other shade-loving houseplants remain in protected spots all summer, because they simply can't tolerate full sun.

Keep in mind that you'll need to water much more frequently when houseplants are outside. Not only are they growing actively, but they also need more water because wind and greater light increase transpiration.

Plants for Wire-Form Topiaries

Trailing abutilon, *Abutilon megapotamicum*

Creeping fig, *Ficus pumila*

Ivy, *Hedera helix*

Jasmines, *Jasminum officinale, J. polyanthum*

Passionflowers, *Passiflora* spp.

Purple bell vine, *Rhodochiton atrosanguineus*

Star jasmine, *Trachelospermum jasminoides*

Plants for Standards

Flowering maples, *Abutilon* spp.

Scented geraniums, *Geranium* spp.

Lantana, *Lantana camara*

Sweet bay, *Laurus nobilis*

Common myrtle, *Myrtus communis*

Rosemary, *Rosmarinus officinalis*

Coleus, *Solenostemon scutellarioides*

Green Sculpture

Whether you want to add height and a formal touch to a container garden or simply create a touch of whimsy, consider growing a topiary. Topiaries are made by clipping plants into various forms — geometric shapes and animals are the traditional ones. In recent years, wire forms have made it very easy to style topiaries in many shapes and sizes. Ivy is the most popular choice for covering wire forms — look for ivy cultivars that feature interesting variegated or deeply cut leaves. Or try creating a topiary that features two different ivies with contrasting leaf patterns and colors. Keep in mind that most ivies need to be overwintered indoors from Zone 6 north. (See the list at left for other plants to consider for wire topiaries.)

Another striking type of green sculpture is the standard, a plant that has been trained so that it has a single, bare stem topped by a dense, rounded, leafy top. (See photo, page 82.) Training a standard takes a bit of patience, but it isn't difficult. Well-stocked garden centers also sell standards. Roses as well as herbs, such as common myrtle *(Myrtus communis),* sweet bay *(Laurus nobilis),* and rosemary *(Rosmarinus officinalis),* are traditional plants for standards. (See chapter 6 for information on many of these plants.)

Creating a Simple Topiary

Training wire-form topiaries is simple to do. Here's how:

1. Select a plant that has long stems, such as ivy, and move it to the container in which you want to grow the topiary. Water it thoroughly.

2. Place the wire form just behind and over the plant (directly over it if you are covering a three-dimensional form, such as an animal). Gently push the base of the form into the soil, making sure the branches of the plant are free and the crown remains uncrushed.

3. Gently wind the stems of the plant around the wire form.

4. As the plant grows, continue to wrap the stems around the form. If short new branches appear along the main stem, either start training them around the form or pinch out the tips to encourage a bushier covering over the wire. Once the main stems have wound two or three times around the form, you may want to pinch the tip of each main stem to encourage branching. Then select the most vigorous new stems and continue training them around the form.

5. Continue pinching and training as necessary to achieve the desired shape.

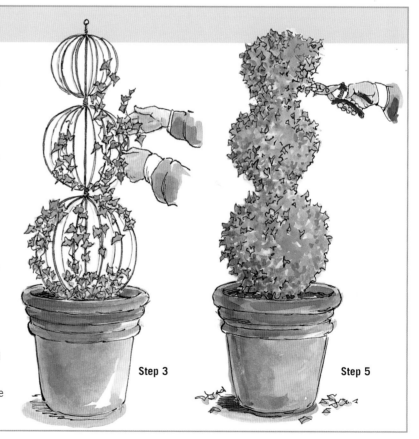

Step 3

Step 5

Training a Standard

1. To train a standard, start with a single-stemmed plant. Since a relatively thin stem supports the top of the plant, most annuals and tender perennials trained as standards require a stake for support. Make sure the stem is not tied too tightly to the stake, or the ties can cut off the supply of water and nutrients to the top of the plant.

2. As the main stem grows, gradually remove any side branches starting at the base of the plant.

3. Once the main stem has reached the height you want, pinch out the tip to encourage branching. Pinch the tips of the branches at the top of the plant regularly to encourage a full, rounded ball of foliage. Continue to remove branches that appear on the bottom part of the trunk as well.

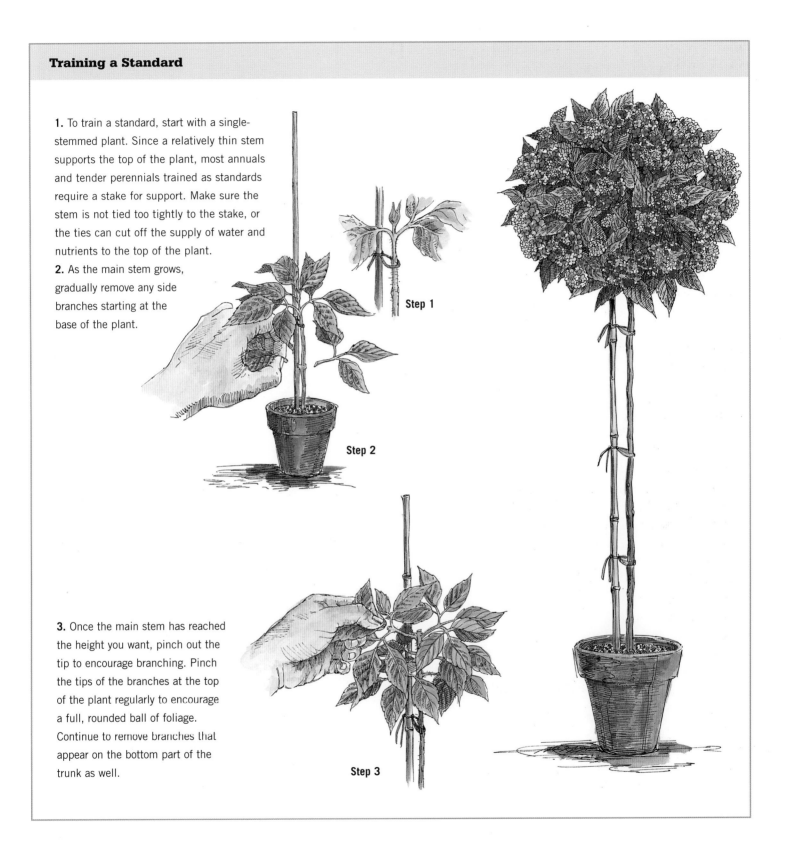

Step 1

Step 2

Step 3

CHAPTER FOUR

Trellises and Arbors

Privacy and shade are essential elements for transforming a deck into an inviting outdoor living space. Vines trained over a sturdy arbor add an island of welcome shade that changes the character of a deck completely. With the right vines and a sturdy structure, you can transform a deck from a hot, sunny space to be avoided to an alluring outdoor refuge. And even a simple trellis that hides an undesirable view can create an intimate enclosure, making a deck more appealing.

Vines also add ambience to a deck simply because they create an atmosphere of rich vegetative abundance. Imagine how appealing your deck would be with flowers and foliage spilling over railings, covering walls and downspouts, and draping from an arbor overhead. An arbor, a trellis, or a fence thickly covered with vines, together with plantings of shrubs and other large landscape plants, also helps muffle noise from the outside world, making your deck retreat seem even more secluded from the outside world. Finally, vines are very effective for softening hardscape elements, such as walls and railings. They will give your deck the charm of an outdoor living space that seems to be right in the middle of the garden.

Creating Shady Retreats

Arbors and other overhead shade structures intended to support vines must be designed so that they safely support the considerable weight of the vegetation. Top-notch construction and heavy-duty materials are especially important if they are to support heavy woody vines. In addition, structures must easily withstand wind and weather. Depending on the size of the structure and the weight it is intended to carry, use posts that measure at least 4 inches by 4 inches — larger is better to support mature vines.

The style of your house and deck will determine the style of arbor that is most appropriate. For our arbor, we used good-sized timbers that echo the timber-frame construction of the addition on our house. The uprights are 6×6 posts that are actually continuations of the structural deck posts that are connected by a 6×6 beam. A series of 4×6 rafters tie into the house and form the roof over the outdoor dining area.

Because the rafters are spaced about 28 inches apart, I use strings to train vines across the top. (I pounded nails into the tops of the rafters and wove strings between them.) Instead of using string to train plants, you could cover the top of the structure with sheets of wood lath and train the vines over the lath. Or you may decide to dispense with vines altogether and simply cover the top of your shade structure with lath or a pattern of 2×2s to provide shade. Before you do this, however, buy a single sheet, set it on top of the arbor, and make sure you like the shade pattern it casts. Some people find the diamond-checkerboard pattern of sun and shade distracting.

Other Options

For a particularly rustic look, build a structure of logs and small saplings. This style is especially appropriate for a log cabin or similar-style house. In some cases, climate may help make your decision. In areas with rainy summers, you may decide to cover a section of your deck with a full-fledged roof so you can spend time outdoors even in inclement weather.

While shade structures made of wood are more attractive, it's possible to make a quite serviceable structure out of galvanized pipe. A frame for an old awning makes a fine vine support, or build your own using standard plumbing connectors to attach the various pieces and glue them

▼ This open-weave lath roof creates an island of dappled shade over this hot tub, but make sure you find the pattern it casts appealing, and not distracting, before you install one.

together with a plumber's adhesive. Instead of covering the frame with canvas, cover the top (and some of the sides, if you like) with wire mesh that has fairly large openings (4 inches or so). Then train vines over the mesh. Deciduous vines, such as Virginia creeper *(Parthenocissus quinquefolia)* and Dutchman's pipe *(Aristolochia macrophylla),* cast welcome summer shade, but also have the advantage of letting in the sun after they've dropped their leaves in winter.

Awnings

Retractable awnings are a practical, if non-horticultural, solution for shading a deck. They are relatively easy to install and extend via a motor or a hand crank. Models that have retractable arms extend about 14 feet; for larger areas, consider models with cross rails and uprights, which can extend to about 20 feet.

Awnings need to be mounted so they have a pitch — 15 degrees is one minimum recommendation — to ensure that they shed rain efficiently. The pitch also allows them to better block late-afternoon sun. To provide a pitch, mount the awning high enough on the wall so its outside edge is still high enough off the deck to allow you to walk under it comfortably. Eight feet is the recommended minimum height for clearance of a ceiling or other overhead structure.

Keep in mind that retractable awnings cannot be left extended when you are not home; they are not designed to withstand heavy rain or high wind. They also do not support snow loads.

▶ Shade cloth stretched on top of an arbor creates a cool, shady spot for dining. (It does not keep out rain, though, as an awning would.) It can be a relatively permanent solution to your shade requirements, or consider using it for a season or two while you are waiting for vines to grow large enough to cover the arbor.

Vines for Shade Structures

To create a deeply shaded retreat, choose large, vigorous vines that will readily cover an arbor or other structure. Because we treat our arbor with a wood preservative every few years, I have avoided vines that stick to the wood via rootlets or holdfasts (see How Vines Climb on page 91), because they would make recoating the arbor too difficult. Instead, I've selected vines that climb by twining stems, such as Dutchman's pipe *(Aristolochia macrophylla)*.

Although without a doubt roses are a romantic choice for clambering over an arbor, I avoid them because of the pruning and training they require. Dealing with long, thorny canes overhead simply is not a task I want to add to my annual gardening routine. Instead, I use roses on deck railings and trellises, where they are simpler to manage. More important, their blooms are more visible and easier to enjoy on those structures. Because roses carry their blooms on the top of the plants, the flowers are not very visible from below when they're on an arbor overhead, anyway. (See Deckside Roses on page 107 for more information.)

Grapes are another romantic-sounding option, and they certainly will grow large enough to cast good shade. However, in late summer, the ripe fruit attracts wasps, which is unpleasant if not hazardous. The fruit also drops and stains deck wood and furniture. On the other hand, grapes that do not bear fleshy fruit are a good choice of vine for shading a deck.

Wisteria is one of the most vigorous vines for covering arbors and other structures, and its fragrant flowers add wonderful appeal to the late-spring garden. Note that wisteria is among the strongest and heaviest of woody vines, so if you set your heart on using it, be sure to erect a structure that will support its weight and withstand its twining habits. Mature wisteria vines will damage or pull apart light- to medium-weight structures made of smaller-sized cuts of wood, such as those used for deck railings. Instead, they require structures made from very heavy timbers or galvanized pipe and steel wire. Keep wisteria and other vigorous vines away from gutters and downspouts, too, because they can actually pull them off the house.

How Vines Climb

When selecting a trellis or other support for a particular vine — or deciding which vine to use for a particular purpose — it's important to know how the plant climbs. That's because some vines attach themselves permanently to their supports with various holdfasts and others climb by winding their stems around structures. Some plants treated as vines — most notably, climbing roses, which aren't really vines — don't attach themselves at all and must be tied in place.

Twining stems. Vines that climb by winding their stems around trellises and other supports range in size from pole beans to enormous woody plants, including wisteria. Plant size greatly affects the size and scale of the trellis or other support that is used. Annual vines with twining stems may need only a string trellis or a lightweight wooden support, but woody twiners need substantial trellises or arbors that can carry their weight.

Tendrils and leafstalks. Both peas and grapes cling to trellises by tendrils; clematis attach themselves by leafstalks that wrap around supports. Vines that climb by these methods need supports small enough for the tendrils or leafstalks to wrap around. These plants can grasp strings, branches, and small slats on a trellis; however, they can't grasp wide slats or large posts. To help tendril and leafstalk climbers cling to larger structures, attach strings, netting, or poultry wire to the supports.

Rootlets and holdfasts. Vines that produce rootlets and holdfasts can cling to any solid surface. Rootlets are small roots that grow along the stems; holdfasts are tendril-like structures that end in round, suckerlike disks. Trumpet vine *(Campsis radicans)*, climbing hydrangea *(Hydrangea petiolaris)*, Japanese hydrangea vine *(Schizophragma hydrangeoides)*, and English ivy *(Hedera helix)* all climb via rootlets. Boston ivy *(Parthenocissus tricuspidata)* attaches itself via holdfasts. All climb with ease but are quite difficult to remove from the surfaces they choose. They're fine clambering up stone walls, trees, or other maintenance-free surfaces, but don't allow them to climb wood surfaces that must periodically be painted or treated with a preservative. Rootlets and holdfasts can mar aluminum siding and will damage mortar in brick or stone walls if it is loose.

Off to a Good Start

Vines need a bit of guidance to get them growing in the right direction. For best results, always install a trellis or other support *before* planting the vine — otherwise, it's likely you'll damage the plant during installation. If your plant is too small to reach the arbor or other structure it will one day cover, install a "training trellis" next to the plant that leans up to its main support. Bamboo canes, a few sticks from a pruned shrub, or lengths of string work well for this purpose.

As the plant grows, gently wrap the stems around the supports. Look carefully at the stems to try to determine which way they want to "wrap" naturally and train them accordingly. Early in the season, you may have to train fast-growing shoots daily to keep up with their growth. They'll slow down later in the season. If the main objective is to train a vine to the top of an arbor, where it will spread out, select two or three main stems and remove side branches that appear so you can direct growth to the main stems. Once the plant has reached the top, you may decide to keep some lower side branches to create fullness.

Trellises and Other Supports

Although vines take a bit more planning than other plants — you have to select both a species and an appropriate support — they are well worth the extra effort. If you do not want or need a full-blown arbor, trellises and other structures offer many creative options for supporting vines. They can be as simple as a string trellis or a sheet of lattice erected on a wall, or as elaborate as a free-form sculpture constructed of recycled metal parts.

Especially where space is at a premium, vines are a wonderful option for adding a sense of seclu-sion and privacy to an outdoor living space. Whereas even a single row of shrubs or trees requires considerable horizontal space in which to grow, vines can be grown in the areas between decks at the back of town houses, along lot lines where space is tight between buildings, and other spots where space is limited.

Vines also make much softer and more friendly screening than does a solid fence or wall. For a permanent screen, erect a sturdy trellis con-structed of wood or wrought iron. Plastic lath products that closely resemble wood (either stained or painted) are also quite attractive. Annual and tender perennial vines make it possible to add privacy during the summer months only. You can fasten plastic mesh or netting to a frame on which to grow these perennial vines. If you use a simple string trellis, just cut down the vines and compost them at the end of the season.

Trellis Benefits

In addition to providing structures for beautiful plants, trellises perform a host of other beneficial functions. Not only do they provide shelter from wind and sun, but they also dress up the deck by covering an unsightly undercarriage, hiding down-spouts that run through the deck, and decorating uninteresting or unattractive walls.

Although overhead arbors and other struc-tures are most effective for casting shade on a sunny deck, a strategically placed vine-covered trellis can provide welcome shade as well. (Think about blocking the heat and glare of the late-after-noon sun, for example.) Trellises offer protection from prevailing winds, too. On an especially windy site, consider erecting two wooden or plastic lath trellises several inches apart to provide a more solid barrier against the wind; vines then provide additional protection. If you have a nice view that

▼ This trellis provides protection from wind and late-day sun, while offer-ing welcome privacy for relaxing in the hot tub.

you don't want to block, create a windowlike opening in the trellis that features the view. You can use a trellis alone or in conjunction with a hedge or a mixed border of shrubs and trees.

To hide ugly, weed-ridden underpinnings of a deck, erect trellises along the base — either attached to deck supports or freestanding — and cover them with vines. Use vines alone or plant them behind shrubs and other vegetation growing in beds around the deck. The vines will add height to deck plantings and an extra layer of screening to hide the undercarriage.

Vines also offer an effective way to dress up downspouts that descend along the corners of the house and through the deck. You can find trellises designed especially to cover downspouts, or you can make your own out of galvanized fencing. Where the downspout is located determines whether you'll have to confine vines to a container or can plant them directly in the ground. Container-grown plants remain smaller than those grown in the ground.

To cover the wall beside the deck with flowers and foliage, mount a trellis directly on the house, then plant vines, either in the ground or in a very large tub or container set at the base, and train the vines onto the trellis. Water and feed the vines regularly for best growth and flower display. Plan for maintenance in advance if you are training a climber against a wall that must be painted or treated periodically. You can set the trellis a foot or two out from the wall, so that you can reach behind it with a paint roller. Or you can try mounting the trellis with hinges at the bottom and a fastener at the top, so that the entire trellis can be moved out of the way when necessary.

▶ Lattice covered with vines and a grouping of containers create an attractive screen for the underside of this deck and the door leading to storage space.

A Question of Scale

In general, trellises and other supports don't need to be as heavy-duty as those designed to supply shade, because they don't have to support as much weight. However, many of the trellises and other supports commonly sold for vines are simply too small. Not only does an average-sized vine overwhelm them, but they are also too small for the average-sized house and deck. Against a two-story wall, a 3- or 4-foot-tall trellis looks like an afterthought; a minimum height of 8 feet is much more appropriate. And a 3- or 4-foot-tall trellis isn't large enough to support most vines, including annuals, which easily reach 5 feet by midsummer and, if not trained, sprawl everywhere by late summer. For these reasons, it's important to consider scale when selecting or designing vine supports.

Materials for Homemade Trellises

Take a few minutes to look around a well-stocked garden center and you'll discover a wealth of trellises and other supports made from a wide range of materials — wrought iron, wood, and plastic, to name a few. You can also create homemade trellises and supports with simple materials.

Wooden and plastic lattice. Sheets of wooden and plastic lattice are very handy to make trellises for vines and screens for privacy. Wooden lattice is available at lumberyards and comes in pressure-treated and untreated wood. For longer life, however, there are some new plastic lattice products. Plastic lattice usually comes with dia-mond-shaped openings of about 2¾ inches. Sheets with smaller openings (about 1¾ inches) are available for use as privacy screens. Although white is the most common color in sheets, fairly natural-looking browns are worth searching for. In my opinion, these colors blend better with the colors of a deck, as well as with the vines trained to cover them.

Standard sheets of plastic lattice are 4 feet by 8 feet. You can buy precast moldings for joining sheets and for finishing the edges. All you need to do is predrill holes along the edges and screw them together. Although moldings that frame and finish the edges make the sheets more rigid, the individual sheets — both plastic and wood — still need to be supported, as they're not designed to stand freely. You can attach lattice sheets at the top and bottom of a board mounted on a wall, or install metal or wooden posts spaced at 2-foot intervals. The posts should be tall enough to support the lattice along the entire length of each sheet.

Wood and wire for a permanent structure. For a fairly easy-to-make trellis that is more permanent than a string trellis, use a traditional design intended to support grapes: Sink posts made from rot-resistant wood into the ground, then stretch 12- to 14-gauge galvanized fence wire between them. (You may want to consider recycled plastic posts for this purpose.) Stretch the lowest wire about 2½ feet above the ground, and then use a stake to train the vine up to the wire. Depending on how high you want the trellis to be, add additional wires at 2-foot intervals.

◄ Sheets of wooden lattice create the feel of a private outdoor room.

Decoration for Railings

Climbing roses and clematis (*Clematis* spp.) are beautiful spilling over deck railings. If you treat railing wood periodically, though, you'll have to remove them or other perennial woody vines before spraying or painting. To apply preservative to railings decorated with roses, untie the roses and secure the canes so they will be out of the way. You can lay them on the ground or tie them loosely to a stake pounded into the ground for this purpose. For other hardy vines, schedule wood treatment for spring to correspond with regular pruning so you can cut back the plants hard, as necessary, before applying preservative. Annual vines are also effective trained over railings. Consider planting scarlet runner beans *(Phaseolus coccineus)*, which will attract hummingbirds, purple bell vine *(Rhodochiton atrosanguineum),* or any of the morning glories (*Ipomoea* spp.). For luminous white, night-scented blooms, plant moonflower *(Ipomoea alba)*. Annual vines make it easy to treat deck railings with wood preservative; just schedule time to apply it in spring before planting.

Wire mesh for a wraparound trellis.
Although this isn't necessarily the most ornamental option, a wire-mesh trellis can be handy and effective, and it's certainly inexpensive. To help vines climb up individual posts or to cover downspouts, wrap the designated surface with pieces of wire fencing or mesh; PVC- or vinyl-coated products are best for this purpose, but you can also use poultry wire. Even though wire mesh rusts — and may leave rust marks on downspouts — it can last for years.

An inexpensive wire pillar. To make a simple, inexpensive pillar to support vines, use the heavy-duty welded-steel mesh designed to reinforce concrete. In terms of beauty, this mesh won't rival the expensive wrought-iron models, but it's a good choice for gardeners on a budget or those who plant so heavily that the structure isn't visible by midsummer.

You'll need a small pair of bolt cutters, protective glasses, baling wire, wooden or metal stakes, and heavy work gloves to handle wire mesh. Be very careful when you work with this material, as the mesh is sold in a roll and springs up with a good deal of force when cut.

Trim short sections of wire mesh and fasten them into cylinders. Three linear feet of mesh makes a nice 1-foot-wide pillar that you can use in a large container or in the ground. Use small pieces of sturdy wire to fasten together the cylinder along the long side.

Set the pillar in position, and use wooden or metal stakes to fasten it in place — otherwise, it may tip over once the vines grow tall enough to cover it. Be sure to fasten the pillar to the stakes with more wire.

▶ Wire mesh is handy for covering downspouts and providing a trellis for pot-grown annual vines placed at its base.

Note: If you need several wire-mesh cylinders, consider making them in incremental sizes with diameters of 6 inches, 5½ inches, and 5 inches (cut from 3-foot, 3½-foot, and 4-foot pieces, respectively). This enables you to nest the cylinders one inside the other for storage and also gives you a range of heights and widths.

Bamboo for a natural look. Strong and lightweight, bamboo is useful for a variety of vine supports. Tie five or more 8-foot-long pieces at the top and you have a sturdy pole teepee suitable for any number of annual and tender perennial vines. Thicker bamboo is strong enough to use as the framework for a string trellis. Another option is to arrange bamboo stalks in a grid or other pattern and lash them together to create a trellis that can be mounted on a wall, attached to a deck railing, or allowed to stand freely in the garden. One of the great advantages of bamboo is that it is extremely strong, yet lightweight. It also provides a natural look. For centuries, in the Orient, it has been fashioned into all manner of structures, including fences and screens. If you are interested in exploring the many uses for bamboo, surf the Internet or consult a book for designs.

String for a Seasonal Trellis

To make a simple string trellis, you still need a fairly sturdy frame, even though you'll use such lightweight structures only for annual or tender perennial vines. Here are some methods to try:

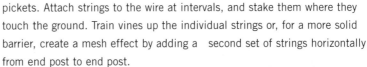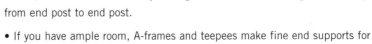

• If you're building a trellis in the ground next to a deck, start with well-anchored end posts, then stretch heavy-gauge wire between the two.

• If you want a string trellis on top of deck railings (a good option for adding privacy), attach the end posts to the railing pickets. Attach strings to the wire at intervals, and stake them where they touch the ground. Train vines up the individual strings or, for a more solid barrier, create a mesh effect by adding a second set of strings horizontally from end post to end post.

• If you have ample room, A-frames and teepees make fine end supports for string trellises.

• If you want to clothe walls with vines, fasten a heavy dowel or broomstick to a windowsill, then tie strings on the dowel, run them down the wall, and tie them to a 2x4 laid underneath the window.

• For an organic approach, use natural-fiber string. Then, at the end of the season, you can cut down all the strings, wrap them up with the vines, and add them to your compost pile.

◄ This simple bamboo trellis provides a support for climbing roses, as well as a handsome backdrop for a perennial border. Openwork screens like this one let in air and light, yet still add a measure of privacy.

Although the most common metal trellises on the market are made of wrought iron, there are other options for those not experienced with welding equipment. Copper plumbing pipe can easily be made into handsome trellises. This project makes a trellis that is perfect for supporting annual vines to add height and drama to a large container. To assemble it, you'll need a flat work space. A table covered with newspaper to protect it from glue, or even the garage floor, works just fine. For best results, cut the pieces and first dry-fit them together. Then adjust pipe lengths, if necessary. Once the pieces fit, glue them together one section at a time.

Materials

- Pipe cutter
- 3 8'-long pieces ½" copper pipe
- 12 T-shaped connectors
- 4 45°-angle connectors
- 4 90°-angle connectors
- Plumber's cement

1. Using the pipe cutter, divide the copper pipe into six 18-inch vertical pieces and four 6-inch horizontal pieces. These sections will make up the main rectangle of the trellis. Dry-fit them together with eight of the T-shaped connectors. In all cases, the pipe fits into the connectors about ½ inch.

2. Cut one 4¾-inch piece, two 4-inch pieces, and two 5-inch pieces of pipe for the top piece. Dry-fit the pieces using the 45-degree connectors. Fit the 4¾-inch center piece last.

3. Cut four 12-inch pieces and four 4-inch pieces of pipe for the center rectangle and dry-fit the pieces using the four remaining T-shaped connectors and four 90-degree-angle connectors.

4. Cut two 1-inch pieces, one 5-inch piece, and one 5¼-inch piece of pipe to connect the center rectangle to the outer one. Dry-fit the short pieces into the existing T-shaped connectors.

5. Make sure the trellis lies flat; if not, adjust the lengths of the pieces to get a proper fit. Once you are sure all the pieces are cut to the proper lengths and fit together well, use plumber's cement (such as Plumber's Goop) to fasten them. Divide the trellis in half vertically (roughly), assemble the sides of the outer rectangle first, and then glue half of the center rectangle and half of the curved top to each side. Glue only two or three pieces at a time and let the glue set before doing the next section. When the two sections have set, glue the halves together. Make sure you apply glue to both the outside of the pipe and the inside of the connector so that there are two sticky surfaces at each joint. Wipe off any excess glue that exudes when you push the pieces together.

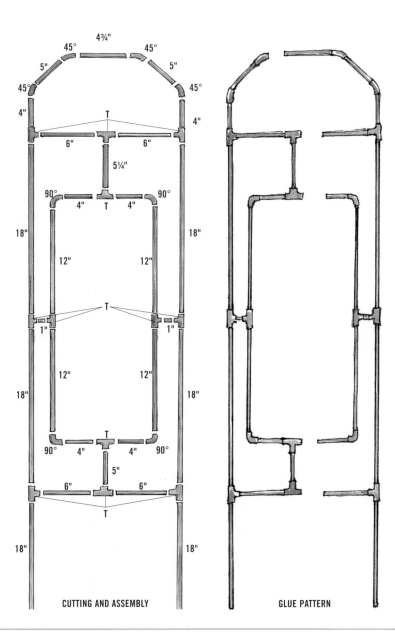

CUTTING AND ASSEMBLY

GLUE PATTERN

Creating Your Own Design

To create your own design, first draw it out on paper. Study the various connectors that are used to join individual lengths of pipe at different angles (90- and 45-degree angles are standard). Copper pipe comes in two standard sizes — ½ inch and ¾ inch. You can design a trellis with just one size of pipe or with both sizes, using connectors that step down from the larger to the smaller size. For instance, try using ¾-inch pipe for the main structural elements and step down to ½-inch pipe for the rest of the design. If you want to get really fancy and include curves in your design, try a pipe bender or flexible copper tubing.

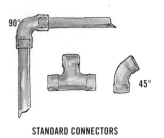

STANDARD CONNECTORS

Large Perennial Vines for Arbors

Kiwis, *Actinidia* spp.

Dutchman's pipe, *Aristolochia macrophylla*

Cross vine, *Bignonia capreolata*

Trumpet vines, *Campsis* spp.

Clematis, *C. montana* 'Elizabeth';
 C. terniflora

Climbing hydrangea, Wood vamp,
 Decumaria barbara

Hops, *Humulus lupulus*

Climbing hydrangea, *Hydrangea petiolaris*

Virginia creeper, *Parthenocissus quinquefolia*

Boston ivy, Japanese creeper, *P. tricuspidata*

Japanese hydrangea vine, *Schizophragma
 hydrangeoides*

Grapes, *Vitis* spp.

Wisterias, *Wisteria* spp.

**Small Perennial Vines for
Trellises and Modest Structures**

Clematis, *Clematis* spp.

Carolina jasmine, Carolina yellow
 jessamine, *Gelsemium sempervirens*

Jasmine, *Jasminum nudiflorum*

Perennial pea, Everlasting pea,
 Lathyrus latifolius

Honeysuckles, *Lonicera* spp.

Passionflowers, *Passiflora* spp.

Roses, *Rosa* spp.

▶ *Wisteria sinensis* provides a shady cover for
this pergola above a hot tub.

Vines for Deckscapes

When it comes to vines, the best choices for your deckscape will depend on what you want them to do and what type of support you have available. To provide islands of welcome shade on an otherwise sunny deck, look to large vines and sturdy arbors. Large vines are also best for covering trellises designed to create privacy from neighbors. For covering smaller trellises, decorating walls, festooning railings, and adding height to container gardens, look to vines that aren't quite as large; otherwise, they'll quickly overwhelm the support you've chosen for them.

Large Perennial Vines for Arbors

The large perennial vines listed on page 100 are vigorous plants that are suitable only for covering arbors or training on large trellises. Keep in mind that when these vines are used to cover an arbor, the flowers of most species won't be readily visible, as they are usually carried on the top of the vine. Wisterias are an exception, because they bear pendent blooms before or as the leaves emerge. (Refer to chapter 6 for detailed information on many of these plants.)

Small Perennial Vines for Trellises and Modest Structures

Vines for deck railings, pillars, obelisks, teepees, and trellises should be smaller and somewhat more manageable. The list on page 100 includes some of the best hardy perennial vines for smaller structures (see page 102 for a list of annual vines that you can train on trellises and other modest structures and see chapter 6 for detailed information on each plant).

▼ *Mandevilla* 'Alice du Pont' provides an easy-to-manage vine for the posts on this deck. The pink geraniums and vinca echo the colors above.

Vines to Avoid

Oriental bittersweet *(Celastrus orbiculatus)* and American bittersweet *(C. scandens).* These rampant woody vines can easily reach 50 feet or more in height. The orange berries are popular with birds, which sow them far and wide, making these vines an uncontrolled weed in many areas. Both species climb by twining stems and can kill shrubs and trees by girdling them.

Silver lace vine, mile-a-minute plant *(Fallopia aubertii,* formerly *Polygonum aubertii).* This commonly sold but extremely invasive, twining climber easily reaches 40 feet. One of its common names — mile-a-minute plant — says it all: Widespread underground rhizomes allow the plant to expand horizontally, and it can get out of hand very quickly.

Japanese honeysuckle *(Lonicera japonica).* This vigorous vine climbs to 30 feet. The species has escaped cultivation and become a quickly spreading, noxious weed in many parts of the country.

Kudzu *(Pueraria lobata).* Kudzu is another vine homeowners should not consider planting. An invasive spreader that can climb to 70 feet, kudzu has made a valiant effort to engulf most of the southern United States.

Annual and Tender Perennial Vines

Balloon vine, Love-in-a-puff,
  Cardiospermum halicacabum

Cup-and-saucer vine, Cathedral bells,
  Cobaea scandens

Pumpkins, *Cucurbita pepo* ('Baby Boo',
  'Jack Be Little')

Chilean glory vine, *Eccremocarpus scaber*

Variegated Japanese hops, *Humulus
  japonicus* 'Variegatus'

Morning glories, *Ipomoea* spp.

Hyacinth beans, *Lablab purpureus*

Sweet pea, *Lathyrus odoratus*

Chickabiddy, Creeping gloxinia,
  Maurandya scandens

Scarlet runner beans, *Phaseolus coccineus*

Purple bell vine, *Rhodochiton
  atrosanguineum*

Potato vine, *Solanum jasminoides*

Black-eyed Susan vine, *Thunbergia alata*

▲ Peas and climbing nasturtiums scale simple trellises to add vertical accents to this collection of ornamental edibles.

Annual and Tender Perennial Vines for Trellises

Annuals and tender perennials are among the best vines for trellises — or anywhere else on the deck, for that matter. The popular selections listed at left are vigorous and bloom from summer to fall. And while you may settle on some favorites that you want to grow every year, these carefree plants make it easy to give your deck a new look each summer, just by changing the vines.

Unless otherwise noted, all of the plants in the list at left grow best in full sun and rich, well-drained, evenly moist soil (see chapter 6 for detailed information on many of these plants). All require a sturdy trellis or other support — under good conditions, they will climb from 8 to 15 feet, depending on the species and the site provided. All are simple to grow from seeds, but many can also be propagated by cuttings — take them in late summer to overwinter the plants indoors.

Combining Vines

Don't think in terms of planting just one vine in a particular spot. Planting two or more vines together can create wonderful, romantic effects.

Annual and perennial vines. I especially enjoy planting annual vines near established perennial ones. For example, once the Dutchman's pipe *(Aristolochia macrophylla)* was well established on our deck arbor, I began planting scarlet runner beans *(Phaseolus coccineus)* near its base each spring. Scarlet runner beans attract hummingbirds and add colorful flowers, as well as edible fruit. The flowers are a benefit, since Dutchman's pipe bears interesting but insignificant blooms. Introducing an annual vine is also a good way to clothe the base of a larger perennial vine with foliage, adding color and textural contrast in the process.

Annual vine combinations. I rarely plant just one species of an annual vine on a trellis. For example, the lacy leaves of love-in-a puff *(Cardiospermum halicacabum)* look wonderful combined with hyacinth beans *(Lablab purpureus)* or morning glories *(Ipomoea* spp.). In addition, annual vines allow you to try new combinations every year to see what works best for your landscape.

Roses and clematis. Climbing roses make very effective living trellises for clematis. Choose plants that flower together or, to lengthen the bloom season, look for a rose and a clematis that blossom at different seasons. Most roses bloom in early summer, so for different bloom times look for late-flowering clematis hybrids, such as 'Ernest Markham', 'Mrs. Cholmondeley', and 'Polish Spirit'. Italian clematis *(C. viticella)* and its cultivars 'Betty Corning' and 'Etoile Violette' also bloom from midsummer to fall. For clematis that bloom with roses, look for early large-flowered hybrids, such as 'Barbara Jackman', 'General Sikorski', and 'Henryi'. (See Clematis for Trellises on page 104 and see chapter 6 for more information on types and bloom seasons, along with recommendations for planting and pruning.)

Vines for Container Gardens

Vines are wonderful for adding height to container combinations, and they function as flags in my container design system (see page 77 for more information). In containers, try any of the annual and tender perennial vines listed on page 102. To use a vine in a container that will be set against a wall, install a trellis toward the back of the pot. If the container will be viewed from all sides, set the trellis in the center of the pot. Train the main stems of the vines to grow up the trellis, and let some others wander among the other plants and spill over the sides.

Containers planted with a single vine or a combination of vines also make striking specimens. To do this, select a pillar- or obelisk-style trellis large enough for the legs to extend nearly to the edges of the container, then plant the vines. Set containers with specimen vines toward the back of a grouping of lower-growing combinations or display them alone in a prominent place. Or use a pair of containers with vines to mark an entrance.

▲ Container-grown scarlet runner beans and morning glories scale the posts and create a lush ceiling for this shady outdoor room. Flowerbeds filled with pink petunias form low walls that ensure a lovely view.

▲ Clematis climb the trellises and Dutchman's pipe covers the arbor to create a sense of enclosure for this shady retreat.

Clematis for Trellises

Gardeners can choose from a wide variety of clematis species and hybrids. Clematis plants are divided by bloom season into three general groups, and those designations determine how a particular plant should be pruned. Most clematis reach from 8 to 12 feet in height; to select a larger one that could be used on a shade structure, see Large Perennial Vines for Arbors on page 100. For the longest season of bloom, select plants from each of the following groups (see chapter 6 for detailed information on many of these plants).

Clematis prefer sites with cool soil conditions, but they bloom best when the tops of the plants are in full sun to partial shade. To give plants these conditions, look for a spot where the roots will be shaded by low-growing shrubs or perennials, such as hostas, or a site on the shaded (north) side of a low wall. Mulch plants to keep the soil cool. These plants also need well-drained soil but will grow in heavy clay provided it has been deeply dug and amply amended with organic matter, such as compost.

Early-blooming clematis. These plants flower in spring to early summer, and usually have single or bell-shaped flowers. They bloom on old wood (growth from the previous year), so prune if necessary immediately after flowering. However, they do not need annual pruning to bloom well. Remove dead or damaged wood and cut back the shoots to shape the plants. Two good choices are Alpine clematis *(C. alpina)* and *C. macropetala,* each of which may bloom again in summer or fall.

Early large-flowered hybrids. These plants bloom from late spring into early summer and again commonly in mid- to late summer. On cultivars that rebloom, the first flush of flowers is on old wood; the second is produced on new wood at the tips of the current year's growth. Early-blooming hybrids usually do not need heavy annual pruning. Just shape up the plants in spring as needed by removing dead or damaged growth and cutting stems back to a strong set of buds. Cultivars in this group are hardy in Zones 3 through 8.

Late-flowering clematis. This group includes large-flowered hybrids that bloom from summer to early fall, as well as several species that go on into late fall. Prune these plants hard each year in the early spring before they begin to grow. Cut them to 8 to 12 inches from the ground, just above a healthy pair of buds. Good choices for this group are Oriental clematis *(C. orientalis),* native Texas clematis *(C. texensis),* and Italian clematis, *C. viticella.*

◄ *Clematis* 'Jackamanii' entwined with *Clematis* 'Ernest Markham' make a nice pair of vines for this trellis, because they bloom at the same time.

Early Large-Flowered Hybrids

'Barbara Jackman'

'Belle of Woking'

'Blue Ravine'

'Elsa Späth'

'General Sikorski'

'Henryi'

'Niobe'

'Pink Champagne'

'The President'

'Royal Velvet'

'Nelly Moser'

Late-Flowering Clematis

'Comtesse de Bouchaud'

'Ernest Markham'

'Gipsy Queen'

'Hagley Hybrid'

'Jackmanii'

'Lady Betty Balfour'

'Mrs. Cholmondeley'

'Polish Spirit'

'Star of India'

'Ville de Lyon'

Deckside Roses

Consider climbing roses for trellises, deck railings, and freestanding structures, such as pillars. The largest climbers can be trained to grow over arbors and up tree trunks as well. Keep in mind that, unlike true vines, climbing roses don't have twining stems or tendrils with which to attach themselves to structures. Instead, they produce long, supple canes that need to be tied to supports with soft yarn or string.

Gardeners generally make a distinction between rambling and climbing roses, but this is not based on any botanical differences. As a result, roses that are labeled ramblers by one source may be listed as climbers by another. The distinction between a rambler and a climber is based on the general growth habit of the plant, how it is used, and what pruning it requires.

Rambling roses. Ramblers usually have thin, flexible canes that are easy to wrap around supports. They tend to be large, exuberant plants and generally bloom once in early to midsummer. They bear one crop of small flowers carried in large clusters on short side shoots borne on year-old canes. After they finish flowering, ramblers send up long canes from the base of the plant. They can be difficult to keep tidy, so plan on pruning annually if you want to keep them contained, or you can leave them to scramble where they will.

Climbing roses. Climbers usually have stiffer, woodier canes that are somewhat harder to wrap around supports. They are also a bit smaller than ramblers and bear fewer but larger blossoms. Climbers generally produce a flush of bloom in early summer and then repeated, smaller flushes

◀ Shrub roses, geraniums, and lavender provide a beautiful mix of color and fragrance.

throughout the season. Like ramblers, they produce vigorous canes from the base of the plant, but they also tend to send up canes from older wood.

Kordesii climbers. Roses with *Rosa kordesii* as one parent are tough, medium-sized climbers with dark green leaves and feature excellent disease resistance. One of the best *R. kordesii* cultivars is red-flowered 'Dortmund', which blooms once if not deadheaded and has handsome red hips in fall. 'Dortmund' produces several flushes of flowers (but no hips) if spent blossoms are removed. Zones 5 through 9. Canadian Explorer Series hybrid 'William Baffin' also boasts *R. kordesii* lineage. It bears bright pink flowers, has excellent disease resistance, blooms through the season, can be grown as a climber or a very large shrub, and is hardy to Zone 3 (or to 2 with protection).

Wichuraiana roses. *Rosa wichuraiana* is another excellent rose parent to look for, as it produces large, vigorous flowers with dark green, very disease-resistant foliage. Most bloom once in early to midsummer. Handsome hips follow the flowers in the fall. Hybrid Wichuraiana roses are large enough that they're usually called ramblers, as they typically reach 15 to 20 feet at maturity. However, they can be kept smaller with pruning. They are hardy in Zones 5 through 9. The following Wichuraiana hybrids make good selections:

• 'Albertine' has salmon-colored buds that open into pink flowers.

• 'American Pillar' bears an abundance of single, white-eyed pink blooms.

• 'Blushing Lucy' is a repeat-flowering rose that reaches about 12 feet and bears clusters of very fragrant, semidouble pink flowers.

• 'Dorothy Perkins' features masses of lovely pink flowers.

▲ This scarlet rambling rose provides a nice contrast for the white lattice trellis beneath it.

Large-flowered climbers. These bear large blooms, usually in clusters, and range from 8 to 12 feet in height. Although some bloom only once per season, many are *remontant* — that is, they produce a main flush of flowers in early summer followed by repeated flushes for the rest of the season.

Because most large-flowered climbers produce new canes on old wood, be sure to choose cultivars that are hardy in your area (plants killed to the ground won't bloom), and don't remove too much old wood when pruning. The following plants exhibit excellent disease resistance and are remontant. Most are hardy in Zones 5 through 9.

▼ Fragrant climbing Hybrid Tea 'High Noon' is a prolific bloomer and has disease-resistant foliage, so it is an excellent choice for trellises and arbors.

• 'Altissimo' produces single rich red flowers.

• 'America' bears double salmon-colored blooms that are fragrant.

• 'City of York' boasts fragrant semidouble white blooms and tolerates some shade.

• 'Dublin Bay' produces fragrant semidouble red blooms.

• 'Eden', a Meilland Romantica Series rose, has fragrant double flowers in pastel pinks, creams, and yellows.

• 'New Dawn' bears an abundance of fragrant double pink flowers.

Shrub roses. Some long-caned, vigorous shrub roses, including 'Alchemist', 'Alex Mackenzie', and 'Butterflies', also can be trained as climbers. Climbing forms of Hybrid Teas, including 'Climbing Shot Silk' and 'Climbing Sutter's Gold', and Polyanthas, such as 'Climbing Cécile Brünner', are also available. Or consider climbing miniature roses, which grow to 6 or 8 feet tall and are the perfect scale for a small deck. These plants may or may not exhibit good disease resistance — an important consideration if you want plants to look their best without resorting to a spray schedule — so do some research before making any selections.

Thornless climbers. Many gardeners are surprised to learn that there are thornless climbers as well, and these are a good option for deck plantings, where roses and people often coexist in close proximity.

• *Rosa banksia* is a large species that reaches 20 or 30 feet, but it's hardy only in Zones 7 and 8. The species bears lightly scented white flowers; 'Lutea' bears yellow blooms.

• 'Zéphirine Drouhin' sports lightly fragrant pink flowers. Its thornless canes climb to about 10 feet.

Growing Roses

When planting roses, select a site in full sun — roses need *at least* 6 hours a day to bloom well. A spot with good air circulation is important, too, because it helps cut down on foliage diseases. Try to protect plants from cold, northwest winds, because winter winds desiccate the canes. A warm, south- or east-facing site is a good location for a rose — especially a climber — that is near the limits of its hardiness.

Roses thrive in well-drained soil that is loose, deeply dug, and amended with plenty of organic matter. Although roses will not tolerate poorly drained soil, they will grow in heavy clay provided it is well drained; they will also grow in sandy soil if it is heavily amended with organic matter. A slightly acidic pH is ideal (pH 6.5 to 6.8), but roses will also grow in more acidic soil (to about pH 5.5), as well as in slightly alkaline conditions (to pH 7.5).

Mulch roses with shredded bark or another organic mulch to keep the soil moist and cool and to control weeds. Water weekly if the plants do not receive 1 inch of rainfall. To prevent foliage diseases, water early in the day so the leaves dry completely by nightfall.

▲ *Rosa* 'Patio Flame' has orange buds that turn to red as they age, creating a lush, dual-color covering for this trellis.

Deadheading and Pruning Roses

Regular deadheading keeps plants neat looking and also encourages roses to produce new flowers. To deadhead, cut just above the first leaf below the spent bloom.

When pruning, always remove dead or diseased wood as well as weak, twiggy growth. Remove up to one third of the oldest canes, and shorten side branches that have already flowered, so that only three or four buds remain.

Feed roses in spring with a balanced organic fertilizer mixed with compost. Or feed them in fall by giving each bush two shovelfuls of well-rotted manure after the plants are dormant and the ground has frozen. Reblooming roses need regular boosts to fuel their flower production, so water them monthly with 1 to 2 gallons of fish emulsion or manure tea.

Many roses are budded or grafted, meaning that the plant producing flowers in your garden grows on the roots of a more vigorous plant, called the rootstock. The rootstock sometimes produces root suckers; if they are not removed, they will outcompete with the rose you planted. Root suckers usually have leaves and thorns that look different from the rose you planted, as well as canes that are more slender and arching. (Roses that spread naturally by suckers, including many species and shrub roses, send up canes that have foliage and flowers identical to the main plant.) To remove unwanted root suckers, dig near the base of the plant where the suckers are attached to the plant, then cut or snap them off. If you can't find where a sucker is attached, just cut it off as deeply as possible. Don't cut off suckers at the soil line, as this encourages new growth.

The best time to prune climbing or rambling roses depends on when they bloom. For climbers that rebloom, prune in late winter or early spring. Prune once-blooming roses immediately after they have finished flowering in summer.

Both climbers and ramblers grow well with a minimum of pruning; however, they do benefit from training, as the canes bloom best if they are positioned horizontally. Tie the canes loosely to their supports with lengths of soft string, but untie them and carefully lay them on the ground before you prune.

Diseases

Roses are subject to a variety of fungal diseases, including black spot, powdery mildew, and rust. The easiest way to control them is to provide good culture by planting disease-resistant roses in locations that receive full sun and good air circulation. With disease-resistant roses, wait to see if foliage diseases crop up before spraying. If just a few leaves show signs of trouble, pick them off and destroy them. If you know diseases are a problem on your plants, spray in spring as soon as the foliage has emerged. Susceptible plants need to be sprayed every two weeks to keep them free from disease. Some rose growers report good control over black spot and powdery mildew by spraying their plants with a mixture of 1 part milk to 7 parts water. Spray weekly for effective control. A few other organic methods are effective for controlling fungal diseases.

Fungicidal soap often works well and is available at garden centers.

Sulfur is sold in both wettable and flowable forms; follow label directions to apply these products. Combining sulfur with an antitranspirant (a spray developed to reduce moisture loss from plant foliage) prolongs sulfur's effectiveness because it helps spread the product out onto the leaves. Spray sulfur in the early morning, and do not apply it when the weather is hot and dry — it will burn the foliage. Instead, spray antitranspirant alone or mix it with 3 teaspoons of baking soda per gallon of liquid.

Horticultural oil can be used as a fungicide. Mix it at a growing-season dilution (read the label to determine the amount of oil per gallon of water) and add 3 teaspoons of baking soda per gallon of water. Dilute the oil even more than recommended if the weather is hot and dry.

Pests

Insect pests can be a headache, but there are steps you can take to keep problems to a minimum. Good cultural practices, such as selecting a good site and watering and feeding regularly, are important first lines of defense. That's because healthy, vigorous plants are less likely to be plagued with problems than are weak, sickly ones. A few pests can still get out of hand. Here are some suggestions for dealing with them organically:

• Handpick Japanese beetles early in the morning, when they are most sluggish, and drop them into a can of soapy water. To help prevent future infestations, apply parasitic nematodes to the soil to control grubs. You can also apply spores of milky disease to lawns to control grubs, which feed on grass roots. Milky disease takes a season or two to really be effective. Ideally, have your neighbors apply it as well to reduce the number of adults that fly in from nearby yards. Spray seriously infested plants with neem, pyrethrins, or rotenone. Do not hang commercial Japanese beetle traps near roses; they attract more pests than they capture.

• Control aphids and spider mites with a strong spray from the garden hose to simply blast them off the plants.

• Encourage good populations of beneficial insects. Fortunately, many of the same garden features that attract butterflies also attract beneficial insects. (See pages 50 to 52 for specifics on plants that make butterflies happy.) Among the plants that beneficial insects especially appreciate are those of the aster family, such as yarrows, and of the mint family, such as catmints (*Nepeta* spp.).

• If infestations of pest insects get out of hand, apply insecticidal soap.

Japanese Beetles

These pests feed on the foliage and flowers of many plants, including roses, and can become a real nuisance if they are not controlled.

CHAPTER FIVE

Decorating
with Style

A thoughtful, practical design and an effective use of plants play major roles in transforming an ordinary deck into a useful outdoor living space. But the style and allure of any area of your home is dependent on the way the entire space is pulled together. For example, your choice of furniture helps set the style for a deck. And although containers overflowing with plants add undeniable appeal to any deck, they can be even more striking when combined with interesting objects. I group my collection of watering cans with containers, and frog and toad sculptures "hop" around the bases of pots. I also position pieces of driftwood and saucers filled with interesting rocks in areas where they can be enjoyed.

Adding a water feature is another surefire way to give your deck magical appeal. Consider using a simple birdbath, a small container water garden, a freestanding fountain, or even a wall fountain to provide a gentle trickle of running water — an especially nice addition if you need a little "white noise" to mask neighborhood sounds. The style you ultimately settle on is a personal decision, as individual as the way you decorate your living room.

Selecting Furniture

Whether you like a rustic or an ultramodern style, make sure the furniture you choose is comfortable, versatile, and inviting, so that you and your family are lured out to the deck for a wide variety of activities. If you haven't already made a list of the furniture you have room for on your deck, as well as what pieces you may need, see What Do I Want My Deck to Be? (page 16).

The architectural design of your house and deck should suggest an appropriate style for outdoor furnishings. The furnishings of indoor rooms, particularly those adjacent to the deck, may also provide clues. Use the same style indoors and out, or select a complementary style. Whatever you choose, make sure the furniture is well built, comfortable, and suited to your needs. You won't be tempted to use elegant chairs — or charming cottage-style ones — if they aren't sturdy and comfortable.

Consider Your Needs and Space

If you have a small deck, a few large pieces of furniture may completely fill it, making it seem cluttered and crowded. By the same token, small-scale furniture may look fussy or even lost on a large deck. Refer to the suggested measurements in How Much Space? (page 13), and consider the size when comparing styles of furniture. For example, although Adirondack chairs are comfortable, they take up a lot of space, and three equally inviting, conventional chairs can fit in the space occupied by two Adirondacks.

Accommodate the view. If you are blessed with a wonderful view from your deck, you may want to invest in bar-height chairs and tables to make the most of it. Deck railing and pickets block much of the view for guests sitting in conventional-height chairs, but in bar-height chairs, they'll be able to see over it easily.

Expansion seating. You can save space and money with expansion seating. For instance, if you need only one table and four chairs on a day-to-day basis but host an occasional outdoor party, don't blow your furniture budget on an enormous table and lots of extra chairs. Instead, buy a top-notch table that seats four or six, and four or six comfortable chairs. For special occasions, consider these ideas to expand your seating and table requirements in a practical and economic way:

• Buy good-quality folding or stacking chairs to use when necessary.

▼ When selecting furniture for a deck, it helps to think in terms of areas for different activities. This deck features furniture for large gatherings as well as benches for more intimate conversation. The cushions can be removed in case of rain.

• Move your dining-room or kitchen chairs outdoors for evening parties or larger groups (a custom we really enjoy).

• Buy a hollow-core door and set it on two sturdy sawhorses. Cover it with an extra-large tablecloth and you've got festive style and seating space to spare. The door and sawhorses are easy to store when not in use.

The wind factor. For a deck where wind may be a problem, the heaviest furniture options are cast aluminum, wrought iron, and teak. Lightweight plastic or extruded aluminum furniture is simply too easily blown around in a strong wind. On a deck like ours, which is a full story off the ground, an upward gust of wind from below is a sure bet in a storm. For this reason, we chose a cast aluminum table that has a cast, not glass, top for our deck.

If you have a windy site, consider carefully before buying a glass-topped table, as a sudden gust of wind can wreak havoc. Wind can either tip over a glass table or actually lift up the glass and break it if it isn't fastened to the base. If you do decide to buy a glass-topped table, be sure to look closely at how the glass is fastened to it — and find out how much it would cost to replace should it break or become scratched. Another consideration is whether indoor winter storage for the glass is recommended, which means you have added the chore of carrying the heavy glass top indoors each winter and figuring out where to store it.

Test-drive. Before buying furniture, try it out! If at all possible, spend some time sitting on various makes and models of chairs at a well-stocked garden center or pool-and-patio supplier. What feels comfortable is a matter of individual taste and body size. Test whether

chairs are the right height and size, and whether they are easy to get into and out of. We love our Adirondack chairs, for example, but older family members and friends sometimes have a great deal of difficulty with them. Although you may ultimately decide to buy furniture from a catalog or over the Internet, testing out various designs will help you focus on what feels most comfortable to you and narrow down the many options that are available.

▲ This elegant glass-topped table is the perfect complement for a modern-looking house and deck. However, avoid using a table like this if you have a windy site.

Outdoor Furniture Choices

Any room needs comfortable furnishings to make it appealing and useful. Deck furniture must meet additional requirements: It has to withstand sun, wind, and rain. For no-maintenance outdoor furniture, consider purchasing cast or extruded aluminum. Teak is another option, provided you're prepared to allow the wood to weather naturally. Here's a rundown of deck furniture materials, along with important factors to keep in mind when buying them.

Wood for a Natural Look

The best wood furniture is constructed with mortise-and-tenon joints rather than screws or other hardware. When comparison shopping, notice the thickness of the wood used in construction; thicker cuts are more expensive, but they're also stronger and longer-lasting.

Teak, redwood, and cedar. Naturally rot-resistant wood, including teak, redwood, and cedar, resists cracking and is the best choice for outdoor wood furniture. All three types of wood can be left untreated to weather naturally or you can use a manufacturer-recommended sealant to

▼ This sitting area on the author's deck takes advantage of shade from the house during the late afternoon. The wooden Adirondack chairs are made from salvaged water-damaged cedar, but a coat of paint conceals the stains completely.

maintain its original color. Follow the label's directions and apply a fresh coat of the sealant once or twice a year.

Pine. Outdoor wood furniture is also made from either natural or pressure-treated pine. Pine is much less expensive than teak, redwood, and other popular woods, so low price is often its main selling point. As a result, the construction quality of pine furniture may be rather poor, so examine pieces carefully before making any purchases.

Pressure-treated wood. If you want to buy furniture made from pressure-treated wood, keep in mind that concerns about its safety continue. At the least, do not set food directly on pressure-treated wood, and always avoid direct contact with skin. In some cases, the legs of chairs and tables, which tend to wick up moisture, may be made of pressure-treated wood and the seats and tabletops may be made of other types. Check with the store or the manufacturer and read labels carefully so you know exactly what you are buying.

Maintenance. Follow the manufacturer's directions for maintaining wood furniture. Clean it with a soft-bristled brush and mild soap and water, or use a mixture of 4 parts laundry detergent or dishwasher soap and 1 part bleach, then add ¼ to ⅓ cup of that solution to 1 gallon of water. Teak and some other woods can be oiled periodically to maintain the color and finish. Do not use polyurethane products on outdoor wood furniture, because these finishes seal the wood pores, tend to blister, and may cause warping.

Mildew can be a problem for furniture that is kept in a damp spot. If you are letting wood furniture age naturally and are also using cushions, turn the cushions on their sides after a rainstorm to allow them — and the wood below them — to dry thoroughly.

Green Consumers

Today, environmentally conscious gardeners have alternatives when it comes to purchasing wood garden furniture. Before you make any purchases, ask about the source of the lumber used in its construction. Companies that sell furniture made from plantation-grown or responsibly harvested wood are proud of that fact and mention it in their literature. In fact, garden furniture built from plantation-grown teak is widely available, and an excellent option.

Forest Stewardship Council. Some companies offer wood and wood products that have been harvested in a sustainable or ecologically friendly manner. The Forest Stewardship Council (FSC), which started the most prominent program for certifying responsibly harvested lumber, is endorsed by a large number of top international environmental groups. The FSC uses independent inspectors to monitor timber operations and verify that they conform to rigorous standards.

To produce FSC-certified wood, landowners must take specific steps to conserve old-growth and mature second-growth forests, biological diversity, and ecologically or socially significant sites. In addition, they cannot replace mature forests with plantations, which significantly reduce biological diversity and forever alter the original ecosystem. During harvest, FSC-certified operations also must conserve water and soil resources and preserve unique ecosystems. Furthermore, they must consider alternatives to chemical pesticides and herbicides, respect the rights of local indigenous peoples, and maintain or improve the social and economic welfare of workers and local communities. FSC-certified lumber is marked with the FSC logo, and companies that offer furniture certified by the FSC display the logo on a tag or in their literature.

SmartWood Program. Developed by the Rainforest Alliance, the SmartWood Program is one of two wood-certification operations in the United States recognized by the FSC. In addition to certifying newly harvested lumber, this program has a SmartWood Rediscovered Program that certifies salvaged and recycled wood. Other FSC-recognized wood-certification organizations in North America include Scientific Certification Systems and Silva Forest Foundation.

Aluminum

For outdoor furniture, one of the most popular metals is aluminum, since it is lightweight and does not rust. Three types are used to make furniture, all of which are good choices for use on decks.

Cast aluminum. Elegant and expensive, cast-aluminum furniture is often styled to resemble old-fashioned cast-iron furniture and can be elaborately detailed. It is much lighter than antique cast-iron furniture and does not rust. Though costly, it is extremely durable and the finishes adhere very well.

Wrought aluminum. Wrought-aluminum furniture is lightweight, low-maintenance, and rust-proof. Although it is hand-forged, wrought-aluminum furniture is not quite as intricate or detailed as is wrought iron.

Tubular aluminum. These frames are constructed of hollow aluminum tubing that is often reinforced for added strength. Baked-on, powder-coated finishes come in a wide variety of colors and textures. Good-quality finishes are durable and do not chip, peel, or crack. Tubular-aluminum chairs come in cushioned, web-backed, and sling styles.

Maintenance. Wash all types of aluminum furniture with mild soap and water. Avoid abrasive cleansers and harsh-bristled brushes.

• You can leave cast-aluminum furniture outdoors year-round. Touch up nicks in the finish with enamel paint, but use a brush, not paint from an aerosol can.

• For tubular aluminum, clean up scratches thoroughly; sand them with wet, fine-grained steel wool or dry, fine-grained sandpaper; then cover the

▶ This set of cast-aluminum furniture on the author's deck is as intricate and detailed as old-fashioned cast-iron pieces, but it is lightweight and does not rust.

spot with several light coats of the matching touch-up paint available from most manufacturers. Aerosol paint is fine to use on most tubular-aluminum and wrought-aluminum finishes. Many manufacturers recommend coating tubular-aluminum frames and straps with car wax once or twice a year. Do not wax textured aluminum finishes.

Tubular Steel

This type of furniture comes with upholstered cushions or has a single layer of fast-drying fabric suspended from the frame. Tubular steel resembles tubular aluminum, but it is much heavier and much less likely to blow around in high winds. Tubular steel frames are also much more durable than aluminum ones, but they do rust if they are not properly maintained.

When buying tubular-steel furniture, notice the type of finish the manufacturer has employed to inhibit rust — enamel and powder coating are both used. The best manufacturers provide care instructions for their finishes. Be prepared to follow them, and you'll have furniture that's nearly indestructible.

Maintenance. Periodically wash tubular-steel furniture with soap and water. Inspect regularly for scratches and signs of rust, and touch them up according to the manufacturer's directions or as you would for wrought-iron furniture (see page 120).

Wrought Iron

True wrought iron used to make the scrolled tables our grandparents enjoyed has not been manufactured in the United States since 1969, as it is a very labor-intensive process. (True wrought iron has iron silicate in it, which makes the metal more malleable, more resistant to corrosion, and more able to withstand stress. It also has a rough, irregular surface that allows it to hold a thick finish more effectively.)

Fortunately, hand-forged, wrought-iron-style furniture is widely available in simple and ornate designs. Like tubular-steel furniture, wrought iron rusts, and a good rust-inhibiting finish is essential for a long life. The best manufacturers have developed a variety of hard-wearing finishes that prevent rust, whereas inexpensive wrought-iron-style furniture is often coated with only spray paint.

▲ Lightweight and versatile, good-quality tubular aluminum furniture features a baked-on powder-coat finish that is very durable.

Maintenance. Wash wrought-iron furniture occasionally with soap and water. Never leave it sitting in water. Depending on the finish, a coating of auto wax or spray furniture wax may be in order (see the manufacturer's recommendations). Coat springs or steel-action mechanisms with WD-40.

Inspect wrought-iron furniture regularly for signs of rust; welded areas are particularly susceptible. Touch up rust spots promptly. Clean the spot thoroughly by spraying with a household grease removal product, then clean off all the rust with a toothbrush. Let the spot dry completely, then apply touch-up paint. Several light coats of paint offer the best protection; let each coat dry completely before applying the next. If the finish has been scratched off to bare metal, sand it with fine-grained sandpaper, then clean and paint it. Store wrought-iron furniture indoors over winter or keep it covered.

Wicker

Traditional wicker or rattan is not suitable for a deck, as it is damaged by direct exposure to sun and rain. A new option is all-weather wicker (tech-nically, *wicker* is the weaving technique, not the specific material used to make it), which is usually constructed over a metal frame. The wicker may be made of extruded polypropylene resin, vinyl, fiberglass, heavily coated natural reed, or other materials. Read the manufacturer's information to determine whether a piece can be used outdoors all season long. Well-made all-weather wicker is as attractive and comfortable as traditional wicker.

Maintenance. Hose off all-weather wicker regularly and wash it with mild soap and water occasionally. Do not scrub it with abrasive powders or silicone cleaners, and do not add chlorine bleach to the wash water.

Plastic

Lightweight and durable, plastic has long been a mainstay for outdoor seating. There are two types of plastic furniture: resin and tubular. Resin plastic furniture is molded into shape; tubular furniture is made of PVC pipe joined with glue. Resin furniture may or may not need cushions; tubular plastic furniture always needs them. Undeniably inexpensive,

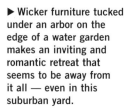

▶ Wicker furniture tucked under an arbor on the edge of a water garden makes an inviting and romantic retreat that seems to be away from it all — even in this suburban yard.

plastic may not be very stylish or comfortable, but it can be a good intermediate step if you are furnishing your deck on a budget. Environmentally conscious gardeners can find plastic furniture made from 100 percent recycled plastic.

Maintenance. Hose off plastic furniture regularly, and wash it periodically with a solution of mild soap and water. Dry it with a soft towel, and do not use abrasive cleansers or products that contain bleach. A layer of car wax will protect the finish.

Outdoor Fabrics

Cushions and chairs with fabric slings, webbing, or upholstery must be covered or taken inside over winter. Regardless of the material of the frame, webbed and sling-style furniture, which have fabric attached to a frame, require less maintenance than do cushioned or padded chairs, which consist of a frame and separate upholstered seats. That's because webbing and fabric slings are designed to dry quickly in place, while cushions may need to be removed from the furniture in order to dry out after a heavy rain.

When shopping for upholstered outdoor furniture or cushions for chairs, look for washable, fade-resistant fabrics that also resist mildew. Two fabrics commonly used to make durable outdoor furnishings are acrylic and polyester. Sunrella is one brand of water-repellent acrylic fabric used in awnings, umbrellas, and outdoor upholstery and cushions. PVC-coated fabric is also used for some outdoor furniture, as are cotton blends.

Cushions should be filled with a fast-drying material that does not absorb water, such as polyester. Move cushions off furniture when they get wet, and allow them to air-dry. They'll dry fastest when set on their sides. This is particularly important for steel and wrought-iron furniture, because dampness from the fabric causes rust on the frames.

Furniture Cover-Ups

Furniture covers come in many shapes and sizes. In addition to covers designed for various chairs and tables, you can purchase them for grills and other items stored on the deck. Look at pool and patio stores or in catalogs. All are made from two main types of material.

Reinforced vinyl. Look for covers made of heavyweight (10- to 12-gauge) material, and be sure a usable temperature range is listed with the product. The best-quality covers can be used in temperatures as low as ¯20°F; however, poor-quality covers are brittle and crack in cold weather.

Tyvek. Furniture covers made of Tyvek are very lightweight, making them easy to put on and take off, yet are quite effective. Tyvek repels rain but also breathes, which allows moisture to escape.

Although most fabrics designed for outdoor use are mildew resistant, mold and mildew will grow on substances such as dirt and suntan oil that build up on the fabric. Therefore, wash cushions periodically with a solution of water and mild detergent, then rinse them and let them air-dry. To store cushions over winter, wash and thoroughly dry them, then store them indoors. Never store outdoor cushions in sealed plastic bags or when they are wet.

Winter Storage

How much winter storage space do you have? Most deck furniture lasts best when protected from the elements over winter, so if your storage space is limited, look for deck furniture that either folds up or can be stacked in a space-efficient manner. Better yet, buy furniture that can be left outdoors year-round. Another option is to invest in furniture covers to protect furnishings from the elements, so that you can leave them outdoors even in winter. Planning on carrying furniture indoors each fall? Consider how heavy each piece is. You'll come to dread this chore if it's too difficult. And keep in mind that for the longest life span, chair cushions should always be stored indoors.

Decorating Your Deck Year-Round

Small decorative touches offer a fun way to give a deck unique appeal that is yours alone. Decorations for the deck can be permanent or temporary. A still life of gourds and pumpkins combined with container-grown kales or mums celebrates fall; a snow sculpture could be a showstopper for a few weeks in winter. Since decks often are visible from indoors, keep in mind that decorations offer a nice way to strengthen the connection between indoor and outdoor rooms. Look for ways to repeat materials or colors indoors and out, or use similar objects in both places. For example, we have watering cans that hang in the rafters of our living room and others that sit out on the deck.

▼ Wreaths and decorations are easy to hang on deck railings to send holiday greetings to your entire neighborhood. Be sure to position some to point toward the house, so that they can be enjoyed from indoors.

▲ For a flat, plain wall, a trompe l'oeil scene of flowers can add wonderful charm and appeal.

Selecting Decorations

When selecting ornaments, keep in mind that they should be able to withstand the weather, and should be either heavy enough not to blow around in the wind or securely fastened down. While bronze, aluminum, and stainless-steel items won't rust outdoors, other metals will. You'll have to decide whether you care — some metal pieces look great when they rust. Use the ideas on these pages as a springboard; the options are as varied as your imagination.

Lighting. While basic safety lighting to illuminate steps and walkways is essential, lights can also become a decorative element all their own. Shining a small spotlight or two up into a nearby tree adds drama to a deck at night (however, make sure spotlights don't shine into your neighbor's yard). Hanging strings of small decorative lights over a dining area or under an arbor creates a festive atmosphere, too.

Table decorations. Dress up an outdoor table with a simple all-weather centerpiece. All summer, a collection of choice cacti and succulents fills our table. A shallow bowl planted with annuals or bulbs is another great choice. (Don't leave wet or potentially wet pots on wrought-iron tables!) For parties, consider candles. Lanterns designed for boats are great, because they're safe on wooden decks and don't blow out on windy evenings. You can also find blown-glass rings designed to hold a flower or two that can be floated in a shallow dish of water. Combine them with floating holders for votive candles and you'll have a wonderful nighttime centerpiece.

Mementos. A deck is a great location to display objects that remind you of special people or places. Tuck a piece of driftwood from a favorite vacation spot or a garden sculpture from a friend next to a container and you'll have a daily reminder of a special memory.

Collections. If you collect certain items, and they can withstand the weather, consider displaying them on your deck. Place items among containers, along the base of railings, or on side tables.

Wall decorations. The walls surrounding a deck cry out for decoration. Try hanging all-weather versions of paintings, metal wall ornaments, and stone plaques. An antique iron gate or section of fence may be just the thing to hang on a wall. Ornamental latticework is also effective. Traditionally, it is made of strips of lath or thin branches cut and fastened to form a grid or another pattern, which can be either simple or complex. Any number of collections can be used to decorate walls, including old garden tools, birdhouses, or floats from crab or lobster pots.

▶ A steel sun-and-moon wall hanging made in Haiti and a mix of houseplants decorate a shady porch on the author's deck. The all-weather plant stand is made from two cast-stone pedestals topped by a bluestone stair tread.

Favorite
Deckside Plants

Wherever your garden and whatever your design, great plants are crucial for creating a wonderful deckscape. Some of my favorites are listed in this chapter and are organized by plant type: annuals and tender perennials; perennials, biennials, and bulbs; shrubs and small trees; and hardy and tender vines. All are easy to grow and offer a long season of interesting features that are attractive for deckscapes.

Don't stop your search for deckscaping candidates here, though; you'll find lots of ideas by visiting other gardens — both public and private — in your area. This is an especially effective way to find plants you like that are hardy in your zone. If you have problem spots in your yard, such as steep slopes or hot, sunny exposures, for example, look for similar sites in other yards and gardens to see which plants might offer good solutions. While you are out looking for new plants to try, make sure you notice effective plant combinations as well. You may discover a wonderful mix of new plants to use when highlighting a particular favorite. Well-stocked garden centers and nurseries, especially those with demonstration gardens, are also fine places to look for ideas. Make a list of your own favorites, too, and try a few new ones each year.

Annuals and Tender Perennials

Both annuals and tender perennials are invaluable for deckscaping, because the most popular ones remain attractive all summer long. The plants listed here include some tried-and-true favorites and a few more unusual selections you'll find at well-stocked garden centers.

Flowering maples

Abutilon spp.

As their common name suggests, these tender shrubs have maplelike leaves and delicate-looking bell- to cup-shaped flowers. Blooms are borne from early summer to fall and come in shades of pink, yellow, orange, red, or white. Where hardy, flowering maples can exceed 10 feet in height, but plants remain much smaller when grown in containers. Selections with variegated leaves are especially handsome.

Abutilon x *hybridum* 'Souvenir de Bonn'

Grower's Choice: Flowering maple, *Abutilon* x *hybridum;* many hybrids are available, including 'Souvenir de Bonn' (white-edged leaves and soft orange flowers). *A. pictum* 'Aureo Maculata' and 'Thompsonii' (variegated leaves and yellow or orange flowers).
Special Features: Good for containers; nice specimens or standards.

Acalyphas

Acalypha hispida and *A. wilkesiana*
Both species are handsome tender shrubs, one grown for its flowers and the other for its showy foliage. Both produce pendent spikes of tiny, densely packed flowers. Where hardy, they reach 6 feet or more.
Grower's Choice: Red-hot cat's-tail, *A. hispida* (green leaves and showy, ropelike, bright red flower clusters). Copperleaf, Jacob's-coat, *A. wilkesiana* (foliage plant with showy, often lobed or wavy-edged leaves variegated with cream, pink, copper, red, and green).
Special Features: Good for containers.

Agastaches

Agastache hybrids
Vigorous relatives of mint, agastaches are 1½–3-foot-tall tender perennials with aromatic leaves and two-lipped flowers. Flowers come in shades of orange, salmon, pink, and rose-purple; plants bloom all summer and into fall.
Grower's Choice: 'Apricot Sunrise', 'Firebird', 'Tutti-Frutti'.
Special Features: Flowers are fragrant and attract butterflies and hummingbirds; leaves are fruity scented; make good container plants.

Agastache, hybrid cultivar, 'Blue Fortune'

Joseph's coat, Parrot leaf

Alternanthera ficoidea
Grown for its colorful foliage, this tender perennial features rounded or narrow leaves marked in many combinations of red, bronze-purple, brown-purple, green, and orange. Plants form loose, 6–12-inch mounds. The flowers are insignificant.
Special Features: Good container plant (filler); good for edgings.

Bacopas

Bacopa spp.
Grown for their dainty flowers and trailing habit, these 3-inch-tall tender

perennials have low branches that spread to 1–1½ feet. Plants bear tiny leaves and an abundance of white flowers all summer long.

Grower's Choice: 'Snowflake' and 'Snowstorm' (heat- and disease-resistant; white flowers); lavender-flowered selections are also available.

Special Features: Good container plants (trailers and weavers).

Begonias

Begonia spp.

Planted either in the ground or in containers, begonias bring striking foliage along with a summerlong display of flowers. The fleshy leaves are commonly rounded or wing-shaped; flowers range from single to double; and plants grow from fibrous roots, tubers, or rhizomes. Consider tuberous begonias for containers or for a spot with rich, moist, well-drained soil. They are best in areas with relatively cool summers. Popular wax begonias, *B. semperflorens,* grow in sun to shade, but partial shade is best. Although most begonias are fine with morning sun, they need shade from midmorning to late afternoon and are ideal for sites in partial shade.

Grower's Choice: *B.* 'Richmondensis Alba' (fibrous rooted, white or very pale pink flowers, dark green, glossy angel-wing-shaped leaves). Sutherland begonia, *B. sutherlandii* (tuberous, bears pale orange flowers). Tuberous begonias, *B.* x *tuberhybrida* (large red, red-orange, orange, pink, cream, or yellow flowers along with bold foliage; both upright and trailing forms are available).

Special Features: All make fine container plants; great for shade.

Swiss chard

Beta vulgaris

Normally confined to the vegetable garden, Swiss chard produces handsome, erect, 1½-foot-tall clumps of edible green leaves, often with stems and veins in a contrasting color.

Grower's Choice: 'Bright Lights' (stems and veins in cream, yellow, pink, or red); 'Rhubarb' (scarlet stems and veins).

Special Features: Makes a good container plant (flag); attractive in kitchen and flower gardens.

Brugmansias, Angel's trumpets

Brugmansia spp.

Grown for their exotic-looking, trumpet-shaped flowers, these tender shrubs or small trees bear enormous blossoms 6–10 inches in length, depending on the species. Plants bloom from summer to fall and can reach 15 feet in height, but usually are smaller in containers. Keep plants in containers year-round or plant them in the garden during the summer and dig up in fall to overwinter indoors. Keep them nearly dry in a cool (45°F), frost-free place over winter.

Grower's Choice: *B.* x *candida* and *B. suaveolens* (fragrant at night). *B. sanguinea* (showy orange-red flowers but not fragrant).

Special Features: Good plants for containers, especially when used as specimens; fragrant cultivars are nice additions to an evening garden.

Brugmansia x *candida*

Caladiums

Caladium bicolor

Caladiums are essential foliage plants for shade, especially in containers. The plants, which grow from tubers, reach 1½–2 feet and feature showy, arrow-shaped leaves in many colors and patterns. Florida Series cultivars are especially good for containers, as they have thicker, more sun-tolerant leaves. Caladiums are fine in a spot with morning sun, but they do best with bright shade during the rest of the day.

Grower's Choice: 'Candidum'; 'Fanny Munson'; 'Little Miss Muffet'; Florida Series cultivars, including 'Florida Cardinal', 'Florida Fantasy', and 'Florida Sunrise'.

Special Features: Grow in partial to full shade; handsome container plants.

Canna 'Durban'

Cannas

Canna x *generalis* hybrids
Cannas produce upright clumps of large leaves topped by clusters of showy, orchidlike flowers that add a tropical flair to the garden. Many of the newest cannas have brilliantly colored foliage in addition to attractive flowers. Dwarf cultivars, such as the ones listed below, reach about 3 feet in height and are effective in containers, beds, and borders.
Grower's Choice: 'China Doll' (green leaves, pink flowers); Pfitzer Series (green leaves; red, pink, and yellow flowers); 'Red Futurity' (burgundy leaves, red flowers); 'Rose Futurity' (burgundy leaves, coral-pink flowers); 'Striped Beauty' (yellow-striped leaves, yellow flowers); 'Tropical Rose' (green leaves, rose-pink flowers).
Special Features: Good container plants (flags); handsome accents for flower beds.

Ornamental peppers

Capsicum annuum
These heat-loving annuals feature starry white or purple flowers, attractive foliage, and shiny fruits in a variety of sizes, shapes, and colors. Fruits, which either point up or hang down, usually start out green and ripen to yellow, red, purple, orange, or chocolate-brown, depending on the cultivar selected. Several selections have colorful leaves marked with purple, green, and cream.
Grower's Choice: 'Holiday Cheer'; 'Poinsettia'; 'Starburst'; 'Thai Hot Ornamental'; 'Marbles'; 'Pretty in Purple'; 'Largo Purple' and 'Trifetti' (variegated-leaved cultivars).
Special Features: Heat tolerant; good container plant (contrast or accent); good for beds and kitchen gardens.

Dusty millers

Centaurea spp., *Senecio cineraria*
These tender perennials are grown for their lacy-looking, white-woolly, fernlike leaves, which add color and contrast to container combinations. Most gardeners remove the small, daisylike flowers.
Special Features: Lacy-textured container plants (fillers); add nice texture to flower beds.

Cosmos

Cosmos spp.
Easy-to-grow cosmos sport showy, daisylike flowers and lacy leaves. *C. bipinnatus* bears flowers in shades of pink, maroon, pinkish red, and white. *C. sulphureus* has yellow, orange, and orange-red flowers.
Grower's Choice: 'Sonata' and Versailles Mix are dwarf plants. *C. bipinnatus* (1½–2 feet tall); *C. sulfureus* 'Klondike' and Ladybird Series (18-inch-tall dwarf selections).
Special Features: Flowers attract butterflies; white cultivars ('Purity' and 'Sonata White' are two) are good in an evening garden; dwarf forms make good container plants.

Cupheas

Cuphea spp.
These shrubby tender perennials are grown for their small, tubular flowers, which are carried from summer to fall either singly or in clusters.
Grower's Choice: Mexican or Hawaiian heather, *C. hyssopifolia* (clusters of pale pinkish purple, pink, or white flowers). Cigar flower, firecracker plant, *C. ignea* (red to red-orange flowers, borne singly, each with a white edge and two dark purple petals at the tip that make them look like a lit cigarette). *C.* x *purpurea* (clusters of pink to red flowers).

Cuphea x *purpurea*

Special Features: Flowers attract hummingbirds; all make good container plants (fillers).

Daturas, Angel's trumpets

Datura metel

Daturas bear large, erect trumpets in white, yellow, or purple all summer long. (Daturas resemble *Brugmansia* species, which bear pendent trumpets.) All parts of this plant are poisonous, so you may want to avoid it if you have small children or pets.

Grower's Choice: 'Evening Fragrance' (scented white flowers).

Special Features: Good in an evening garden; flowers are fragrant.

Fuchsias

Fuchsia spp.

In areas with cool summers, few plants surpass fuchsias for summertime display. Grow them as standards, as contrast or accent plants, or as trailers in hanging baskets. The pendent, tubular flowers may be single, semidouble, or double. They often feature two or more colors and usually come in shades of red, purple, pink, or cream. Give fuchsias partial shade or morning sun and afternoon shade plus rich, well-drained, evenly moist soil. Shade and daily watering are essential in most areas, even those with mildly warm summers.

Grower's Choice: Hundreds of cultivars are available, all wonderful. Choose the colors that appeal to you.

Special Features: Flowers attract hummingbirds; good container plants (contrasts or accents; specimens); grow in partial shade.

Curry plants, Licorice plants

Helichrysum spp.

Helichrysums are grown primarily for their foliage, which is sometimes aromatic. The small, daisylike flowers are insignificant, and many gardeners remove them as they appear. Cut back curry plants as required to keep them looking neat and compact. Curry plant, *H. italicum* ssp. *serotinum,* is grown for its lacy-textured aromatic leaves. Licorice plant, *H. petiolare,* bears on branched stems small, woolly, ornamental leaves that are not fragrant.

Grower's Choice: Curry plant, *H. italicum* ssp. *serotinum* (highly aromatic, currylike, gray-white leaves on mounding, 1–1½-foot plants). Licorice plant, *H. petiolare* (heart-shaped, non-fragrant, gray-green leaves); 'Limelight' (silvery lime-green leaves); 'Variegatum' (gray-green and cream leaves); miniature cultivars are also available.

Special Features: All make nice container plants (trailers and weavers).

Heliotrope

Heliotropium arborescens

Also called cherry pie, heliotrope is a tender perennial shrub with dark green leaves that set off showy, rounded, 3–4-inch-wide clusters of tiny fragrant flowers. Blooms come in shades of violet and lavender, as well as white. Plants can reach 4 feet in height.

Grower's Choice: Many cultivars feature a rich, vanilla-like fragrance, but not all are scented, so it pays to sniff before you buy. As it's name implies, 'Alba' has white flowers.

Special Features: Flowers attract butterflies; makes a good container plant (contrast or accent); flowers are fragrant; white cultivars are good in an evening garden.

Heliotropium arborescens

Ornamental sweet potatoes

Ipomea batatas

Normally found in vegetable gardens, these tender perennials feature heart-shaped leaves and small, pale purple flowers that are insignificant. The cultivars that follow were developed especially for ornamental purposes.

Grower's Choice: 'Blackie' (dark, purple-black, maplelike leaves); 'Margarita' (chartreuse leaves); 'Pink Frost' (green leaves marked with white and pink).

Special Features: Attractive foliage plant for containers (trailers and weavers); excellent ground cover in flower beds.

Beefsteak plant, Painted blood leaf

Iresine herbstii

These annual or short-lived tender perennials are grown for their colorful leaves variously marked with green, yellow, red, purple-red, and orange-red. Plants usually stay about 1 foot tall but can reach 5 feet where hardy.

Grower's Choice: 'Aureoreticulata' (green leaves with yellow veins); 'Brilliantissima' (red-pink leaves blotched with purple-brown).

Special Features: Good container plant (filler); good edging plant.

Lantanas

Lantana camara

Tender shrubs reaching 3–6 feet, lantanas are grown for their showy clusters of tiny flowers that often have several colors in each head. Blooms come in shades of yellow, pink, red, cream, lilac, and purple. Trailing lantana, *L. montevidensis,* is a spreading species that makes a nice trailer.

Grower's Choice: 'Dwarf Yellow' (yellow flowers); 'Radiation' (red and yellow-orange clusters); 'Snow White' (white flowers).

Special Features: Good in containers and flower beds; effective as a standard.

Lantana camara 'Dwarf Yellow'

Edging lobelia

Lobelia erinus

These popular trailing or bushy tender perennials grow 4–9 inches tall and bear an abundance of very small (½-inch) blue, violet, pink, red, or white flowers from early summer to frost. Plants have green leaves that are sometimes flushed with maroon-bronze.

Special Features: Grows in shade; makes a good container plant (trailer and weaver).

Parrot's beak, Lotus vine

Lotus berthelotii

A prostrate or trailing tender perennial, parrot's beak grows 6–8 inches tall and spreads to several feet. Plants bear silver-green, needlelike leaves in clusters and small orange-red to red-scarlet flowers all summer.

Special Features: Makes a good container plant (trailer and weaver).

Stocks

Matthiola spp.

Common stock and night-scented stock are cool-weather annuals that produce beautiful spikes of spicy-scented blooms in early summer. In areas that do not have cool summers, they will need replacing with more heat-tolerant plants once warm weather arrives.

Grower's Choice: Common stock, *M. incana.* Night-scented stock, *M. longipetala.*

Special Features: Flowers are fragrant; good for an evening garden.

Nicotianas, Flowering tobaccos

Nicotiana spp.

Nicotianas bear tubular flowers in shades of pink, red, white, and chartreuse that may or may not be fragrant. Modern hybridizers have concentrated on developing cultivars with blooms that remain open during the day (flowers of most species open only in the evening) and come in a broader color range, and the result is that most cultivars are scentless. Fortunately, some (see the following list) are worth growing for their fragrance. Plants self-sow.

Nicotiana alata 'Nicki'

Grower's Choice: Flowering or jasmine tobacco, *N. alata* (aromatic, greenish yellow, trumpet-shaped flowers); Nicki Series (dwarf hybrids with fragrant flowers); *N. sylvestris* (white, sweetly scented white flowers especially fragrant in the evening).

Special Features: Fragrant flowers attract hummingbirds, butterflies, and moths; dwarf cultivars are good container plants; scented and white-flowered cultivars are good plants for an evening garden.

Geraniums

Pelargonium spp.

Many geraniums are outstanding plants for deck gardens. Scented geraniums usually bear small, relatively inconspicuous flowers but richly aromatic foliage; the better-known zonal or bedding geraniums are grown for their round clusters of flowers in shades of scarlet, orange-red, pink, and white that appear from summer to frost. Many have a distinct maroon-brown band, or zone, on their leaves that adds interest to the foliage.

Other geraniums feature smaller flowers but handsomely colored foliage.

Grower's Choice: To choose scented geraniums, it's best to rub leaves and pick your favorites; fragrances include lemon, coconut, nutmeg, apple, and mint. For zonal geraniums with colorfully patterned leaves, look for 'Bird Dancer' (dark-zoned, maplelike leaves); 'Mr. Henry Cox' (leaves in shades of green, cream, yellow, purple-maroon, and red); and 'Vancouver Centennial' (gold leaves marked with maroon-brown).

Special Features: Good container plants (contrasts or accents); handsome in flower beds.

Petunias

Petunia spp.

These popular bedding and container plants bear showy trumpet-shaped flowers in a wide range of colors. In addition to popular hybrids, *P. integrifolia* is a species with small, dark-centered, magenta-pink flowers from spring to frost that is an

especially good weaving plant, both in the ground and in containers.

Grower's Choice: Fantasy Series (abundant 1–1½-inch-wide flowers blooming all summer on 2–4-inch-tall plants that spread to 8 inches); Supertunia and Surfinia groups (also very vigorous, especially with weekly or biweekly feeding).

Special Features: Good container plants (trailers and weavers); flowers attract hummingbirds.

Petunia, hybrid cultivar, 'Fantasy Pink Morn'

New Zealand flax

Phormium tenax

These tender perennials form clumps of sword-shaped leaves 3–6 feet in height. Many variegated cultivars are available.

Grower's Choice: 'Bronze Baby' (2–3-foot-tall, arching bronze leaves); 'Dazzler' (3-foot, bronze-maroon leaves striped with red and pink); 'Sundowner' (6-foot leaves striped in pink, bronze, and green).

Special Features: Handsome container plant (flag).

Plectranthus

Plectranthus spp.

Several species of these tender perennials are grown for their leaves, which are both aromatic and attractive. The spikes of tiny, pale-colored flowers, which are borne in summer, are relatively insignificant. Cuban oregano or Mexican mint, *P. amboinicus,* is attractive and edible. It has rounded, spicy-scented leaves that make a delicious accompaniment to many dishes. Gray-green-leaved *P. argentatus* is another handsome, widely available species.

Grower's Choice: For special foliage interest, look for variegated selections such as *P. amboinicus* 'Variegatus' (also sold as 'Marginatus') and *P. forsteri* 'Marginatus' (also sold as 'Iboza'), both of which have white-edged leaves.

Special Features: All of these plants make handsome, robust container plants (fillers); excellent for sites in partial shade.

Common mignonettes

Reseda odorata

These annuals bear clusters of insignificant greenish and brownish flowers but with an extremely sweet scent. Blooms are most fragrant when grown in poor soil and full sun. Sow seeds in beds in spring or start them in containers on the deck.

Grower's Choice: Newer hybrids with showier blooms aren't as aromatic as the species.

Special Features: Flowers are extremely fragrant; grows well in partial shade.

Sages, Salvias

Salvia spp.

Sages bear their clusters of two-lipped, tubular flowers in a variety of colors, most notably red, purple-red, blue, purple, and pink. Although many sages aren't hardy north of Zone 7, common sage *(S. officinalis)* is an exception; it's hardy in Zones 5–9). Sages are easy to grow as annuals or tender perennials. Just plant them after danger of frost has passed. To keep sages blooming all summer, deadhead regularly. If plants become too leggy, cut them back hard in midsummer, then water and feed them, and they'll produce new flowers and foliage within a few weeks.

Grower's Choice: Texas sage, *S. coccinea* (spikes of pink, red, or white flowers); 'Coral Nymph' (salmon-and-white flowers) and 'Lady in Red' (scarlet flowers), both 1½ feet tall. Scarlet sage, *S. splendens* (a popular, long-blooming annual; brilliant red cultivars are most common, but attractive violet, mauve-

Salvia 'Purple Majesty'

purple, creamy white, and pink selections are available). Gregg sage, *S. greggii* (red, purple, violet, pink, and yellow flowers). *S. guaranitica* (rich blue flowers).

Special Features: Flowers attract hummingbirds; make good container plants (flags); many have aromatic foliage.

Creeping zinnias

Sanvitalia procumbens

These mat-forming annuals produce an abundance of small golden yellow daisies with dark centers from early summer to fall. Selections with yellow, orange, and gold flowers are available, too. Plants reach 6–8 inches in height but can spread to several feet.

Grower's Choice: 'Mandarin Orange' and 'Yellow Carpet' (dwarf selections; grow up to 4 inches tall).

Special Features: Nice edging or ground cover plant; effective in containers (contrast or accent plant).

Dusty miller

Senecio cineraria; see *Dusty millers, Centaurea cineraria*

Coleus

Solenostemon scutellarioides

These popular foliage plants come in a staggering array of colors and leaf shapes; once the bug bites, you'll want to collect them all. Give coleus rich, evenly moist, well-drained soil in partial to full shade. So-called "sun coleus" cultivars thrive in full sun with evenly moist soil. Remove the erect spikes of flowers as they appear, to direct energy to the plants' amazing

Solenostemon scutellarioides 'Frogsfoot Purple'

foliage. To overwinter your favorites, take cuttings in early fall and grow them indoors.

Grower's Choice: 'Alabama Sunset', 'India Frills', 'Inky Fingers', 'Japanese Giant', 'The Line'.

Special Features: Outstanding and showy container plant (contrast or accent); thrives in shady beds.

Marigolds

Tagetes spp.

These hardworking, popular annuals are as great in containers as they are in the garden. French marigolds, *T. patula*, bear orange, yellow, or bronze flowers in many patterns and forms. They tend to stop blooming in very hot weather but will resume later in the season when temperatures cool. Signet marigolds, *T. tenuifolia*, produce 1-foot mounds of lacy, aromatic foliage topped by an abundance of dainty gold, yellow, or orange flowers all summer long. Triploid marigolds (the result of crosses between French and African marigolds) are especially vigorous dwarf (1-foot) plants with showy 2–3-inch flowers. These continue blooming right through hot, stressful weather and don't set seeds.

Grower's Choice: Gem Series signet marigolds, *T. tenuifolia* ('Lemon Gem' and 'Tangerine Gem'); triploid marigolds (Zenith and Nugget Series).

Special Features: Flowers attract butterflies and hummingbirds; good container plants (contrasts or accents); flowers are edible.

Common nasturtiums

Tropaeolum majus

These popular annuals bear nearly round leaves and spurred 2–2½-inch flowers in shades of red, orange, and yellow. In addition to the bushy

Tropaeolum majus 'Whirlybird Cherry Rose'

cultivars listed here, see Nasturtiums (page 155) for information on climbing nasturtiums.

Grower's Choice: Alaska Series (green leaves splotched and speckled with cream); 'Tip Top Mahogany' (stunning chartreuse leaves, mahogany flowers); Whirlybird Series (compact, bushy plants; spurless flowers).

Special Features: Good container plant (trailer and weaver); attractive spilling over walls and sprawling out of beds; flowers and foliage are edible.

Verbenas

Verbena spp.

Trailing forms of verbena make handsome, long-flowering additions to containers. They produce showy clusters of small, trumpet-shaped flowers in a range of shades from purples and violets to red, rose, maroon-red, and white. Plants usually stay under 1 foot and spread to about 2 feet.

Grower's Choice: 'Peaches and Cream' (apricot and salmon flowers); Novalis and Romance Series (compact plants with flowers in a range of colors); 'Silver Ann' (pink flowers). Moss or cut-leaf verbena, *V. tenuisecta* (aromatic leaves, and clusters of flowers in shades of lavender to purple, mauve, lilac-blue, and white).

Special Features: All make good container plants (trailers and weavers); flowers attract hummingbirds and butterflies.

Perennials, Biennials, and Bulbs

For a progression of color from spring to fall, plant a variety of perennials, biennials, and bulbs in the flower beds surrounding your deck. The following list includes plants for both sun and shade. All of them are dependable and feature long-lasting flowers and/or handsome foliage.

Achilleas, Yarrows

Achillea spp.

Achilleas bear flat-topped or slightly rounded clusters of tiny flowers in shades of yellow, pink, red, and white all summer, provided the spent blooms are removed. The plants produce mounds of aromatic, feathery leaves and attract beneficial insects as well as butterflies. Dry or sandy soil is best, but plants tolerate richer conditions if the soil is well drained. Zones 3–8, depending on the cultivar.

Achillea, hybrid cultivar, 'Coronation Gold'

Grower's Choice: Galaxy Hybrids (including 'Appleblossom' with lilac-pink flowers, 'Fanal' with red flowers, and 'Summerwine' with dark red blooms); 'Coronation Gold' and 'Moonshine' (yellow flowers). *A. millefolium* 'Cerise Queen' (magenta flowers). *A. millefolium* 'Summer Pastels' (compact plants in a range of pinks, lavenders, and creams).
Special Features: Flowers attract butterflies and beneficial insects; leaves are slightly aromatic.

Bugleweeds

Ajuga spp.

These vigorous perennials are grown for both their showy foliage and their short spikes of tiny, densely packed flowers. Blossoms are borne in spring and early summer and come in shades of blue-purple to pink and white. Plants produce ground-hugging rosettes of rounded, spinachlike leaves that are evergreen or semievergreen. They can be extremely vigorous spreaders. Zones 3–8.
Grower's Choice: Blue or geneva bugleweed, *A. genevensis* (moderately fast-spreading species with indigo flowers in spring). Pyramid bugleweed, *A. pyramidalis* (slow-spreading, compact species); 'Metallica Crispa' (crinkled, dark green leaves flushed with bronze-purple). Common or carpet bugleweed, *A. reptans* (fast spreaders, especially 'Catlin's Giant' and 'Jungle Beauty'); 'Burgundy Glow' and 'Multicolor' (moderate spreaders with variegated leaves marked with white, pink, and green).
Special Features: Good ground covers; grow in shade.

Aquilegia flabellata 'Mini-Star'

Columbines

Aquilegia spp.

Although they flower best and stay more compact when grown on sunny sites, columbines will bloom in partial shade and actually appreciate the cooler conditions offered by a spot with morning sun and afternoon shade. Columbines are an important nectar source for hummingbirds from late spring into early summer, when the birds are migrating into most areas. All columbines are short-lived perennials, so plan on replacing them every few years. Many self-sow, but seedlings may not resemble their parents; pull up any that you find unattractive. Zones 3–9, depending on the cultivar.

Grower's Choice: Native wild columbine, *A. canadensis* (red-and-yellow flowers). Golden or yellow columbine, *A. chrysantha* (yellow flowers, heat tolerant). Fan columbine, *A. flabellata* (lilac- to purple-blue flowers). Long-spurred columbine, *A. longissima* (yellow flowers); McKana Hybrids (all colors).

Special Features: Flowers attract butterflies and hummingbirds; grow in shade.

Wild gingers

Asarum spp.

Handsome, low-growing perennials for shade, wild gingers are prized for their large, kidney-shaped leaves. Their spring-borne flowers are generally inconspicuous and are carried under the foliage near the ground. Plants spread steadily to form broad drifts or mounds.

Grower's Choice: Canada wild ginger, *A. canadense* (native wildflower with deciduous leaves, Zones 3–8). European wild ginger, *A. europaeum* (glossy evergreen leaves, Zones 4–8). *A. hartwegii* and *A. shuttleworthii* (evergreen leaves marbled with silver, Zones 5–9).

Special Features: Good ground covers; thrive in shade.

Asarum europaeum

Coreopsis, Tickseeds

Coreopsis spp.

Coreopsis are sturdy, easy-to-grow perennials bearing daisylike single or double flowers in summer. Blooms usually come in shades of yellow and gold, and plants flower for weeks provided spent blooms are removed regularly either by deadheading or by shearing.

Grower's Choice: Large-flowered coreopsis, *C. grandiflora* (hardy perennial or warm-weather annual, blooms late spring through summer; yellow to yellow-orange, daisylike flowers from spring to late summer; easy to grow from seed). Lance-leaved coreopsis, *C. lanceolata* (yellow flowers from late spring to midsummer). Pink coreopsis, *C. rosea* (rosy pink flowers from summer to early fall). Thread-leaved coreopsis, *C. verticillata* (blooms all summer); cultivars 'Moonbeam' (pale yellow flowers) and 'Zagreb' (deep yellow flowers).

Special Features: All attract butterflies; *I. grandiflora* makes a good container plant (contrast or accent).

Coreopsis lanceolata 'Sterntaler'

Dianthus gratianopolitanus 'Baker's variety'

Pinks

Dianthus spp.

Pinks bear single, semidouble, or double flowers that often feature a rich spicy-sweet scent, plus foliage that is often evergreen. Blooms come in all shades of pink as well as white and maroon; bicolors are common. When buying pinks (or any perennials) specifically for fragrance, read the label or catalog descriptions carefully, or buy plants in bloom so you can sniff before you buy. Zones 3–9.

Grower's Choice: Cheddar pinks, *D. gratianopolitanus,* and cottage pinks, *D. plumarius* (both have fragrant flowers).

Special Features: Good for sunny flower beds; evergreen foliage; nicely fragrant flowers.

Bleeding hearts

Dicentra spp.

Several species of these popular perennials are ideal additions to shade gardens. They bear arching racemes of dainty, pendent, heart-shaped flowers, primarily in shades of pink or in white. Fringed bleeding heart, *D. eximia,* and Western bleeding heart, *D. formosa,* are native species that form handsome mounds of fernlike leaves and bloom from spring through fall, provided the soil remains moist.

Grower's Choice: Fringed bleeding heart, *D. eximia,* and its cultivars, including 'Bountiful' (rose-red flowers); 'Langtrees' (white flowers); 'Luxuriant' (cherry red flowers); and 'Snowdrift' (white flowers). Western bleeding heart, *D. formosa.* Common bleeding heart, *D. spectabilis* (rose-pink, rose-red, or white flowers in late spring or early summer; plants go dormant after blooming).

Special Features: Grow in shade; long bloom season; handsome leaves.

Purple coneflowers

Echinacea purpurea

Tough, native wildflowers, purple coneflowers bear daisylike blooms with conelike centers and drooping purple, purple-pink, or white petals from early to midsummer. Deadheading prolongs bloom. Plants self-sow. Zones 3–9.

Grower's Choice: 'Kim's Knee-High' (pink flowers, 2 feet tall); 'Bright Star' or 'Leuchtstern' (purplish red flowers); 'Magnus' (extra-large flowers); 'White Lustre' and 'White Swan' (both have white flowers).

Special Features: Flowers attract butterflies and beneficial insects; seedheads feed birds in winter; white cultivars are nice in an evening garden.

Echinacea purpurea 'Magnus'

Epimediums

Epimedium spp.

Also called barrenworts, epimediums feature showy, wiry-stemmed clusters of small flowers in early spring. Most gardeners treasure these tough, easy-to-grow perennials for their delicate-textured foliage that remains handsome from spring through early winter. While plants prefer evenly moist soil, they will tolerate dry shade as well once established. Zones 4–8.

Grower's Choice: Long-spurred epimedium, *E. grandiflorum,* and its cultivars 'Rose Queen' and 'White Queen'. Bicolor epimedium, *E. x versicolor* (pinkish red and yellow flowers with red spurs and evergreen to semievergreen leaves). Warley epimedium, *E. x warleyense* (brick- to orange-red flowers and evergreen to semievergreen leaves). Young's epimedium, *E. x youngianum* (white or rose-pink flowers and evergreen to semievergreen, fernlike leaves, 6–8 inches tall); look for 'Niveum' (white flowers) and 'Roseum' (pale mauve-pink flowers).

Special Features: Grow in shade; good ground covers; tolerate dry shade and competition from tree roots once established.

Cranesbills, Hardy geraniums

Geranium spp.

These versatile perennials produce mounds of exceptionally handsome, finely cut leaves topped by loose clusters of five-petaled flowers from late spring to midsummer, depending on the species. Many species also exhibit good fall foliage color. Most do best in full sun or partial shade with rich, evenly moist, well-drained soil; shade during the hottest part of the day is best in warm climates. After the main flush of flowers fades, cut plants to within 1 inch of the ground to encourage new leaves to form and discourage flopping. Many geraniums are evergreen in mild climates. All feature attractive, lobed leaves. Unless otherwise noted, all of the following species are hardy in Zones 4–8.

Grower's Choice: Grayleaf cranesbill, *G. cinereum* (gray-green leaves, purple-pink flowers in late spring to early summer) and its cultivar 'Ballerina' (dark-eyed, purplish red flowers all summer); Zones 5–8.

Dalmatian cranesbill, *G. dalmaticum* (pink flowers in late spring and early summer; red-orange fall foliage; grows in sun as well as shade).

Lilac cranesbill, *G. himalayense* (violet-blue flowers in early summer; red-orange leaves in fall); 'Ann Folkard' (hybrid with dark-eyed, magenta flowers in midsummer to fall; chartreuse leaves on trailing stems); Zones 5–9.

Bigroot geranium, *G. macrorrhizum* (pink to purple-pink flowers in spring; mound forming; aromatic leaves; spreads vigorously); Zones 3–8.

Wild cranesbill, spotted geranium, *G. maculatum* (pink flowers from late spring to midsummer).

G. x oxonianum (pink flowers spring to fall); hybrids 'Claridge Druce' (rose-pink flowers and gray-green leaves) and 'Wargrave Pink' (salmon-pink flowers).

Armenian cranesbill, *G. psilostemon* (dark-eyed, magenta flowers; red leaves in fall); Zones 5–8.

Bloody cranesbill, *G. sanguineum* (pink flowers spring into summer; scarlet leaves in fall). Good cultivars include 'Album' (white flowers); 'Elsbeth' (pink flowers); 'New Hampshire Purple' (purple flowers); and 'Shepherd's Warning' (rosy purple flowers).

G. sanguineum var. *striatum* (also listed as *G. sanguineum* var. *lancastriense;* bears pale pink flowers; all are suitable for sun as well as shade); Zones 3–8.

Wood cranesbill, *G. sylvaticum* (violet-blue flowers in spring; deeply cut leaves; grows best in partial shade).

Geranium maculatum

Hellebores, Lenten roses

Helleborus x *hybridus* (often listed as *H. orientalis*)

These dependable, shade-loving perennials produce handsome clumps of 1–1½-foot-tall dark green, leathery leaves that are evergreen. Loose, showy clusters of saucer-shaped flowers appear in late winter to early spring. Typically, flowers are creamy to greenish white spotted with maroon, but hybridizers are developing many new selections, including ones with pure white, mauve, mauve-purple, maroon, and black-purple blooms. Zones 4–9.

Grower's Choice: Look for any of the new hybrids. All are seed-grown, so self-sown seedlings generally are attractive plants as well.

Special Features: Grows in shade.

Daylilies

Hemerocallis spp.

Tough and versatile, daylilies produce clumps of arching, sword-shaped leaves topped in summer by trumpet-shaped

Hemerocallis, hybrid cultivar, 'Barbary Corsair'

flowers. Thousands of cultivars are available, and the best selections are worth searching out, as they produce lots of buds and bloom over a period of 3–4 weeks. Colors include all shades of yellow, orange, and peach, as well as maroon, red, orange-red, pinkish lavender, plum, and nearly white. Surprisingly, quite a few daylilies bear blooms that remain open in the evening. Plants tolerate poor soil and drought conditions but will bloom less. Deadhead daylilies regularly to keep the faded flowers from detracting from the new ones that are about to open. (Tetraploid daylilies especially need regular deadheading.) Daylilies are also classified by bloom season, so select a mix of plants that are described as early, midseason, and late blooming. Zones 3–10.

Grower's Choice: 'Apricot Sparkles', 'Big Time Happy', 'Bitsy', 'Butterpat', 'Eenie Weenie', 'Fragrant Treasure', 'Fairy Tale Pink', 'Happy Returns', 'Little Grapette', 'Pardon Me', 'Rosy Returns', 'Gentle Shepherd', 'Joan Senior', 'Stella D'Oro', and 'Scentual Sundance'. For the best show, look for cultivars described as reblooming or continuous blooming. Fragrant daylilies include lemon daylily, *H. lilioasphodelus,* and the cultivar 'Hyperion', both with fragrant flowers.

Special Features: Flowers (especially red, orange, and pink) attract hummingbirds.

Heucheras

Heuchera spp.

Until recently, coral bells, *H.* x *brizoides* and *H. sanguinea,* both noted for their

flowers, were the most commonly grown plants from this genus of North American plants. Coral bells produce low mounds of rounded, lobed leaves topped by airy clusters of tiny, bell-shaped flowers from late spring to early summer in shades of pink, coral, red, rose-red, and white. Today, a variety of heucheras grown for their foliage have become popular. Also called alumroots, these are hybrids of *H. americana* and *H. micrantha.* Foliage cultivars produce clusters of tiny white or greenish flowers in early summer (many gardeners remove them) but feature handsome mounds of lobed or ruffled leaves that can be richly marked with a mix of silver, purple-brown, rose-burgundy, maroon-green, and purple-red. Leaves featuring contrasting veins and blotches also are common. Zones 4–8.

Grower's Choice: 'Palace Purple' is most popular; other cultivars include 'Chocolate Ruffles', 'Chocolate Veil', 'Dale's Strain', 'Garnet', 'Persian Carpet', 'Pewter Veil', 'Ruby Ruffles', and 'Velvet Knight'.

Hostas

Hosta spp.

Classic perennials for shade, hostas come in an amazing variety of sizes and shapes. By planting several different cultivars, you can use them to add bold foliage, brightly patterned leaves, and showy flowers to shade gardens. When selecting hostas, mix up sizes, foliage colors, and variegati to ensure an interesting array of plants. Zones 3–8.

Hosta plantaginea 'Big Daddy'

Grower's Choice for Large Hostas (2½–3 feet tall; at least 4 feet wide): 'Big Daddy' (enormous clumps of heart-shaped leaves and white flowers); 'Blue Angel' (blue-gray leaves and white flowers in midsummer); 'Blue Umbrellas' (blue to blue-green leaves and pale lavender flowers in early summer); 'Krossa Regal' (blue-gray leaves and lavender flowers in midsummer); 'Regal Splendor' (blue-gray leaves marked with creamy white and yellow); 'Sagae' (formerly *H. fluctuans* 'Variegata'; blue-gray leaves edged with cream; white flowers in midsummer); 'Sum and Substance' (chartreuse leaves and pale lilac flowers in mid- to late summer); *H. sieboldiana* 'Elegans' (blue leaves) and 'Frances Williams' (variegated leaves).

Grower's Choice for Medium-Sized Hostas (2 feet tall; 2–3 feet wide): 'Blue Cadet', 'Blue Wedgwood', and 'Halcyon' (all with blue leaves); 'Birchwood Parky's Gold' and 'Zounds' (both with chartreuse leaves); 'Brim Cup', 'Francee', 'Gold Standard', 'Golden Tiara', 'Great Expectations', and 'Wide Brim' (all with variegated leaves).

Grower's Choice for Small Hostas (under 1 foot): 'Ginkgo Craig' (green leaves edged in white; lavender flowers bloom in late summer); 'Gold Edger' (pretty chartreuse leaves); 'Kabitan' (greenish yellow leaves edged in darker green).

Grower's Choice for Fragrance: August lily, *Hosta plantaginea* (green leaves; good for evening gardens); 'Fragrant Bouquet' (leaves edged in creamy yellow); 'Honeybells' (green leaves); 'So Sweet' (leaves edged in creamy white).

Special Features: Grow in shade.

Lamiums, Deadnettles

Lamium spp.

These low-growing perennials bear small clusters of two-lipped flowers, but most are enjoyed for their attractive variegated leaves. Give lamiums a spot in partial to full shade, but be aware that some selections spread vigorously, especially in rich, moist soil. They are best kept away from less vigorous perennials.

Grower's Choice: Yellow archangel, *L. galeobdolon* (green leaves and yellow flowers in summer; extremely vigorous); 'Hermann's Pride' (less invasive cultivar; leaves streaked with silver); Zones 4–8.

Outstanding cultivars of *L. maculatum* include 'Beacon Silver' (silver, green-edged leaves and pink flowers); 'Beedham's White' (chartreuse leaves and white flowers); and 'White Nancy' (green-edged, silver leaves and white flowers); Zones 3–8.

Special Features: Good for shade gardens; excellent ground covers.

Lamium maculatum 'Pink Nancy'

Lavender

Lavandula angustifolia

A well-known herb, lavender is grown for its mounds of aromatic gray-green, needlelike, evergreen leaves and spikes of fragrant flowers in summer. Plants tolerate drought and absolutely require well-drained soil. Lavender is ideal in terraced or raised beds. Shear or cut back after the main flush of bloom is finished in summer. Zones 5–9.

Grower's Choice: 'Hidcote' (dark purple flowers); 'Munstead' (compact, to 1½ feet); 'Jean Davis' (pink flowers).

Special Features: Both foliage and flowers are fragrant.

Lavandula angustifolia 'Lavender Lady'

Lilies

Lilium spp.

Lilies are among the showiest bulbs of summer, and because they bloom when deck use is at its peak, they're perfect for adding color and fragrance to deckscapes. Hummingbirds visit the trumpet-, cup-, or bowl-shaped flowers of many hybrid lilies. For lilies that shine during the evening, look for white-flowered fragrant cultivars. As most lilies aren't all that attractive once they have finished blooming, combine them with annuals or perennials to help hide their yellowing foliage. Zones 3–8, depending on the cultivar.

Grower's Choice: There are hundreds of lilies to choose from in a rainbow of colors. Look through a catalog or visit your local garden center and pick the ones that appeal. To attract hummingbirds, consider planting Canada lily, *L. canadense,* or Turk's-cap lily, *L. superbum,* both native species with red to orange-red flowers. Fragrant, white-flowered lilies are terrific for an evening garden. Look for Madonna lily, *L. candidum;* white regal lily, *L. regale* 'Album'; white Japanese lily, *L. speciosum* 'Album'; trumpet and Aurelian hybrid 'Bright Star'; and Oriental hybrid 'Casa Blanca'.

Special Features: Flowers attract hummingbirds; many are fragrant; white-flowered plants are good in an evening garden.

Lilyturfs

Liriope spp.

These vigorous ground covers produce drifts of grassy, evergreen leaves and spikes of small, densely packed flowers in late summer or fall. Flowers are usually violet to white. For added interest, look for cultivars with variegated leaves.

Grower's Choice: *L. muscari* 'John Birch' (gold-edged leaves) and 'Variegata' (creamy white leaf margins), both hardy in Zones 6–9; *L. spicata* is hardy in Zones 5–10.

Special Features: Good ground cover; plants grow in shade.

Nepetas, Catmints

Nepeta spp.

These sturdy plants produce mounds of aromatic leaves topped by spikes of small, two-lipped flowers throughout the summer. Cut back plants hard after the first main flush of bloom to encourage rebloom. Zones 3–8, depending on the cultivar.

Grower's Choice: *N.* x *faassenii* (lavender-blue flowers; silvery gray leaves; 1–2 feet tall). Look for 'Six Hills Giant' (violet-purple flowers).

Special Features: Flowers are attractive to bees, butterflies, and beneficial insects.

Penstemons, Beardtongues

Penstemon spp.

These spring- and summer-blooming perennials bear loose, graceful clusters of tubular red, purple, lavender-blue, yellow, or white flowers. Because most penstemons dislike hot, humid summers, the

Penstemon 'Ruby'

hybrids listed here are Grower's Choice for gardens in the eastern United States. Gardeners in the West can grow a wide range of species plus the hybrids.

Grower's Choice: Look for hybrids 'Garnet', 'Prairie Fire', and 'Ruby', as well as hairy beardtongue, *P. hirsutus.*

Special Features: Flowers attract hummingbirds.

Perovskia, Russian sage

Perovskia atriplicifolia

A tough, shrubby plant 3–5 feet tall, perovskia is grown for its aromatic, ferny-textured leaves, which are silver to gray-green in color. In addition to having handsome foliage all summer, plants produce showy clusters of small, violet-blue flowers from late summer through fall. To keep plants compact, cut them back hard in late fall; from Zone 5 north, they are generally killed to the ground each winter but will resprout. Zones 5–9.

Special Features: Adds airy, cloudlike texture to perennial gardens.

Phlox

Phlox spp.

Phlox bear rounded clusters of five-petaled flowers in a variety of colors, including red, pink, lavender, purple, and white. There are species for sun and shade, and ones that bloom in spring, early summer, and midsummer.

Grower's Choice for Shade: Wild blue phlox, *P. divaricata* (lavender or white flowers in spring and early summer; Zones 3–9). Creeping phlox,

Phlox divaricata 'London Grove'

P. stolonifera (pink, white, or lavender flowers in spring; Zones 3–8).

Grower's Choice for Sun: Carolina phlox, *P. carolina* (purple to pink flowers; Zones 4–9). Wild sweet William, *P. maculata* (fragrant mauve-pink blooms; 'Miss Lingard' and 'Omega' are white cultivars; Zones 4–8). Old-fashioned garden phlox, *P. paniculata* (comes in a range of colors); 'David' (outstanding disease-resistant white cultivar); 'Shortwood' (pink-flowered, disease-resistant sport of 'David'; Zones 3–8).

Special Features: Flowers attract hummingbirds; white cultivars are good in an evening garden.

Platycodon, Balloon flower

Platycodon grandiflorus

Tough and dependable, this sturdy perennial forms clumps and sports inflated balloonlike buds that open into bell-shaped flowers from early to midsummer. Flowers come in shades of purple, blue-violet, lilac, pink, and

white. The blue-green leaves turn a nice yellow in fall. Removing spent blooms keeps plants flowering all summer. Self-sows. Plants are slow to emerge in spring, so mark the clumps to avoid digging into them accidentally. Zones 3–8.

Grower's Choice: *P. grandiflorus* f. *albus* (white blooms; compact, blue-flowers. Forms include Balloon Series plants, *P. grandiflorus* f. *mariesii*, and 'Sentimental Blue'). 'Shell Pink' (very pale pink flowers).

Special Features: White cultivars are good in an evening garden; very long-blooming.

Solomon's seals

Polygonatum spp.

Sturdy, shade-loving perennials, Solomon's seals are grown primarily for their handsome leaves, which resemble arching green feathers. Use them to add contrasting shape and habit to the shade garden by combining them with plants such as hostas. The small, bell-shaped, creamy white flowers, which appear in spring, are relatively insignificant, as they are borne under the leaves. Pendent black berries follow the flowers in fall. Plants spread steadily by rhizomes to form large drifts. Zones 4–8.

Grower's Choice: Variegated Solomon's seal, *P. odoratum* var. *thunbergii* 'Variegatum' (leaves striped with white; 3 feet tall).

Special Features: Thrives in shade.

Pulmonarias

Pulmonaria spp.

Also called Bethlehem sages and lungworts, pulmonarias bring small clusters of tiny bell-shaped flowers to the shade garden from late winter into late spring. Attractive leaves are arranged in rosettes and are usually mottled or blotched with silver. They remain attractive from spring into early winter, and some are evergreen in mild climates. An old standby cultivar, *P. saccharata* 'Mrs. Moon', with silver-spotted leaves, is most commonly grown, but many outstanding newer hybrids are available and well worth planting. Zones 4 or 5–8.

Rudbeckia laciniata

Grower's Choice: 'Janet Fisk' (pink flowers aging to blue; white-marbled leaves); 'Roy Davidson' (sky blue flowers; green leaves blotched with silver); 'Spilled Milk' (pink flowers aging to blue; silver-white leaves).
Special Features: Grow in shade.

Rudbeckias, Orange coneflowers

Rudbeckia spp.

Tough and tolerant, rudbeckias are native wildflowers that bear daisylike flowers in summer; most have yellow-orange petals and dark centers. Popular black-eyed Susans, *R. hirta,* are biennials or short-lived perennials, so start new plants each year. The other species listed here are dependable perennials. Zones 3–9.
Grower's Choice: *R. fulgida* var. *sullivantii* 'Goldsturm'. *R. hirta* (red-brown, yellow, gold, bronze, and rust flowers). 'Indian Summer' (cultivar with large yellow flowers). Ragged coneflower, *R. laciniata* (towers 3–6 feet with yellow flowers and green centers). Look for double-flowered 'Golden Glow' or 'Goldquelle'.
Special Features: Attract birds and butterflies.

Sedums

Sedum spp.

Tough, drought-tolerant sedums have clusters of small star-shaped flowers and fleshy leaves. There are species and hybrid cultivars suitable for perennial beds and borders as well as for ground covers. Unless otherwise noted, sedums are hardy in Zones 4–9.

Sedum spectabile

Grower's Choice for Beds and Borders: 'Autumn Joy' and 'Herbstfreude' (8-inch-wide flowers, initially green, then dark pink, then red-brown; flowers stand through winter; Zones 3–9); 'Vera Jameson' (rose-pink flowers in fall; purplish to burgundy leaves). 'October Daphne', *S. sieboldii* (pink flowers in fall; blue-green leaves edged in pink; Zones 3–8). Showy stonecrop, *S. spectabile* (blooms late summer); 'Brilliant' (hot pink flowers); 'Carmine' (dark pink flowers); 'Variegata' (creamy yellow leaves); Zones 3–9. *S. telephium* spp. *maximum* 'Atropurpureum' (pink flowers in late summer or fall; purple leaves and stems).
Grower's Choice for Ground Covers: 'Ruby Glow' (pinkish red flowers in midsummer to early fall; purplish green leaves; Zones 5–9). *S. kamtschaticum* (golden flowers in late summer); 'Variegatum' (white-edged

leaves). *S. spathulifolium* (yellow flowers in summer; slow-spreading evergreen); 'Cape Blanco' (blue-green leaves); 'Purpureum' (purple leaves); Zones 5–9. Two-row sedum, *S. spurium* (pinkish-purple or white flowers in late summer; fast-spreading evergreen); 'Dragon's Blood' (also sold as 'Schorbuser Blut'; dark pink flowers and purple-tinted leaves); 'Elizabeth' (bronze and maroon leaves); 'Tricolor' (pink-, white-, and green-striped leaves).

Tiarellas, Foamflowers

Tiarella spp.

Tiarellas are native woodland wildflowers that bear fluffy spikes of tiny white or pink flowers in late spring or early summer. The plants produce mounds of leaves that range from maplelike to deeply cut. Happily, this is another genus that has received lots of attention from hybridizers in recent years. Hybrids of both Allegheny foamflower *(T. cordifolia)* and Wherry's foamflower *(T. wherryi)* are available. Although the flowers are lovely, the foliage is the big attraction here. Zones 3–8.

Grower's Choice: 'Dunvegan' (deeply lobed leaves and pink flowers); 'Eco Red Heart' (maplelike leaves with a reddish central blotch); 'Iron Butterfly' (deeply cut leaves with maroon-black stripes); 'Oakleaf' (oakleaf-shaped leaves and pink flowers); 'Slickrock' (deeply cut, dark green leaves); 'Tiger Stripe' (red-veined leaves with a prominent central stripe).
Special Features: Thrive in shade.

Spiderworts

Tradescantia spp.

Spiderworts bear clumps of long, straplike leaves and clusters of three-petaled flowers that last only one day. After plants finish producing their main flush of bloom, cut them to the ground to keep them neat. This also encourages them to rebloom and discourages self-sowing. Many cultivars are available and, in recent years, hybridizers have released some new ones that bloom from early summer to fall and feature more attractive foliage and more compact habits than those of older hybrids. Zones 4–9.
Grower's Choice: 'Bilbury Ice', 'Concord Grape', 'Hawaiian Punch', 'Little Doll', 'Purple Dome', 'Red Cloud', 'Snowcap'.
Special Features: Grow in shade.

Yucca, Adam's needle

Yucca filamentosa

This tough native plant bears large, showy, erect spikes of creamy white, bell-shaped flowers above a mound of sword-shaped, evergreen leaves. Selections with variegated leaves are attractive year-round. Zones 4–10.
Grower's Choice: 'Bright Edge' and 'Color Guard' (both with green leaves edged in yellow); 'Garland Gold' and 'Golden Sword' (both with yellow leaves edged in green).

Tradescantia 'Concord Grape'

Shrubs and Small Trees

By surrounding your deck with flowering shrubs, roses, and even small trees, you can bring the garden right up to the edge of the railings. Here are some of the best woody plants for summer deckscapes, in both sun and shade. All feature long seasons of color and interest from flowers, foliage, berries, bark, and other characteristics.

Butterfly bush, Summer lilac

Buddleia davidii
Grown for its liliac-like trusses of lavender, rose-purple, violet, and white flowers, butterfly bush blooms from summer into fall, especially if you deadhead regularly. This plant is a 10-foot-tall shrub in the southern

Buddleia davidii 'Black Knight'

United States but is routinely killed to the ground over winter in Zone 6, and thus remains smaller. Even in warmer climates, it is best to cut it within several inches of the ground in spring to keep it nice and compact. Where butterfly bush is not hardy, you can grow it in a container overwintered indoors, as you would tender perennials, by keeping it nearly dry in a cool (40°F), sunny spot. Zones 6–9.
Grower's Choice: 'Black Knight' (purple-black flowers); 'Harlequin' (variegated leaves and red-purple flowers); Nanho Series ('Nanho Blue', 'Nanho Purple', 'Nanho White'; cultivars are somewhat dwarf, reaching only 4–5 feet); 'Pink Delight' (pink flowers).
Special Features: Flowers very attractive to butterflies.

Sweetshrub, Carolina allspice

Calycanthys floridus
In summer, this old-fashioned shrub bears small, maroon-red flowers that have a sweet, fruity fragrance. The scent varies from plant to plant, so look for specimens in flower so you can sniff before you buy. Sweetshrub grows in sun or shade and reaches 6–9

feet in height. It may exhibit good yellow fall color. Zones 5–9.
Special Features: Fragrant flowers in early summer.

Dogwoods

Cornus spp.
By far the best-known member in this genus is flowering dogwood, *Cornus florida,* but a number of excellent shrubs that are worthy of attention also belong

Cornus florida 'Alba'

here. Dogwoods bear their small, starry flowers in clusters, and the showy "petals" are actually petal-like bracts surrounding the clusters. In addition to spring flowers, dogwoods bring other features to the landscape, including berries, colorful fall foliage, and attractive bark. They also tolerate a range of growing conditions; the selections that follow are suitable for shaded sites.

Grower's Choice: Silky dogwood, *C. amomum* (yellowish white flowers in late spring or early summer; bluish berries; moist to wet soil; grows in shade; Zones 5–8). Cornelian cherry, *C. mas* (large, multistemmed shrub or small tree; clusters of tiny yellow flowers in late winter followed by showy red fruit in summer; purple-red foliage in fall; scaly, exfoliating bark attractive in winter; thrives in partial shade but tolerates full shade); 'Golden Glory' (heavy flowering) and 'Pioneer' (large, showy, dark red fruit); Zones 4–8. Pale dogwood, *C. obliqua* (flat-topped clusters of white flowers; bluish berries; moist to wet soil; grows in shade; Zones 3–8).
Special Features: Berries are attractive to birds and other wildlife.

Cotoneasters

Cotoneaster spp.

These utilitarian plants range from low-growing ground covers to large shrubs and feature small spring flowers followed in summer by fruits that often are showy. Some species of cotoneasters are evergreen; others are deciduous.

Grower's Choice: Bearberry cotoneaster, *C. dammeri* (evergreen to semievergreen; white flowers; red fruits; red-purple leaves in fall; 1½ feet tall and 6 feet wide; Zones 5–8). Rockspray cotoneaster, *C. horizontalis* (mounding ground cover; about 3 feet tall, at least 5 feet wide, often wider; pink flowers; showy red fruits; red-purple leaves in fall; interesting branching habit, somewhat like fish

Cotoneaster horizontalis

bones; Zones 5–7). Many-flowered cotoneaster, *C. multiflorus* (10–15-foot-tall species that is suitable for hedges, privacy screening, and along the back of beds surrounding a deck; white spring flowers; abundant red fruits; somewhat blue-green, deciduous leaves; Zones 4–7).
Special Features: Four-season interest; fruits attract birds.

Fothergillas

Fothergilla spp.

These often-overlooked shrubs feature fragrant white flowers in spring, handsome foliage in summer, and very showy yellow, orange, or red foliage in fall. Both of the commonly cultivated species require well-drained, acidic soil rich in organic matter. Fothergillas will tolerate

partial shade but bloom best in a spot with full sun.
Grower's Choice: Dwarf fothergilla, *F. gardenii* (2–3 feet tall). Large fothergilla, *F. major* (9–10 feet tall).

Fothergilla gardenii

Hydrangeas

Hydrangea spp.

These easy-to-grow plants bring color to the garden from early summer into fall, at a time when few other shrubs are in bloom. Hydrangeas bear large, very showy clusters of many small individual flowers; each cluster contains tiny fertile (seed-producing) flowers and larger, petal-like sterile ones. Although most hydrangea species will grow in sun to partial shade, oakleaf hydrangea in particular grows very well in shade; however, it will bloom less in a shaded site.

Hydrangea quercifolia

Grower's Choice: Smooth hydrangea, *H. arborescens* (5 feet tall; creamy white flowers from early summer to fall; Zones 4–9). Bigleaf hydrangea, *H. macrophylla* (6 feet tall; pink, blue, or purplish flowers bloom early to midsummer; popular cultivars include 'Blue Billow', 'Blue Wave', 'Pia', and 'White Wave'; Zones 6–9). Panicle hydrangea, *H. paniculata* (10–20 feet tall; white flowers bloom in midsummer that turn purplish pink by fall; Zones 4–8). Oakleaf hydrangea, *H. quercifolia* (4–6 feet tall, spreads by suckers; showy panicles of white flowers in summer that turn purplish pink, then brown by fall; oak-shaped leaves turn spectacular shades of red, orange, and purple-maroon in fall; cinnamon-colored, exfoliating bark; grows in shade but may not bloom well without some sun, Zones 5–9).
Special Features: Very showy flowers throughout summer.

Hollies

Ilex spp.

The best-known hollies are broad-leaved evergreens with spiny foliage, but this genus contains tough, handsome deciduous shrubs as well. Among the best of the shrub-sized evergreen species are the blue, or Meserve, hybrid hollies *(I. x meserveae),* which feature exceptional hardiness along with glossy dark green leaves and heavy crops of red fruits. With all hollies, you need both male and female plants to obtain fruit set.
Grower's Choice for Deciduous Hollies: Common winterberry, *I. verticillata* (deciduous, showy red fall fruits). Look for 'Winter Red' and 'Southern Gentleman' (a suitable male pollinator), as well as 'Sparkleberry' and 'Apollo' (a suitable pollinator); Zones 3–9.
Grower's Choice for Evergreen Hollies: Japanese holly, *I. crenata* (black fruits and small, rounded

Ilex verticillata

leaves; Zones 5–9). Inkberry holly, *I. glabra* (native species; black fruits; small, rounded leaves; Zones 5–9). Blue (Meserve) hollies, *I. x meserveae.* Look for 'Blue Girl', 'Blue Maid', and 'Blue Princess' and their suitable male pollinators 'Blue Boy' and 'Blue Prince'. In the southeastern United States, look for heat-tolerant cultivars 'China Boy', 'China Girl', and 'Nellie R. Stevens'; Zones 5–7. Longstalk holly, *I. pedunculosa* (large shrub or small tree; dark green, nonspiny leaves; showy red fruits; Zones 6–9).
Special Features: Showy berries in fall and winter; attractive to birds; evergreen selections add winter color.

Magnolias

Magnolia spp.

Most magnolias are large trees; however, two species that bear fragrant flowers remain small enough to fit into plantings around a deck: star magnolia and sweet bay magnolia.

Grower's Choice: Star magnolia, *M. stellata* (fragrant white flowers in late winter or early spring; handsome dark green leaves that turn yellow in fall; attractive smooth gray bark; Zones 5–9). Sweet bay magnolia, *M. virginiana* (lemon-scented, creamy-white flowers from spring or early summer through early fall; leaves silvery underneath, some with yellow fall foliage; in warm climates, grows to 60 feet or more, evergreen; in cool climates, grows 10–20 feet tall and wide and is semideciduous or deciduous; Zones 6–9).

Malus 'Indian Summer'

Magnolia stellata 'Rubra'

Crabapples

Malus spp.

Crabapples, with their clusters of often fragrant spring flowers and ornamental late-summer to fall fruits, make nice additions to any deck planting. Although most crabapples are 20–25 feet tall when mature, dwarf selections also are available — ones that mature at 10 feet are hardly bigger than shrubs. If you want to attract birds, look for small-fruited cultivars (¼–⅓-inch fruits are best), so birds will be able to fit the fruits into their beaks. Zones 5–8.

Grower's Choice: Select crabapples resistant to common foliage diseases, because they remain attractive all summer and are healthier and longer-lived than ones without that trait. Hybridizers are introducing new disease-resistant plants annually, so talk to your local Cooperative Extension Service, surf the Internet, or discuss your options with experts at a nearby nursery or botanical garden to determine which cultivars are best for your area. The seriousness of a particular disease depends on where you live, so local recommendations are valuable.

Special Features: Flowers are often fragrant; ornamental fruits; fruits attract birds and other wildlife.

Mock oranges

Philadelphus spp.

The white early summer blooms of mock oranges are legendary for their sweet scent, which resembles that of orange blossoms. Make your choices carefully, however, as many cultivars are only slightly fragrant or not scented at all. Plant these sturdy, 5–10-foot-tall shrubs toward the back of a deck border. Most cultivars are hardy in Zones 5–8, but 'Minnesota Snowflake' is hardy into Zone 4.

Grower's Choice: 'Avalanche'; 'Belle Etoile'; 'Fleur de Neige'; 'Innocence'; 'Manteau d'Hermine' (about 3 feet tall); 'Minnesota Snowflake'; 'Sybille'; 'Virginal'.

Special Features: Flowers of the cultivars listed above are fragrant.

Rosa rugosa 'Alba'

Roses

Rosa spp.

When selecting roses for landscape plantings, it's hard to look beyond their flowers, but there are other criteria worth considering. Roses described as "reblooming" (or *remontant*) produce their main show in early summer, followed by smaller flushes of bloom later in the season. Flower fragrance also is important, especially for roses that will surround a deck. Many roses feature showy hips that add color to the late-summer and fall garden. Because performance of different types and cultivars of roses varies from one part of the country to another, it's a good idea to get recommendations from local gardeners, rosarians, or experts at botanical or other public gardens before you make a selection.

Roses with disease-resistant foliage are more attractive landscape plants than are finicky hybrid teas, so keep disease resistance near the top of your list. Catalogs describe disease resistance with such adjectives as *some, good,* and *excellent*. Ideally, you want highly disease-resistant roses that look great with minimal care.

Unfortunately, many rose gardens keep their plants attractive by sticking to a biweekly, summerlong spray program with chemical pesticides and fungicides — not something that's good for the environment. Plus, spraying is not a pleasant gardening chore and such chemicals are best kept away from places where people eat, such as a deck. See Deckside Roses on page 107 through 111 for general information on growing roses, plus ideas on selecting and using climbing roses effectively.

Grower's Choice for Shrub Roses: Alba roses, *R. alba;* eglantine roses, *R. eglanteria;* red-leaved roses, *R. glauca* (also listed as *R. rubrifolia*); Meidilland Series shrub roses, including 'Coral Meidilland', 'Royal Bonica' and 'Sevillana'; moyes rose, *R. moyesii;* rugosa roses, *R. rugosa;* Scotch briar, *R. spinosissima.*

Special Features: All of the roses listed here are sturdy and disease resistant; many have showy hips in fall.

Yews, Taxus

Taxus spp.

These needled evergreens, which grow in sun or shade, bring rich, dark green foliage to the garden and also have graceful and attractive growing habits. Use them for screening and informal hedges. They demand well-drained soil and do not tolerate heat. (Plum yews, *Cephalotaxus* spp., are similar-looking plants that are also heat tolerant and good yew substitutes for warm climates.) Cultivars of both species listed here are the best choices for any landscape; named selections with compact or spreading habits are ideal for deckscapes.

Grower's Choice: English yews, *T. baccata* (60 feet tall; dwarf forms include 'Nana', 'Pygmaea', and 'Repandens'; Zones 5 or 6–7). Japanese yews, *T. cuspidata* (40 feet tall; dwarf forms include 'Cross Spreading', 'Dark Green Spreader', 'Densa', 'Emerald Spreader', 'Nana'; Zones 4–7).

Special Features: Grow in sun or shade; berries attract birds; evergreen foliage.

Blueberries

Vaccinium spp.

Often overlooked as landscape plants, blueberries bring white, urn-shaped flowers to deckscapes in spring, followed by succulent berries in summer. They also boast spectacular fall foliage — the leaves turn shades of scarlet, bronze-red, orange, and yellow — so these plants are worth growing even if you don't get a harvest. Although they bloom and bear fruit best in full sun, blueberries grow well in partial shade, too. Plants require acidic soil for best growth. Keep in mind that for good fruit set, you'll need to plant more than one cultivar. You'll also need bird netting if you want to keep the berries for yourself.

Grower's Choice: Lowbush blueberry, *V. angustifolium* (Zones 2–8); rabbiteye blueberry, *V. ashei* (Zones 8–10);

highbush blueberry, *V. corymbosum* (Zones 3–7).

Special Features: Edible fruits; all-season interest; grow in shade.

Viburnums

Viburnum spp.

Premier landscape shrubs, viburnums bring multiseason features to the garden. In addition to spring or early-summer flowers, they produce summer to fall fruit that attracts birds and may or may not be showy. Most also exhibit excellent fall foliage color. If you spend time on your deck in spring, fragrant viburnums are certainly worth growing — or cut the flowers and take them indoors to enjoy. Depending on the species, plants may be evergreen or deciduous. All are valuable plants for screens, natural hedges, and background plants along the base of a deck. Give viburnums full sun to partial shade and rich, evenly moist, well-drained soil.

Grower's Choice: Mapleleaf viburnum, *Viburnum acerifolium* (grows in shade; Zones 4–8).

Burkwood viburnum, *V.* x *burkwoodii* (round, spicy-scented clusters of pink buds that open into white flowers in spring). Look for 'Mohawk' (flowers heavily; disease-resistant foliage turns orange-red in fall); Zones 4–8.

Fragrant viburnum, *V.* x *carlcephalum* (clusters of fragrant white flowers from late spring to early summer; red-purple fall foliage; Zones 6–8).

Koreanspice viburnum, *V. carlesii* (rounded clusters of pinkish buds and fragrant white flowers in spring; Zones 5–8).

Arrowwood viburnum, *V. dentatum* (native shrub; clusters of white flowers from late spring to early summer; blue-black fruits; yellow, red, and red-purple leaves in fall; grows in shade; Zones 3–8).

Linden viburnum, *V. dilatatum* (clusters of white flowers from late spring to early summer; rust-red fall foliage; clusters of bright red fruits that stay on the plant into early winter; grows in partial shade; Zones 5–8).

Judd viburnum, *V.* x *juddii* (rounded clusters of fragrant white flowers in spring; Zones 5–9).

European cranberry-bush viburnum, *V. opulus* (clusters of white flowers from late spring to early summer; showy red fruits; some yellow- to purple-red fall foliage color). Look for 'Compactum' (4–6 feet) and 'Xanthocarpum' (showy yellow fruits); Zones 4–8.

Doublefile viburnum, *V. plicatum* var. *tomentosum* (horizontal branches covered with flat-topped clusters of white flowers in late spring; red berries ripen in mid- to late summer and attract birds; leaves turn stunning red-purple in fall). Look for 'Shasta' (compact; flowers abundantly); 'Summer Stars' (compact; blooms from spring to fall; bears red fruit); and 'Mariesii' (showy flower clusters on horizontal branches); Zones 4–8.

Blackhaw viburnum, *V. prunifolium* (native; pinkish fruit ripens to blue-black; dark green leaves turn red-purple in fall; partial shade; Zones 3–9).

V. x *rhytidophylloides* (semievergreen; reddish fruits in summer that ripen to black; grows in shade). Look for

'Allegheny' (dense, rounded habit; abundant flowers; red fall fruit; handsome foliage); Zones 5–8.

Leatherleaf viburnum, *V. rhytidophyllum* (grows in full sun or heavy shade; clusters of white flowers in spring or early summer; evergreen; Zones 6–8).

Sargent viburnum, *V. sargentii* (showy red fruit from late summer to fall; bronze-purple spring foliage that turns dark green in summer; good yellow to red fall color; Zones 4–7).

American cranberry-bush viburnum, *V. trilobum* (native; bright red, edible fruits in fall; yellow to red-purple fall foliage; Zones 2–7).

Special Features: Showy spring or summer flowers (some are fragrant); colorful fruits attract birds and wildlife; nice summer foliage; spectacular fall color; interesting winter branching habit.

Viburnum plicatum var. *tomentosum* 'Mariesii'

Hardy and Tender Vines

Whether they are trained up trellises, over arbors, or along railings, or simply allowed to spill out of containers, vines add a lush, abundant feel to deckscapes unlike any other plants. You can even train them over shrubs, or plant several vines together to add color and textural contrast to plantings. The species listed here are some of the best annual and tender perennial vines for deckscapes; they are ideal for growing alone or in combination with hardy species. Hardy species need a permanent trellis or other support, while annuals do not. Unless otherwise noted, all grow best with full sun and rich, well-drained soil.

Kiwis

Actinidia spp.
This genus contains both hardy and tender species, all of which are vigorous, twining climbers that bear edible, berrylike fruits. Plants grow in poor to rich soil and sun or partial shade; poor soil helps slow down the plants' rapid growth. Prune plants hard in late winter, cutting back stems to 8–10 strong buds. (Follow pruning guidelines for grapes.) Most kiwis require male and female plants for fruit set, but *A. arguta* 'Issai' is self-fertile.

Grower's Choice: Hardy kiwi, *Actinidia arguta* (vigorous to rampant woody vine; reaches 25–30 feet; handsome dark green leaves; small greenish white flowers in spring; 1-inch, sweet-tasting, yellow-green fruits; Zones 3–8).

Variegated kiwi, *A. kolomikta* (large, handsome leaves blotched with deep pink, pale pink, and white; 15–20 feet; white, early-summer flowers are fragrant; small, sweet-tasting berries; Zones 5–8). Look for 'Arctic Beauty' (hardy to Zone 4; especially handsome variegated leaves).

Fiveleaf akebia

Akebia quinata
Fiveleaf akebia is a vigorous 20–40-foot vine that climbs by twining stems. The plant produces clusters of fragrant brownish purple flowers in spring followed by purplish 4-inch-long fruit in fall. The handsome blue-green leaves remain on the plant until early winter. The plant grows in sun or shade and in any soil. Prune as necessary in early summer after it flowers to keep it in bounds. Can be very invasive. Zones 4–8.

Dutchman's pipe

Aristolochia macrophylla (formerly *A. durior*)
Dutchman's pipe is a vigorous 25–30-foot native vine that climbs by twining stems and bears large, heart-shaped leaves. The plant produces unusual-looking pipe-shaped, yellowish green flowers in early summer. This species grows in any moist, well-drained soil and full sun or partial shade. Zones 5–8.

Cross vine

Bignonia capreolata
Cross vine is a 30–50-foot native, semievergreen to evergreen vine that climbs via tendrils that end in adhesive disks. In late spring, it bears clusters of fragrant, trumpet-shaped flowers that are red-brown on the outside and yellow-orange on the inside. Any well-drained soil is suitable. The plant blooms best in full sun but tolerates heavy shade. Prune heavily in late winter as necessary. Zones 6–9.
Special Features: Flowers attract hummingbirds.

Trumpet vines

Campsis spp.
These rampant climbers cling to walls and supports by adhesive holdfasts. They bear compound leaves with leaflets arranged in a featherlike fashion and clusters of trumpet-shaped flowers. Give them sun and any type of soil. Prune back plants to a few buds in late winter or early spring to keep them in bounds. Zones 5–9.

Campsis tagliabuana 'Mme Galen'

Grower's Choice: Common trumpet vine, *C. radicans* (2½–3-inch-long orange to orange-red flowers from late summer to fall; 30–40 feet; Zones 5–9). Look for 'Flava' (yellow flowers). *C.* x *tagliabuana* 'Mme. Galen' (showy clusters of orange-red, 3-inch-long flowers; Zones 5–9). **Special Features:** Flowers attract hummingbirds.

Balloon vine, Love-in-a-puff

Cardiospermum halicacabum
Balloon vine, or love-in-a-puff, is an old-fashioned, warm-weather annual that climbs by tendrils and bears lacy, fernlike leaves. The insignificant greenish white flowers are followed by inflated, balloonlike seedpods that gave the plant one of its common names.

Clematis

Clematis spp.
These popular vines are grown for their showy flowers and climb via twining leafstalks. Early-blooming clematis bloom in spring to early summer, and usually have single or bell-shaped flowers. They bloom on old wood, so prune immediately after flowering. However, they do not need annual pruning to flower well. Remove dead or damaged wood and cut back shoots to shape the plants.

Early large-flowered hybrids produce blooms from late spring into early summer and also commonly rebloom in mid- to late summer. The first flush of flowers is on old wood; the second flush is produced on new wood at the tips of the current year's growth. Some cultivars produce two flushes of blooms, one on the old wood and a second on new wood. These early-blooming hybrids usually do not need heavy annual pruning. Just shape up the plants in spring as needed by removing dead or damaged growth and cutting back stems to a strong set of buds.

The late-flowering clematis group includes large-flowered hybrids that bloom from summer to early fall, as well as several species that continue into late fall. Prune these plants hard each year in early spring before they begin to grow: Cut them down to 8–12 inches from the ground just above a healthy pair of buds.

Clematis prefer cool soil conditions but bloom best when the tops of the plants are in full sun to partial shade. To give plants these conditions, look for a spot where the roots will be shaded by low-growing shrubs or perennials, or a site on the shaded (north) side of a low wall. Mulch plants to keep the soil cool. Clematis need well-drained soil, so dig deep and amend the soil with organic matter at planting time.

Grower's Choice for Early-Blooming Clematis: Alpine clematis, *C. alpina* (bell-shaped, blue-and-white blooms followed by silky seedheads; Zones 6–9). *C. macropetala* (lavender- to violet-blue, bell-shaped flowers; Zones 4–9). *C. montana* (15–35 feet; 2–2½-inch-wide white or pink flowers in late spring or early summer; Zones 5–7). Look for 'Elizabeth'.

Grower's Choice for Early Large-Flowered Hybrids: 'Barbara Jackman', 'Belle of Woking', 'Blue Ravine', 'Elsa Späth', 'General Sikorski', 'Henryi', 'Nelly Moser', 'Niobe', 'Pink

Clematis 'Elsa Späth'

Champagne', 'The President', and 'Royal Velvet'; Zones 3–8
Grower's Choice for Late-Flowering Clematis: 'Comtesse de Bouchaud', 'Ernest Markham', 'Gipsy Queen', 'Hagley Hybrid', 'Jackmanii', 'Lady Betty Balfour', 'Mrs. Cholmondeley', 'Polish Spirit', 'Star of India', and 'Ville de Lyon' (all hybrids); Zones 3–8.

Oriental clematis, *C. orientalis* (bell-shaped yellow flowers, silky seedheads late summer to late fall; Zones 5–9). Look for 'Bill MacKenzie'.

Sweet autumn clematis, *C. terniflora* (formerly *C. maximowicziana, C. paniculata;* to 20 feet; starry, fragrant white flowers late summer to fall; silky seedheads; self-sows; can become quite invasive).

Texas clematis, *C. texensis* (bell-shaped, red to red-orange flowers in summer). Look for 'Dutchess of Albany', 'Etoile Beauty', and 'Gravetye Beauty'; Zones 3–9.

Italian clematis, *C. viticella* (small, purple-blue or rose-red, bell-shaped flowers from midsummer to fall; Zones 5–9). Look for 'Betty Corning' and 'Etoile Violette'.

Cup-and-saucer vine, Cathedral bells

Cobaea scandens

This tender perennial or warm-weather annual is a vigorous tendril climber that reaches 10–15 feet in the north but up to 40 feet in frost-free climates. Plants bear fragrant, bell-shaped flowers, each carried in a ruffled green cup. Blooms open greenish white and age to purple. 'Alba' bears greenish white flowers.

Pumpkins

Cucurbita pepo

Annual pumpkins make surprisingly nice climbers, especially the miniature-fruited types. The vigorous, attractive vines are large enough to provide considerable screening. They have large, handsome, lobed leaves that can exceed 8 inches across and showy trumpet-shaped, yellow-orange flowers. Check periodically to make sure the vines and fruit are well supported and tie them with soft yarn or string as necessary. Choose vining, not bush-type, cultivars.

Grower's Choice: 'Baby Boo', 'Jack Be Little'.

Chilean glory vine

Eccremocarpus scaber

A tender perennial or warm-weather annual, Chilean glory vine is an exotic-looking tendril climber that bears dark green leaves divided into leaflets and showy clusters of tubular flowers in shades of orange, orange-red, pink, or yellow.

Special Features: Flowers attract hummingbirds.

Carolina jasmine, Carolina yellow jessamine

Gelsemium sempervirens

Carolina jasmine is a 10–20-foot-tall vine with twining stems and small, glossy, evergreen leaves. The plant bears 2–3-inch clusters of fragrant yellow flowers in spring and summer. It grows in sun or shade, although it flowers less in shade. For best results, plant Carolina jasmine in rich, well-drained soil. Zones 6–9.

Gelsemium sempervirens

Hops

Humulus spp.

Hops, *H. lupulus,* is a twining, 20-foot-tall vine with hairy shoots and large lobed, toothed leaves. The plant bears small spikes of mildly fragrant green flowers in summer. Variegated Japanese hops, *H. japonicus,* is a vigorous tender perennial vine that is large enough to cover privacy screens. This plant grows in full sun or partial shade and self-sows. It can become weedy, but the seedlings are easy enough to pull up where they are not wanted.

Grower's Choice: *H. lupulus* 'Aureus' (ornamental chartreuse leaves; Zones 4–8). Variegated Japanese hops, *H. japonicus* 'Variegatus' (deeply lobed leaves splashed and streaked with white; insignificant spikes of greenish flowers; cool-weather annual).

Climbing hydrangea

Hydrangea petiolaris (formerly *H. anomala* ssp. *petiolaris*)

A vigorous woody vine, climbing hydrangea attaches itself to supports by aerial roots and easily reaches 50 feet or higher. The plant has ornamental red-brown, exfoliating bark; attractive rounded leaves; and showy clusters of white flowers that bloom in early to midsummer.

Climbing hydrangea is a large, heavy vine with somewhat brittle stems that require substantial support. The plant needs rich, well-drained, moist soil and grows in both sun and shade. It is slow to establish after transplanting. Zones 4–8.

Morning glories

Ipomoea spp.

Summertime favorites, morning glories are classic tender perennials or warm-weather annuals with funnel-shaped or tubular flowers that open in the morning and close later in the day. The plants listed climb by twining stems.

Ipomoea quamoclit

Grower's Choice: Moonflower, *I. alba* (large heart-shaped leaves; fragrant white, 5-inch-wide flowers that open at dusk from early to midsummer to frost; flowers attract night-flying moths).

Red or star morning glory, *I. coccinea* or *Quamoclit coccinea* (ovate or deeply toothed leaves; clusters of small scarlet trumpets).

Spanish flag, *I. lobata* (formerly *Mina lobata, Ipomoea versicolor,* and *Quamoclit lobata;* lobed leaves; showy, dense, one-sided racemes of tubular ½–¾-inch-long flowers that initially are red but turn orange, yellow, and then cream as they age). Look for 'Citronella' (lemon yellow flowers that age to white).

Cardinal climber, *I.* x *multifida* (deeply lobed leaves; small, brilliant red, trumpet-shaped flowers).

Morning glory, *I. nil* (15 feet; 2–4-inch-wide flowers from midsummer to fall in shades of pale to deep blue, plus red, purple, or white). Look for 'Chocolate' (pale red-brown flowers); 'Early Call Mix' (a fast-growing form good for areas with short growing seasons); and 'Scarlett O'Hara' (red flowers).

Morning glory, *I. purpurea* (2½-inch-wide trumpets in shades of blue, purple-blue, pink, red, and white; white flowers with stripes of color also are available).

Morning glory, *I. tricolor* (vigorous 3-inch-wide flowers with white throats in shades ranging from pale blue to purple). Look for 'Heavenly Blue' (sky blue flowers with white throats) and 'Pearly Gates' (white flowers).

Cypress vine, star glory, *I. quamoclit* (20 feet; deeply cut leaves; ¾-inch-wide scarlet flowers).

Special Features: Flowers attract hummingbirds.

Winter jasmine, Hardy jasmine

Jasminum nudiflorum

Unlike most jasmines, winter or hardy jasmine can be grown in Zones 6–9 and into Zone 5 in a very protected location. This plant is actually a shrub with arching green branches that can reach 10 feet high and wide; they must be tied to trellises like roses. Winter jasmine has dark green, three-leaflet leaves and reddish buds that open into solitary yellow flowers in late winter or early spring. The flowers are not fragrant. Stems root and produce new plants wherever they touch the soil. Plants grow in sun or shade, although they bloom less in shade, and tolerate a range of well-drained soils.

Hyacinth bean

Lablab purpureus (formerly *Dolichos lablab, Dolichos purpureus*)

Hyacinth bean is a fast-growing, twining, tender perennial grown as an annual for its showy rose-purple flowers and unusual glossy purple-maroon pods. The plant can reach 20 feet in a single season. The flat ornamental pods are edible but extremely strong-tasting, and some people may have an allergic reaction to them.

Lablab purpureus

Lonicera sempervirens

Honeysuckles

Lonicera spp.

Climbing honeysuckles can be moderate- to fast-growing vines. All climb by twining stems and bear clusters of two-lipped flowers. Some are fragrant. Give the plants full sun and average to rich, well-drained soil. They will tolerate partial shade. Prune plants after flowering (they bloom on old wood). Cut back stems to encourage branching and to keep the plants in bounds.

Grower's Choice: Goldflame honeysuckle, *L.* x *heckrottii* (red buds open into red-and-yellow, lightly fragrant flowers from spring to summer; 10–20 feet tall; blue-green leaves are evergreen in the southern United States; Zones 5–9). Woodbine honeysuckle, *L. periclymenum* (white to yellow fragrant flowers on 10–20-foot plants; Zones 5–9). Trumpet honeysuckle, *L. sempervirens* (10–20 feet; orange-red, red, or yellow unscented flowers in summer; Zones 4–9).

Special Features: Flowers attract hummingbirds.

Virginia creeper, Boston ivy, Japanese creeper

Parthenocissus spp.

These vigorous vines climb by adhesive holdfasts and easily reach 50 feet or more. Both species described here are tough, tolerant plants that grow in sun or shade, as well as in very poor to rich soil. They produce insignificant flowers in summer, outstanding red fall foliage, and small blue or black berries. Birds relish the seeds and bird- "planted" seedlings may become a nuisance in the garden.

Grower's Choice: Virginia creeper, *P. quinquefolia* (glossy five-lobed leaves turn scarlet in fall; Zones 3–9). Boston ivy, Japanese creeper, *P. tricuspidata* (large three-lobed leaves turn bright red to purple in fall; Zones 4–8).

Passiflora caerulea

Passionflowers

Passiflora spp.

Passionflowers are usually tropical plants suitable only for container culture in the northern United States, but there are hardy species that will add an exotic touch to trellises. Both species described here bear flowers followed by egg-shaped yellow-orange fruit that is edible. Passionflowers climb by tendrils. Give them average to rich soil in full sun or partial shade.

Grower's Choice: Blue passionflower, *P. caerulea* (20–30 feet; 3–4-inch-wide white flowers flushed with purple from summer to fall; Zones 6–9). Maypop, *P. incarnata* (native species; 6 feet tall; pale purple to white 3-inch flowers are lightly scented; Zones 6–8).

Scarlet runner beans

Phaseolus coccineus

Scarlet runner beans are twining tender perennial climbers grown as annuals that can exceed 12 feet in a single season. Plants bear three-part leaves and clusters of scarlet, pea-shaped flowers followed by edible pods and seeds.

Grower's Choice: 'Albus' (white flowers); 'Painted Lady' (red-and-white flowers).

Special Features: Flowers attract hummingbirds, butterflies, and bees.

Purple bell vine

Rhodochiton atrosanguineum

Purple bell vine is an exotic-looking, tender perennial grown for its showy blooms. Individual flowers consist of a bell-shaped mauve-purple calyx (the "bell") with a tubular dark purple flower (the "clapper") that hangs from the center. The plant bears showy heart-shaped leaves that are often blushed with purple, and the showy calyxes remain on the plant long after the true flowers drop. The plant climbs by both twining stems and tendril-like leafstalks.

Potato vine

Solanum jasminoides

Potato vine is a tender perennial climber grown for its small clusters of fragrant, dainty bluish white flowers, which are followed by small black berries.

Grower's Choice: 'Album' (white flowers); 'Aurea' (leaves variegated with green and yellow).

Solanum jasminoides

Nasturtiums

Tropaeolum spp.

Nasturtiums are grown for their showy, spurred flowers and can be bushy, trailing, or climbing plants. See Common nasturtiums on page 133 for more on nasturtiums.

Grower's Choice: Common nasturtium, *T. majus* (climbing or bushy annual; nearly round leaves; 2–2½-inch flowers in shades of red, orange, and yellow). Look for 'Jewel of Africa' (climbs to 8 feet; leaves variegated with creamy white).

Canary vine, canary creeper, *T. peregrinum* (tender perennial; 8 feet long; gray-green leaves; small yellow flowers with fringed petals).

Flame flower, flame nasturtium, *T. speciosum* (tender perennial; 10 feet long; dark green leaves; scarlet flowers; partial shade).

Grapes

Vitis spp.

Grapes are woody vines that attach themselves to supports via tendrils. Although grapes grown for fruit are generally too messy to use over a deck, some ornamental species that do not bear large, fleshy fruit can be used to cover an arbor.

Grower's Choice: Crimson glory vine, *V. coignetiae* (climbs to 50 feet; bears up to 10-inch-long heart-shaped, lobed leaves that turn rich scarlet in fall; small blue-black fruit; Zones 5–9). Purple-leaved grape, *V. vinifera* 'Purpurea' (reaches 20 feet or more; large purple leaves turn dark purple in fall; small purple grapes in summer; Zones 6–9).

Wisterias

Wisteria spp.

Wisterias are vigorous to rampant woody vines that climb by twining stems and easily exceed 30 feet in height. For best flowers on Japanese wisterias, select a named cultivar propagated by cuttings rather than a seed-grown plant. Wisterias are extremely vigorous and need very sturdy supports. Once you have established a main stem that reaches an arbor or other support, cut back shoots hard in late winter, leaving only three or four buds per shoot. Prune as necessary throughout the summer to keep plants in bounds.

Grower's Choice: Japanese wisteria, *W. floribunda* (pendent, 12-inch-long clusters of fragrant, pea-shaped flowers in late spring before or as the leaves emerge; cultivars have flowers in shades of lilac, purple, violet, pink, and white; Zones 5–9). American wisteria, *W. frutescens* (native species with 6-inch-long clusters of lilac flowers in early summer after the leaves have emerged, as well as intermittently throughout the season; Zones 6–9). Chinese wisteria, *W. sinensis* (fragrant, pale lilac to white flowers in late spring as the leaves emerge; Zones 5–8).

Special Features: Flowers are fragrant.

Wisteria floribunda

Zone Map

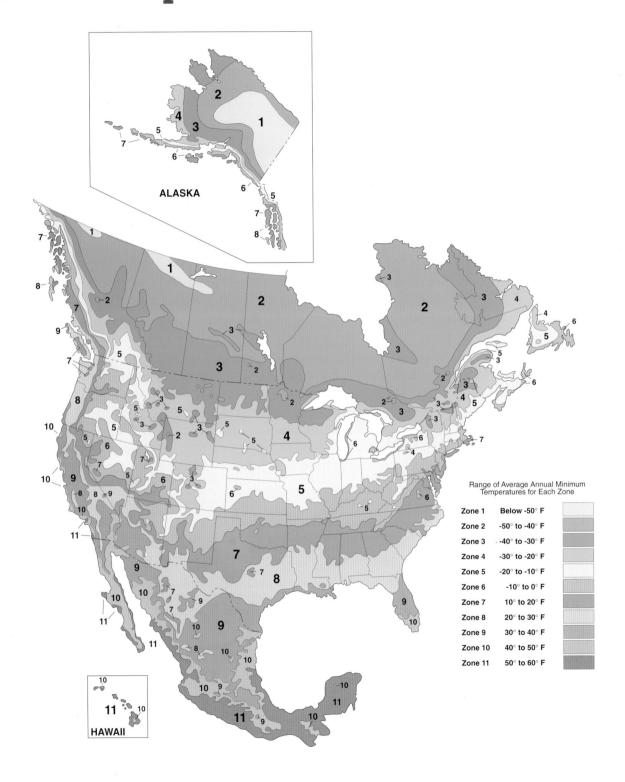

ALASKA

HAWAII

Range of Average Annual Minimum
Temperatures for Each Zone

Zone 1	Below -50° F
Zone 2	-50° to -40° F
Zone 3	-40° to -30° F
Zone 4	-30° to -20° F
Zone 5	-20° to -10° F
Zone 6	-10° to 0° F
Zone 7	10° to 20° F
Zone 8	20° to 30° F
Zone 9	30° to 40° F
Zone 10	40° to 50° F
Zone 11	50° to 60° F

Photograph Credits

© All American Selection: 140 (center left)

© Mark Bolton/gardenIMAGE: 41

© Gay Bumgarner: 43, 101

© Gay Bumgarner/Positive Images: 10, 89, 103

© Rob Cardillo Photography: viii, 9 (bottom right), 27, 35, 62, 69, 79, 83 (bottom left), 98, 116, 118, 123

© Crandall & Crandall Photography: 11, 44, 64, 72, 76, 88, 92, 95, 108, 122 (top right)

© Grace Davies Photography: 78

© R. Todd Davis Photography: 12, 40, 65

© Barbara Ellis: v, 9 (bottom left and top right), 132, 139 (top left), 142 (top right), 146 (top right), 149

© Derek Fell: 93, 105, 107, 109

© Forest Stewardship Council: 117

© Global Book Publishing: 126 (bottom left and top right), 127, 128 (top left and bottom right), 129, 131 (top and center right), 133 (top left and bottom center), 134

(bottom left), 136 (top center and center right), 137, 138, 139 (bottom center), 142 (bottom left), 144 (center right), 145 (center top), 146 (center left), 147 (top right), 151, 153 (bottom right), 154 (center), 155 (bottom right)

© Jeffrey Gracz/Elemental Images: 145 (bottom right)

© Harry Haralambou: ii, vii (bottom left), 22, 26, 60, 82, 124

© Grant Heilman Photography, Inc.: 33, 57

© Saxon Holt Photography: 30, 31, 53, 63 (bottom right), 115, 119, 120

© Jerry Howard/Positive Images: vi (center left), 24, 49

© Frances Litman Photography, Inc.: Cover, 94

© Janet Loughrey Photography: i, vii (top left), 28, 36, 39, 50, 77, 86, 104, 106

© Craig Lovell/Eagle Visions Photography: vi (top left), 4

© MACORE Company, Inc.: 130, 134 (center right), 135 (bottom right), 140 (bottom right), 141, 144 (bottom left), 147 (bottom left), 148, 150, 152, 153 (top left), 154 (top left), 155 (center left)

© Arthur N. Orans: 46

© Jerry Pavia Photography, Inc.: 15, 16, 61, 67

© Ben Phillips/Positive Images: 75

Giles Prett: 8, 14, 135 (top center), 143

© Martha Storey: 81

© Mark Turner: 7, 34, 45, 63 (top right), 100

© Deidra Walpole: vi (bottom left), vii (center left), 20, 55, 58, 66, 112

© judywhite/GardenPhotos.com: 3, 80, 97, 102, 114

© Terry Wild Studio, Inc.: 90, 122 (bottom left)

Illustrations by Elayne Sears except for that of the plant chart on page 32, which is by Ann Kremers.

Garden Design Credits

Robert Chestnut: 44

Chris Jacobson: 63,

Gordon Kurtis Landscape Design: vii (center left), 112

Lefever/Grushow: 33, 57

Mark David Levine Design Group: 55

Ruby Begonia Fine Gardens: vi (bottom left), 20, 58, 66

Ken Ruzicka: vii (bottom left), 22, 124

Philip Thornburg: i, vii (top left), 28, 36, 86, 106

Index

Page numbers in **bold** indicate boxed material. Page numbers in *italics* indicate photos or illustrations.

A

Abelia × *grandiflora,* 40

Abutilon × *hybridum,* 82, 126, *126*

Abutilon megapotamicum, 84

Abutilon pictum, **78,** 126

Abutilon spp., 84, 126

    trailing, 84

Acalyphya hispida, 126

Acalypha spp., 76, 126

Acalypha wilkesiana, 76, 126

Achillea millefolium, 134

Achillea spp., 38, 52, 134, *134*

Actinidia arguta, 150

Actinidia kolomikta, 150

Actinidia spp., 100, 150

Adam's needles, 38, 52, 143

Adirondack chairs, 114, 115, *116*

Aesculus pavia, 49

Agapanthus spp., 82

Agastache hybrids, 76, 126, *126*

Agastache spp., 50, 54

Ageratum houstonianum, 52

Ajuga genevensis, 134

Ajuga pyramidalis, 134

Ajuga reptans, 37, 134

Ajuga spp., 42, 134

Akebia quinata, 150

alba roses, 148

Alcea rosea, 52

alfalfa, 51

Allegheny foamflower, 143

Allium spp., 52

Alpine clematis, 105, 151

aluminum, for deck furniture, 115, 116, 118–119, *118, 119*

Alternanthera ficoidea, 77, 126

alumroots, 138

Amaryllis belladonna, 55

American bittersweet, **101**

American cranberry-bush viburnum, 149

American wisteria, 155

Amorpha spp., 51

Anethum graveolens, 51

angelonia, 76

Angelonia angustifolia, 76

angel's trumpets, 56, 82, 127, 129

Anisodontea × *hypomandarum,* 76

annuals

    for butterflies, 52

    cold-tolerant, 74

    in container gardens, 73

    for evening gardens, 57

    fragrant, 55

    for hummingbirds, 48, 80

    shade-tolerant, 42

annual sages, 80

Antirrhinum majus, 48

Antirrhinum spp., 52

aphids, 111

Apiaceae (Parsley family), 50, **52**

apothecary's rose, 54

apples, 49

Aquilegia canadensis, 135

Aquilegia chrysantha, 135

Aquilegia flabellata, 134, 135

Aquilegia longissima, 135

Aquilegia spp., 43, 48, 134–135

arbors, 87–91, 100–101

Arctium lappa, **52**

Aristolochia durior. See *Aristolochia macrophylla*

Aristolochia macrophylla, 37, 89, 90, 100, **102,** 150

Aristolochia spp., **52**

Armenian cranesbill, 137

arrowwood viburnum, 149

Artemisia spp., 38

arugula, *80*

Asarum canadense, 135

Asarum europaeum, 135, *135*

Asarum hartwegii, 135

Asarum shuttleworthii, 135

Asarum spp., 42, 135

Asclepiadaceae family, 50, 51

Asclepias curassavica, 50, 51

Asclepias incarnata, 50, 51

Asclepias spp., **52**

Asclepias tuberosa, 50, 51

Asimina spp., **52**

Asimina triloba, 44

Asteraceae (Aster family), 51

Aster family, 50, 51, **52,** 111

Aster novae-angliae, 50

Aster novae-beglii, 50

Astilbe spp., 52

Athyrium felix-femina, 42

Athyrium niponicum, 42

Athyrium spp., 42

August lily, 54, 57

Aurelian Hybrid lily, 54

Aurinia saxatilis, 51

autumn fern, 42

awnings, **89**

azaleas, 40, 44, 49

B

Bacopa spp., 78, *78,* 83, 126

balloon flowers, 38, 57, 141

balloon vine, 102, 151

bamboo, as trellis material, 97, *97*

Barberton daisy, 77

barrenworts, 136

basils, 46, 47, **47,** 71, 80, *80*

basket-of-gold, 51

baskets, wire, as containers, 64

beans, 46

bearberry cotoneaster, 145

beardtongues, 48, 140–141

beds, garden

    shaping and sizing of, 29

    width of, for viewing, **29**

bee balm, 48, 50

beefsteak plant, 77, 130

"before" photos, 9, *9*

beggar-ticks, **52**

Begonia semperflorens, 42, 127

    B. × *semperflorens* hybrids, 48

Begonia spp., 42, 77, 82, 127

Begonia sutherlandii, 82, 127

Begonia × *tuberhybrida,* 82, 127

begonias, tuberous, 82

belladonna lily, 55

bellflowers, 52

benches, for storage, 14

berries, 74

Beta vulgaris, 76, 127

Bethlehem sage, 142

bicolor epimedium, 137

Bidens spp., **52**

biennials, 134–143

    for hummingbirds, 48

    for partial shade, 42

bigleaf hydrangea, 146

Bignonia capreolata, 100, 150

bigroot geranium, 137

binoculars, for observing wildlife, 52

birds, attracting, **48,** 74
black-eyed Susan, 77, 102, 142
blackhaw viburnum, 149
blanket flowers, 50
blazing stars, 48
bleeding hearts, 43, 136
 common bleeding heart, 136
blood grass, 38
bloodflower, 50, 51
bloody cranesbill, 137
bloom, length of, 30
blue bugleweed, 134
blue daisy, 77
blue fescue, 38
blue (Meserve) hollies, 146
blue oat grass, 38
blue passionflower, 154
blue spruce, *40*
blueberries, 44, 148–149
bok choy, 46
Boston ivy, **91,** 100, 154
bouncing bet, 48
boxes, for deck storage, 14
boxwoods, 40
Brassicaceae (Mustard family), 51
broad beans, 51
broad-leaved evergreens, 40
broccoli, 51
Browallia americana, 42
Browallia speciosa, 42
Brugmansia x *candida,* 127, *127*
Brugmansia sanguinea, 127
Brugmansias spp., 56, 82, 127
Brugmansia suaveolens, 127
Buddleia davidii, 50, 51, 144, *144*
Buddleia family, 51
Buddleia spp., 49, 50
bugleweeds, 42, 134
 common bugleweed, 37, 134
bulbs, 38, *73,* 134–143
 in container gardens, 73
 fragrant, 55, 56

 for hummingbirds, 48
burdock, **52**
burkwood viburnum, 149
bush clovers, 51
bush peas, 74
bush violets, 42
butterfly bush, 49, 50, 51, 144
butterfly gardens, 50–52. *See also*
 individual plant descriptions in
 chapter six
butterfly weed, 50, 51
Buxus spp., 40

C

cabbages, 46, 51, 74
cacti, in container gardens, *83*
Caladium bicolor, 77, 127
Caladium spp., 77, 82, 127
Calendula officinalis, 74
Calocephalus brownii, 77
Calycanthys floridus, 44, 54, 144
camera, using for design, **8,** 9
Campanula spp., 52
campions, 48
Campsis radicans spp., 49, **91,**
 151
Campsis spp., 100, 150–151
Campsis tagliabuana, 150, 151
Canada lily, 140
Canada violet, 51
Canada wild ginger, 135
canary creeper, 155
canary vine, 155
Candidum Hybrid lilies, 54
candles, as deck decorations, 123
Canna x *generalis* hybrids, 76, 128
cannas, *78, 128*
cape fuchsias, 76
Capsicum annuum, 77, 128
Capsicum spp., 46
cardinal climber, 153
cardinal flower, 48, 52

Cardiospermum halicacabum, 102,
 102, 151
Carex conica, **42**
Carex morrowii, **42**
Carex oshimensis, **42**
Carex siderosticha, **42**
Carex spp., **42**
carnations, 48
Carolina allspice, 54, 144
Carolina jasmine, 100, 152
Carolina phlox, 141
Carolina yellow jasmine, 100, 152
carpet bugleweed, 134
carrots, 50, 51, **52**
Cassia spp., 51
cast stone containers, 63
catchflies, 48
Catharanthus roseus, 42, 77
cathedral bells, 102, 151
catmints, 38, 50, 54, 111, 140
catnips, 50
cauliflower, 51
cedar, for deck furniture, 116–117
ceilings, outdoor, 11
Celastrus orbiculatus, **101**
Celastrus scandens, **101**
cement containers, 63
Centaurea cineraria, 77
Centaurea spp., 52, 128
Centranthus ruber, 38, 52
Cephalotaxus harringtonia, 44
Cephalotaxus spp., 148
Ceratostigma plumbaginoides, 37
Cercis spp., 51
Cestrum spp., 56
chart, of plant characteristics, 32,
 32
Chasmanthium latifolium, **42**
cheddar pinks, 136
Cherianthus spp., 51
cherries, **52**
cherry pie, 52, 129

chickabiddy, 102
children's garden, 45
Chilean glory vine, 102, 152
Chinese wisteria, 155
chives, 46, 47, 80
Christmas fern, 42
cigar flower, 128
cilantro, 46
cinnamon fern, 42
Cirsium spp., **52**
citron daylily, 54
Clematis alpina, 105, 151
Clematis macropetala, 105, 151
Clematis maximowicziana. See
 Clematis terniflora
Clematis montana, 53, 100, 151
Clematis orientalis, 105, 151
Clematis paniculata. See *Clematis*
 terniflora
Clematis spp., **91, 95,** 100, **102,**
 104, 104–105, *105,* 151, *151*
Clematis terniflora, 100, 151
Clematis texensis, 105, 151
Clematis viticella, **102,** 105, 151
Cleome hasslerana, 48, 52, 57
Clethra alnifolia, 54
climbing hydrangea, **91,** 100, 152
clovers, 51
Cobaea scandens, 102, 151
Colchicum spp., 37
coleus, 42, 77, *78,* 84, 132
colors of plants, in garden design,
 31, 73–74
columbines, 43, 48, 134–135
combinations. *See also* interest,
 adding; contrast, in design;
 and individual plant descriptions
 in chapter six
 in container gardens, 76
 in garden design, 31, 43, 113
 of vines, **102,** 104
common impatiens, 42

common mignonette, 42, 132

common myrtle, 84

common nasturtium, 78, 133

common sage, 132

common stock, 130

common trumpet vine, 151

common winterberry, 146

conifers, 40

Consolida ajacis, 37

Consolida spp., 48

construction
  of arbors, 88–89
  of trellises, **93,** 94–99

container gardening, 59–85
  vines for, 103

container plants. *See also* container gardening *and individual plant descriptions in chapter six*
  weight of, 15

containers, false-bottom, **65,** *65*

contractor
  finding a, 23
  insurance of, 23

contrast, in design, 34, 39, 40, 47, 73, 78, **102.** *See also* interest, adding; combinations; *and individual plant descriptions in chapter six*

"contrast and accent plants," 76–77, 78

cool-season grasses, 38

copper, as trellis material, **98,** *98*

copperleaf, 76, 126

coralbells, 48

Coreopsis grandiflora, 77, 135

Coreopsis lanceolata, 135, *135*

Coreopsis rosea, 135

Coreopsis spp., 38, 50, *57,* 135

Coreopsis verticillata, 135

cornelian cherry, 145

cornflowers, 52

Cornus amomum, 145

Cornus florida, 144, *144*

Cornus mas, 145

Cornus obliqua, 145

Cornus spp., 44, **52,** 144–145

Coronilla varia, 51

Cortaderia selloana, 82

Corylopsis pauciflora, 54

Cosmos bipinnatus, 128

Cosmos spp., 50, 57, 77, 128

Cosmos sulphureus, 128

Cotoneaster dammeri, 145

Cotoneaster horizontalis, 145, *145*

Cotoneaster multiflorus, 145

Cotoneaster spp., 37, 40, 145

cottage pinks, 136

covers
  for furniture, **121**
  for pots, **62,** *62*

crabapples, 40, 49, 147

Crambe maritima, 51

cranesbills, 38, 137

creeping fig, 84

creeping phlox, 141

creeping zinnia, *61,* 78, 132

crimson glory vine, 155

criniums, 55

Crinum spp., 55

Crocosmia spp., 48

Crocus chrysanthus, 55

crocuses, 37, 73

cross vine, 100, 150

crown vetch, 51

Cuban oregano, 132

Cucurbita pepo, 102, 152

culinary containers, 80

cup-and-saucer vine, 102, 152

Cuphea hyssopifolia, 128

Cuphea ignea, 128

Cuphea × *purpurea,* 128, *128*

Cuphea spp., 71, 77, 128

curry plants, 77, 129

cushionbush, 77

cushions of deck furniture, 121

cut-leaf verbenas, 133

cypress vine, 153

D

daffodils, 37, 38, 73

Dahlia hybrids, 48, 81

Dahlia spp., 77, *81*

daisies, *57*

dalmatian cranesbill, 137

dame's rocket, 51

datura, 56, 129

Datura metel, 56, 129

Daucus carota, 51, **52**

daylilies, 38, 48, 52, 138. *See also* lilies

deadheading, 80, 81, **110**

deadnettles, 139

decks
  designing, 5–23
  evaluating safety of, **15**
  gardens for, 25–57

decorating, 62, **95,** *95,* 113–123

Decumaria barbara, 100

design, principles of, 34

designing
  container plantings, **70,** *70*
  with containers, 66, **70**
  deck gardens, 25–57
  decks, 5–23

Dianthus barbatus, 48, 52

Dianthus gratianopolitanus, 136, *136*

Dianthus plumarius, 136

Dianthus spp., *37,* 48, 52, 54, 136

Dicentra eximia, 136

Dicentra formosa, 136

Dicentra spp., 43, 136

Dicentra spectabilis, 136

Digitalis spp., 48

dill, 46, 50, 51, **52**

dining, considerations for, 12–13

diseases of roses, 111

docks, **52**

dogwoods, 44, **52,** 144–145

Dolichos lablab. See *Lablab purpureus*

Dolichos purpureus. See *Lablab purpureus*

doors, effect on design, 20

doublefile viburnum, 149

drawing, working. *See* working drawing

drip-emitting system of watering, **69,** *69*

drooping leucothoe, 40

Dryopteris erythrosora, 42

Dryopteris filix-mas, 42

Dryopteris spp., 42

dusty miller, 77, 128, 132

Dutchman's pipe, 37, **52,** 89, 90, 100, **102,** *104*

dwarf cannas, 76

dwarf conifers, 40, *40*

dwarf dahlias, 77, 81

E

Easter lilies, 54

Eccremocarpus scaber, 102, 152

Echinacea purpurea, 57, 136, *136*

Echinacea spp., 38, 50

edging lobelia, 76, 78, 130

edging strips, 26

edible flowers, 46, 47

eggplants, 46

eglantine roses, 148

Egyptian star cluster, 48, 77, 81

endive, 46

English ivy, **91**

English yews, 148

entertaining, considerations for, 12–13, **16**

environmentally friendly furniture, **117,** 121

Epimedium grandiflorum, 137

Epimedium spp., 43, 136–137

Epimedium versicolor, 137

Epimedium × *warleyense,* 137
Epimedium × *youngianum,* 137
Erigeron spp., 50
escarole, 46
Euonymus spp., 44
Eupatorium spp., 52
Euphorbia characias spp., *45*
European cranberry-bush
    viburnum, 149
European lady fern, 42
European wild ginger, 135
evergreens, broad-leaved, 40
everlasting pea, 100
Exacum affine, 77
exposure of site, 29

F

Fabaceae (Pea family), 51
fabrics, for deck furniture, 121
Fallopia aubertii, **101**
false indigos, 51
fan columbine, 135
fan flower, 78
feather reed grass, 38, 39
Felicia amelloides, 77
fences, 46. *See also* trellises
   as deck decorations, 123
fennel, 50, 51, 57
ferns, *41*
   for shade, 42, 43, 83
fertilizing container gardens, 71
Festuca glauca, 38
Ficus pumila, 84
Filipendula spp., 52
"filler" plants, 76–77, 78. *See also*
    individual plant descriptions in
    chapter six
firecracker plant, 128
fiveleaf akebia, 150
"flag" plants, 76–77, **77**, *77,* 78.
   See also individual plant descrip-
   tions in chapter six

flame flower, 155
flame nasturtium, 155
fleabanes, 50
flowering maple, *78,* 82, 84,
   126
flowering tobaccos, 42, 48, 52,
    55, 56, 77, 130, 131
   for hummingbirds, 81
flowers, designing with, 78
foam packing "peanuts," 65
foamflowers, 143
Foeniculum vulgare, 51
foliage, in garden design, 31, 78
food, serving considerations for,
   12–13
Forest Stewardship Council, **117**
Fothergilla gardenii, 145, *145*
Fothergilla major, 145
Fothergilla spp., 40, 145
found objects, as containers, 64
fountain grass, 38, *78,* 82
fountains, 10, 11, **48,** 49
four-o'clock, 48, 52, 55, 56
foxgloves, 48
fragrance gardens, 53–55. *See also*
    individual plant descriptions in
    chapter six
   container gardens, 67, 80
   evening gardens, 56-57
fragrance of plants, 30
fragrant viburnum, 149
French marigolds, 133
fringed bleeding heart, 136
fruit trees, 144–149
Fuchsia spp., 77, 129
fungicidal soap, 111
furniture, selecting, 114–121

G

Gaillardia spp., 50
Galanthus spp., 55
Galtonia candicans, 55

galvanized fencing, for downspout
   trellises, 93
galvanized pipe, as arbor material,
   88
gaps, filling, in container gardens, **74**
garden impatiens, 77
garden phlox, 141
garden verbenas, 48
gardens
   in containers, 59–85
   designing, 25–57
garlic, 52
gayfeathers, 48, 52
gazebos
   for shade, 11
   weight of, 15
Gelsemium sempervirens, 100, 152,
   152
geneva bugleweed, 134
geraniums, *37, 76, 81, 82, 101,*
   107. See also Geranium spp.
   and *Pelargonium* spp.
Geranium cinereum, 137
Geranium dalmaticum, 137
Geranium himalayense, 137
Geranium macrorrhizum, 137
Geranium maculatum, 137, *137*
Geranium × *oxonianum,* 137
Geranium psilostemon, 137
Geranium sanguineum, 137
Geranium spp., 38, 43, 52, 137. See
   also *Pelargonium* spp.
   hardy, *37,* 43, 52, 137
   scented, 84
Geranium sylvaticum, 137
Gerbera jamesonii, 77
giant horsetail, *63*
giant hyssops, 76
gladiolas, 56
Gladiolus callianthus, 56
Gladiolus tristis, 56
glass, as deck table top, 115

glazed clay containers, 61
glossy abelia, 40
gloxinia, creeping, 102
goldband lily, 54
golden thyme, *80*
golden (yellow) columbine, 135
goldenrods, 52
goldflame honeysuckle, 154
Gomphrena spp., 77
grape hyacinth, 55
grapes, as arbor and trellis vines,
   90, 100, 155
grass, removing, 37
grasses. *See also* ornamental grasses
   in butterfly gardens, **52**
   medium to small, 38
   for shade, **42**
grayleaf cranesbill, 137
greater periwinkle, 78
Gregg sage, 132
grill, planning for, **13**
ground covers, 37, 82. *See also*
    individual plant descriptions in
    chapter six
   for shade, 42, 43
grubs, 111

H

hairy beardtongue, 141
hakone grass, *39*
Hakonechloa macra, 39, **42**
Hamamelis spp., 44, 54
hardening off, 83
hardscaping, 20
Hawaiian heather, 128
Hawaiian hibiscus, *60*
hayracks and wire baskets, as con-
   tainers, 64
Hedera helix, 84, **91**
height of plants, in design, 34
Helenium autumnale, 50
Helianthus annuus, 57

Helianthus spp., 50, 129

Helichrysum italicum, 77, 129

Helichrysum petiolare, 78, 83, 129

Helictotrichon sempervirens, 38

Heliopsis helianthoides, 50

heliotrope, 55, 56, 77, 80, 129

Heliotropium arborescens, 52, 55, 56, 77, 80, 129, *129*

hellebores, 37, 43, 138

Helleborus x *hybridus,* 37, 138

Helleborus orientalis, 138

Helleborus spp., 43

Hemerocallis citrina, 54

Hemerocallis lilioasphodelus, 54, 138

Hemerocallis spp., 38, 48, 52, 138, *138*

hemlocks, 44

herbs
   in containers, 80
   fragrant, 54
      for kitchen gardens, 46–47, 80
   as standards, 84

Hesperis matronalis, 42, 51, 56

heucheras, *43*

Heucheras americana, 138

Heucheras x *brizoides,* 138

Heucheras micrantha, 138

Heucheras sanguinea, 138

Heucheras spp., 43, 48, 138

Hibiscus moscheutos, 38

Hibiscus spp., 48, 52, *82*

highbush blueberry, 149

hollies, 40, 146

hollyhock, 52

honeysuckles, 49, 100, 154

hops vines, *94,* 100, 152

horned violet, 51

horticultural oil, 111

Hosta fluctuans, 139

Hosta plantaginea, 54, 57, 139, *139*

Hosta sieboldiana, 139

Hosta spp., 43, *43,* 48, 138–139

hot peppers, 80

hot tubs, 15

houseplants, in outdoor container gardens, 83

hummingbird gardens, 48–49, 52, 81, **95,** 102. *See also individual plant descriptions in chapter six*

Humulus japonicus, 102, 152

Humulus lupulus, 100, 152

Humulus spp., 152

hyacinth beans, 102, **102,** 153

hyacinths, 55, 73, **73**

Hyacinthus orientalis, 55

Hydrangea anomala. See *Hydrangea petiolaris*

Hydrangea arborescens, 146

Hydrangea macrophylla, 146

Hydrangea paniculata, 146

Hydrangea petiolaris, **91,** 100, 152

Hydrangea quercifolia, 146, *146*

Hydrangea spp., 44, 146

Hymenocallis spp., 55

Hypoestes phyllostachya, 42, 77

hyssops, 50, 54

I

Ilex crenata, 146

Ilex glabra, 146

Ilex x *meserveae,* 146

Ilex pedunculosa, 146

Ilex spp., 40, 146

Ilex verticillata, 146, *146*

Impatiens spp., 57

Impatiens wallerana, 42, 77

Imperata cylindrica, 38

Indigofera spp., 51, **102**

indigos, 51

inkberry holly, 146

insects. *See also* pests
   beneficial, attracting, 51

interest, adding, 62, 78, 82. *See also* combinations; contrast, in

design; *and individual plant descriptions in chapter six*

Ipomoea alba, 37, 55, **95,** 153

Ipomoea batatas, 78, 130

Ipomoea coccinea, 153

Ipomoea lobata, 153

Ipomoea x *multifida,* 153

Ipomoea nil, 153

Ipomoea purpurea, 153

Ipomoea quamoclit, 153, *153*

Ipomoea spp., **95,** *102,* **102,** *152–153*

Ipomoea tricolor, 153

Ipomoea versicolor. See *Ipomoea lobata*

Iresine herbstii, 77, 130

ironweeds, 52

Italian clematis, **102,** 105, 151

Itea virginica, 44

ivy
   for topiary, 84
   variegated, 73, *82*

J

Jacob's-coat, 76, 77, 126

Japanese beetles, 111, *111*

Japanese creeper, 100, 154

Japanese holly, 146

Japanese honeysuckle, **101**

Japanese hydrangea vine, **91,** 100

Japanese lily, 54, 56

Japanese painted fern, 42

Japanese pieris, 40

Japanese wisteria, 155

Japanese yews, 148

jasmine tobacco, 56, 131

jasmines, 84, 100

Jasminum nudiflorum, 54, 100, 153

Jasminum officinale, 84

Jasminum polyanthum, 84

jessamines, 56

Joe-Pye weeds, 52

Johnny-jump-ups, 51, 73

Joseph's coat, 77, 126

Judd viburnum, 149

K

kales, 46, 47, 51, *74*

Kalmia latifolia, 40

kitchen gardens, 45, 46–47
   care of, **47**
   in containers, 80
   cool-weather, in container gardens, 74

kiwis, 100, 150

Kniphofia spp., 48

Koreanspice viburnum, 149

kudzu, **101**

L

Lablab purpureus, 102, **102,** 153, *153*

lady ferns, 42

Lamiaceae (Mint family), 50, 51

Lamium galeobdolon, 139

Lamium maculatum, 139, *139*

Lamium spp., 43, *65,* 139

lance-leaved coreopsis, 135

Lantana camara, 82, 84, 130, *130*

Lantana montevidensis, 78, 130

Lantana spp., 52, 82, 130

lanterns, as deck decorations, 123

large-flowered coreopsis, 135

large fothergilla, 145

larkspurs, 37, 48

Lathyrus latifolius, 100

Lathyrus odoratus, 102

lattice
   as deck decoration, 123
   as trellis material, 94–95

Laurus nobilis, 82, 84

Lavandula angustifolia, 38, 54, 140, *140*

Lavandula spp., 50

Lavatera trimestris, 57

lavenders, *30, 38, 47, 50, 54, 74, 107,* 140

layered plantings, 37

leatherleaf viburnum, 149

lemon balm, 80

lemon daylily, 138

lemon lily, 54

lemongrass, 80

Lenten roses, 138

Leonotis leonurus, 76

Lespedeza spp., 51

lesser periwinkle, 42

lettuces, 46, *46,* 47, *74,* 80

Leucanthemum x *superbum,* 50

Leucanthemum vulgare, 50

Leucojum vernum, 55

Leucothoe fontanesiana, 40

Liatris spp., 48, 52

licorice plant, *60,* 78, 83, 129

lighting, 14, 122, 123

lilac cranesbill, 137

lilacs, 49, **52,** 54

lilies. *See* daylilies and *Lilium* spp.

Lilium auratum, 54

Lilium canadense, 140

Lilium candidum, 54, 56, 140

Lilium longiflorum, 54

Lilium regale, 54, 56, 140

Lilium spp., *43,* 48, 49, *49,* 54, 56, 140

    fragrant, 54, 80

Lilium speciosum, 54, 56, 140

Lilium superbum, 140

lilyturfs, 42, 140

Limonium spp., 52

linaria, 38

Linaria purpurea, 38

linden viburnum, 149

lion's ear, 76

Liriope muscari, 140

Liriope spp., 42, 140

Liriope spicata, 140

Lobelia cardinalis, 42

Lobelia erinus, 42, 78, 130

Lobelia spp., 42, 52

Lobularia maritima, 51

locusts, 51

Loganiaceae (Buddleia family), 50

Longiflorum Hybrid lilies, 54

long-spurred columbine, 135

long-spurred epimedium, 136

longstalk holly, 146

Lonicera fragrantissima, 54

Lonicera x *heckrottii,* 154

Lonicera japonica, **101**

Lonicera periclymenum, 154

Lonicera sempervirens, 154, *154*

Lonicera spp., 49, 100, 154

Lotus berthelotii, 78, 130

lotus vine, 78, 130

love-in-a-mist, 37, 74

love-in-a-puff, 102, **102,** 151

lowbush blueberry, 148

Lunaria annua, 42

lungworts, 43, 142

lupines, 51

Lupinus spp., 51

Lycoris spp., 48

M

Madagascar periwinkle, 77

madonna lily, 54, 56, 140

magic lilies, 48

Magnolia spp., 40, 147

Magnolia stellata, 147, *147*

Magnolia virginiana, 147

Mahonia spp., 40

maiden grass, *60*

maintenance of plants, 30

male fern, 42

mallow, 38

Malus spp., 40, 49, 147, *147*

Malva alcea, 38

Mandevilla, 101

many-flowered cotoneaster, 145

map, for planning, 18

mapleleaf viburnum, 149

marigolds, 38, 46, 48, 50, 77, 133

    for kitchen gardens, 46, 47

marjoram, 80

Matteuccia struthiopteris, 42

Matthiola incana spp., 55, 56, 130

Matthiola longipetala, 56, 130

Matthiola spp., 130

Maurandya scandens, 102

maypop, 154

meadow rues, 52

Medicago sativa, 51

Melilotus spp., 51

Mentha spp., 50

Meserve hollies, 146

mesquites, 51

Mexican heather, 128

Mexican mint, 132

Mexican sunflower, 48, 50

microclimates, in container gardens, 67

mignonette, 55, 74

mildew, 117, 121

mile-a-minute plant, **101**

Milkweed family, 50, 51, **52**

Mint family, 46, 50, 51, 111

mints, 50

Mirabilis jalapa, 48, 52, 55, 56

Miscanthus, 34, 39

Miscanthus sinensis, 38

mix-and-match system, 76–78

mock oranges, 56, 147

mold, 121

Molinia caerulea, 38

Monarda didyma, 48

Monarda spp., 50

money plant, 42

montbretias, 48

moonflower, 37, 55, **95,** 153

morning glories, **95,** 102, **102,** *103,* 152–153

moss verbena, 133

mountain laurel, 40

moving plants, 35

moyes rose, 148

Muscari armeniacum, 55

Mustard family, 46, 51

Myrtle communis, 84

N

nasturtiums, *61, 63, 74, 102,* 155

    for kitchen gardens, 46, 47

native Texas clematis, 105

native wild columbine, 135

Nepeta x *faassenii,* 140

Nepeta spp., 38, 50, 54, 111, 140

nettles, **52**

New England aster, 50

New York aster, 50

New Zealand flax, *63,* 76, 131

Nicotiana alata, 52, 56, 77, 131, *131*

Nicotiana x *sanderae,* 56

Nicotiana spp., 42, 48, 55, 81, 130

Nicotiana sylvestris, 56, 131

nigella, 57

Nigella damascena, 37, 57, 74

night-blooming plants, 31

night-scented stock, 56, 130

northern sea oats, **42**

notebook for design, 6

notes, organizing, 21

O

oakleaf hydrangea, 146

Ocimum basilicum, 46

old-fashioned weigela, 49

onions, 52

orange coneflowers, 38, 142

oreganos, 46, 47, 54, 80

Oreganum vulgare, 54

organizing notes, 21

Oriental bittersweet, **101**

Oriental clematis, 105, 151

Oriental hybrid lilies, 54, 80, 140

Oriental poppies, 57

ornamental grasses, 34, 38–39, 74, 82

ornamental kales, 74

ornamental leaf lettuces, 74

ornamental peppers, 38, 47, 77, 128

ornamental salad greens, 46

ornamental sweet potato, 78, *78,* 130

Osmunda cinnamomea, 42

Osmunda regalis, 42

Osmunda spp., 42

ostrich fern, 42

overwintering container plants, 80, 84

oxeye, 50

ox-eye daisy, 50

P

PVC coating
for fabric, 121
for wire, 96

PVC pipe, for deck furniture, 120–121

Pachysandra spp., 42

Paeonia spp., 54

painted blood leaf, 77, 130

painting, around trellises, 93

pale dogwood, 145

pampas grass, 82

panicle hydrangea, 146

Panicum virgatum, 38

panorama photographs, **8,** *8*

pansies, 42, 73, 74

Papaver orientale, 57

paperless garden design, 35

parrot leaf, 77, 126

parrot's beak, 78, 130

Parsley family (Apiaceae), 50, **52**

parsleys, 46, 47, 51, 80

Parthenocissus quinquefolia, 89, 100, 154

Parthenocissus spp., 154

Parthenocissus tricuspidata, **91,** 100, 154

Passiflora caerulea, 154, *154*

Passiflora incarnata, 154

Passiflora spp., **52,** 84, 100, 154

passionflowers. See *Passiflora* spp.

Pastinaca sativa, 51

paths
decking, *41*
stepping-stone, **27,** *27*

pawpaws, 44, **52**

Pea family, 51

peas, *102*

Pelargonium hortorum, 63

Pelargonium spp., 131. See also *Geranium* spp.
zonal (bedding) geraniums, 48, *49,* 77, 131
scented geraniums, 77
variegated-leaved geraniums, 82

Pennisetum alopecuroides, 38

Pennisetum setaceum, 76, 82

Penstemon hirsutus, 141

Penstemon spp., 48, 52, 140–141, *140*

Pentas lanceolata, 48, 77, 81

peonies, *37, 38,* 54

peppers, 46
ornamental, 47
hot, 80

perennial pea, 100

perennials, 38–40, 126–133, 134–143
for butterflies, 52
for evening gardens, 57
fragrant, 54
herbs for kitchen gardens, 46–47
for hummingbirds, 48

for shade, 43
tender for partial shade, 42
vines, 100–103

periwinkle, 42

Perovskia, 141

Perovskia atriplicifolia, 38, 54, 141

Persian shield, 42, 77

Persian violet, 77

Peruvian daffodils, 55

pests. *See also* insects
in butterfly gardens, 50, 51
of roses, 111, *111*

Petroselinum crispum, 46, 51

Petunia x *hybrida,* 48, 81

Petunia integrifolia, 131

Petunia spp., 48, 52, 57, 78, 83, *103,* 131, *131*

Phaseolus coccineus, 37, 51, **95,** 102, **102,** *154*

Philadelphus spp., 56, 147

Phlox carolina, 141

Phlox divaricata, 57, 141, *141*

Phlox maculata, 141

Phlox paniculata, 57, 141

Phlox spp., 48, 52, 57, 141

Phlox stolonifera, 141

Phormium cookianum hookeri, 63

Phormium tenax, 76, 131

photographs, as part of planning, **8,** *8*

Phygelius spp., 76

Pieris japonica, 40

pincushion flower, 48

pine, for deck furniture, 117

pink coreopsis, 135

pinks, 48, 52, 54, 136

Pinus strobus, 40

pinxterbloom azalea, 56

planning
for deck usage, **16**
organizing notes for, 21
for plant growth, 66
plantings, 32, *33,* **70,** *70*

problems, identifying, 23
space, 12–13, **13**
working drawing, 18, 20, **21**

planning a deck, 5–23

plant characteristics, chart of, 32, *32*

plant growth, planning for, 66

Plantago spp., **52**

plantain lilies, 48

plantains, **52**

plants
choosing, 30–33
for decks, 125–155
heights of, in design, 34
shapes of, in design, 34–35

plastic
for deck furniture, 120–121
as lattice material, 94
and polyethylene containers, 62

Platanus spp., **52**

Platycodon grandiflorus, 38, 57, 141

Plectranthus amboinicus, 132

Plectranthus argentatus, 132

Plectranthus forsteri, 132

Plectranthus spp., 42, 77, 132

plum yew, 44, 148

plumbago, 37

plums, **52**

poisonous plants, 129

Polianthes tuberosa, 55, 80

polka-dot plant, 42, 77

Polygonatum odoratum, 141

Polygonatum spp., 43, 141

Polygonum aubertii. See *Fallopia aubertii*

polymers, water-retaining, 68–69

Polystichum acrostichoides, 42

polyurethane foam, 64

pontic azalea, 56

poplars, **52**

Populus spp., **52**

pot covers, **62,** *62*

pot marigolds, 74

potato vine, 102, 155

potting mix, in container gardens, 70

privacy, creating feeling of, 10, 92, 94

problem spots, effect on design of, 21

problems, identifying potential, 23

professional advice, 23

Prosopis spp., 51

prostrate conifers, 40

pruning, 44, **71**, *71, 110*

Prunus spp., **52**

Pueraria lobata, **101**

Pulmonaria saccharata, 142

Pulmonaria spp., 43, 142

pumpkins, 102, 152

purple basil, *46*

purple bell vine, 84, **95**, 102, 154

purple coneflowers, 38, 50, 57, 136

purple fountain grass, 76, *78, 82*

purple heart, 78

purple-leaved grape, 155

purple moor grass, 38

Pyracantha coccinea, 40

pyramid bugleweed, 134

Q

Queen Anne's lace, 51, **52**

queen-of-the-prairies, 52

R

rabbiteye blueberry, 148

ragged coneflower, 142

railings, plants for, **95**, *95*

rattan, as deck furniture, 120

recycled furniture materials, **117**, 121

red buckeye, 49

red morning glory, 153

red valerian, 38, 52

redbuds, 51

red-hot-cat's-tail, 76, 126

red-hot pokers, 48

red-leaved orache, 46

red-leaved roses, 148

redwood, for deck furniture, 116–117

regal lily, 54, 56

remontant bloomers, 108, 148

repetition, in design, 34, 78

Reseda odorata, 42, 55, 74, 132

Rhodochiton atrosanguineum, 84, **95**, 102, 154

Rhododendron arborescens, 56

Rhododendron luteum, 56

Rhododendron periclymenoides, 56

Rhododendron prinophyllum, 56

Rhododendron schlippenbachii, 56

Rhododendron spp., 40, 44, 49

Robinia spp., 51

rockspray cotoneaster, 145

roots, planting near, 41, **41**

possible damage to tree, **11**

Rosa alba, 54, 148

Rosa banksia, 108

Rosa eglanteria, 148

Rosa gallica, 54

Rosa glauca, 148

Rosa kordesii, 107

Rosa moyesii, 148

Rosa rubrifolia, 148

Rosa rugosa, 148, *148*

Rosa spp., 40, 100, 148

Rosa spinosissima, 148

Rosa wichuraiana, 107

rose mallow, 38, 76

roses, 37, 40, *53*, 84, *97, 107*, 148

as arbor and trellis vines, 90, **91**, 100, **102**, 107–108, *107, 108, 109*

care of, 109–110, **110**

for decks, 107

fragrant, 54, *55*

for railings, **95**

rugosa, 54, *148*

roseshell azalea, 56

Rosmarinus officinalis, 50, 84

rosemary, 50, 80, 84

rot-resistant woods, 14

royal azalea, 56

royal fern, 42

Rudbeckia fulgida, 142

Rudbeckia hirta, 77, 142

Rudbeckia laciniata, 142, *142*

Rudbeckia spp., 38, 50, 142

rugosa roses, 54, 148

Rumex spp., **52**

Russian sage, 38, 54, 141

rust

of deck furniture, 119–120, 121

of outside decorations, 122

S

safety

of children, **16**

evaluating deck structure, **15**

with hot tubs, 15

with lighting, 14

sages, 46, 47, 48, 50, 76, 80, 132

Salix spp., **52**

Salvia coccinea, 81, 132

Salvia greggii, 132

Salvia guaranitica, 132

Salvia officinalis, 132

Salvia spp., 48, 50, 71, 76, 81, 132, *132*

Salvia splendens, 81, 132

Sanvitalia procumbens, 61, *78*, 132

Saponaria officinalis, 48

Sargent viburnum, 149

Scabiosa caucasica, 48

Scabiosa spp., 52

scaevola, *60*

Scaevola aemula, 78

scale, of trellises, **93**

scarlet firethorn, 40

scarlet runner beans, 37, 51, **95**, 102, **102**, *103*, 154

scarlet sage, 81, 132

scented geraniums, 77, 84

Schizophragma hydrangeoides, **91**, 100

Scotch briar, 148

Scotch crocus, 55

screens, for privacy, 10

sea kale, 51

sea lavenders, 52

seasonal considerations, 30–31, 32, 37, 38, 40

of decorating decks, 122–123

for trellis material, **97**, *97*

for trellis plants, 92

seating

deck boxes as, 14

expandable, 114

seclusion, with trellises, 92

sedges

in butterfly gardens, **52**

for shade, **42**

Sedum kamtschaticum, 142–143

Sedum sieboldii, 142

Sedum spathulifolium, 143

Sedum spp., 34, 52, 142–143

Sedum spectabile, 52, 142, *142*

Sedum spurium, 143

Sedum telephium, 142

Senecio cineraria, 77, 128

sennas, 51

shade. *See also* sun and shade *and individual plant descriptions in chapter six*

from arbors, 88–91

for container gardens, 67, 68

ferns for, 42, 83

grasses and sedges for, **42**

ground covers for, 42

perennials for, 43

planning for, 11

plantings in, 41

shrubs for, 44

specimen plants for, 82

from trellises, 92

vines for, 37

shade cloth, *89*

shapes of plants, in design, 34

shaping and sizing of garden beds, 29, **29**

shaping of plants. *See* pruning

Shasta daisy, 50

shrubs, 20, 40, 144–149

fragrant, 54

for hummingbirds, 49

for shade, 44

signet marigolds, 133

Silene regia, 48

Silene virginica, 48

silky dogwood, 145

silver lace vine, **101**

siting considerations, 29, 30, 42, 43

for container gardens, 67

for hummingbird gardens, 49

for kitchen gardens, 47

for roses, 109

size of plants, 30

SmartWood Program, **117**

smooth hydrangea, 146

snapdragons, 48, 52

sneezeweed, 50

snowdrops, 55

snowflake, 55

soil considerations, 11, 29, 40

for kitchen gardens, 47

for roses, 109

soil improvement, **37,** *37*

Solanum jasminoides, 102, 155, *155*

Solenostemon scutellarioides, 42, 63, 76, 77, 84, 132, *133*

Solidago spp., 52

Solomon's seals, 43, 141

space, planning, 12–13, **13,** 44

Spanish flag, 153

specimen plants, 82

spider flower, 48, 52, 57

spider lilies, 48

spider mites, 111

spiderworts, 43, 143

spinach, 46

spotted geranium, 137

squash, 46

standards, 84–85, **85,** *85. See also* "Special Features" *for individual plants in chapter six*

star glory, 153

star jasmine, 84

star magnolia, 147

star morning glory, 153

steel, tubular, furniture, 119

stepping-stones, **27**

stocks, 55, 56, 130

stonecrop, 142

storage, 14

of deck furniture, 121

of heavy items, 15

planning, **17**

under-deck, 15

string, as trellis material, **97,** *97*

Strobilanthes dyeranus, 42, 77

succulents in container gardens, *83*

sulfur, 111

summer hyacinth, 55

summer lilac, 51, 144

summersweet, 54

sun and shade. *See also* siting considerations; shade; *and individual plant descriptions in chapter six*

effect on design of, 21

patterns, 27

sunflowers, 50

supports for vines. *See* arbors *and* trellises

sutherland begonias, 82, 127

swamp milkweed, 50, 51

sweet alyssum, 51, *76*

sweet autumn clematis, 151

sweet azalea, 56

sweet bay, 82, 84

sweet bay magnolia, 147

sweet pea, 102

sweet pepperbush, 54

sweet rocket, 42, 56

sweet scabious, 52

sweet violet, 51

sweet William, 48, 52

sweetshrub, 44, 54, 144

Swiss chard, 46, 47, 76, 80, 127

switch grass, 38

sycamores, **52**

Syringa pubescens, 54

Syringa spp., 49, **52**

T

tables

decorations for, 123

planning for, 13, **13**

Tagetes patula, 133

Tagetes spp., 47, 48, 77, 133

Tagetes tenuifolia, 133

Taxus baccata, 148

Taxus cuspidata, 148

Taxus spp., 44, 148

teak, for deck furniture, 115, 116–117

terra-cotta containers, 61, **61**

Texas clematis, 151

Texas sage, 132

Thalictrum spp., 52

theme gardens, 45, 80

thistles, **52**

thornless climbing roses, 108

thread-leaved coreopsis, 135

Thunbergia alata, 102

thymes, 46, 47, 50, 54

Thymus spp., 50, 54

Tiarella cordifolia, 143

Tiarella spp., 143

Tiarella wherryi, 143

tickseeds, 135

Tithonia rotundifolia, 48, 50

tomatoes, 46

dwarf cherry, 80

patio, 80

topiary, 84–85, **84,** *84*

Torenia fournieri, 42

Trachelospermum jasminoides, 84

Tradescantia pallida, 78

Tradescantia spp., 42, 43, 143, *143*

traffic

designing for, 12, **23**

patterns, effect on design of, 21

"trailers and weavers," 76–77, 78. *See also individual plant descriptions in chapter six*

trailing lantana, 130

Transvaal daisy, 77

tree mallow, 57

trees, 144–149

effect on design of, 20

for hummingbirds, 49

incorporating into design, **11,** 40

roots of, 41, **41,** *41*

for shade, 11

trellises, **91,** 91–111

triangulation, **18**

Trifolium spp., 51

Tropaeolum majus, 47, 78, 133, *133,* 155

Tropaeolum peregrinum, 155

Tropaeolum spp., 155

Tropaeolum speciosum, 155

trumpet honeysuckle, 154

trumpet hybrid lily, 54, 140

trumpet vine, 49, **91,** 100, 150–151

Tsuga spp., 44

tuberoses, 55, 80

tuberous begonias, 82, 127
Tulbaghia violacea, 82
tulips, *31,* 73
Turk's-cap lily, 140
two-row sedum, 143
Tyvek, for furniture covers, **121**

U

Uniolia latifolia, see *Chasmanthium latifolium*
Urtica spp., **52**
usage considerations, 12, **16–17**
utilities
    effect on design of, 21
    planning for, **17,** 66

V

Vaccinium angustifolium, 148
Vaccinium ashei, 148
Vaccinium corymbosum, 149
Vaccinium spp., 44, 148–149
variegated hakone grass, **42**
variegated Japanese hops, 102, 152
variegated society garlic, 82
variegated Solomon's seal, 141
vegetables. *See* kitchen gardens
Verbena spp., 48, *60, 61,* 78, 133
Verbena tenuisecta, 133
Vernonia spp., 52
Viburnum acerifolium, 149
Viburnum x *burkwoodii,* 149
Viburnum x *carlcephalum,* 149
Viburnum carlesii, 149
Viburnum dentatum, 149
Viburnum dilatatum, 149
Viburnum x *juddii,* 149
Viburnum opulus, 149
Viburnum plicatum, 149, *149*
Viburnum prunifolium, 149
Viburnum x *rhytidophylloides,* 35, 149
Viburnum rhytidophyllum, 35, 149
Viburnum sargentii, 149

Viburnum spp., 37, 40, *41,* 44, 149
Viburnum trilobum, 149
Vicia faba, 51
views
    from deck, 7
    effect on design of, 21
    furniture for, 114
vinca, 42, *65, 101*
Vinca major, 78
Vinca minor, 42
vines, 37, 150–155
    for arbors and trellises, **77,** *77,* 89, 90–93, **91,** *91, 93, 94, 96,* **101,** 100–105, *102*
    for container gardens, 103, *103*
vinyl
    for furniture covers, **121**
    as wire coating, 96
Viola canadensis, 51
Viola cornuta, 51
Viola odorata, 51
Viola spp., 42
Viola tricolor, 51
Violaceae (Violet family), 51
Violet family, 42, 51
Virginia creeper, 89, 100, 154
Virginia sweetspire, 44
Vitis coignetiae, 155
Vitis spp., 100, 155
Vitis vinifera, 155

W

walkways, with container gardens, 66
wallflowers, 51
warley epimedium, 137
warm-season grasses, 38
water
    for birds, **48**
    as a decorating element, 113
    garden, weight of, 15
    surface, effect on design of, 21

watering
    container gardens, 60–61, 67, 68, **68,** *68,* 73
    drip-emitting system, **69,** *69*
    emergency treatment, 69
    while hardening off, 83
    houseplants outside, 83
    premoistening potting mix, 70
    soaker hoses, 43
    water-retaining polymers, 68–69
watering wand, *69*
wax begonia, 42, 48
weeping conifers, 40
weeping lantana, 78
Weigela florida, 49
weight, of heavy items, 15, 65
    of arbor and trellis vines, 88, 90, **91**
Western bleeding heart, 136
Wherry's foamflower, 143
white Japanese lily, 140
white pine, 40
white regal lily, 140
wicker, for deck furniture, 120, *120*
wild blue phlox, 141
wild cranesbill, 137
wild gingers, 42, 135
wild parsnip, 51
wild sweet William, 141
wildlife, attracting, **48,** 74
willows, **52**
wind protection considerations, 27, 53, 67, 92, 109, 115
windows, effect on design, 20
winter greens, in container gardens, 74
winter hazel, 54
winter honeysuckle, 54
winter jasmine, 54, 153
winter, plantings for, 31

winter storage of deck furniture, 121
wire, as lattice material, 95
wire mesh, as lattice material, 96, *96*
wishbone flower, 42
Wisteria floribunda, 155, *155*
Wisteria frutescens, 155
Wisteria sinensis, 100, 155
Wisteria spp., 51, 155
    as arbor and trellis vines, 90, *90,* 100, 101
witch hazels, 44, 54
wood
    containers, 63
    for deck furniture, 116–117
    as lattice material, 94–95
    as roof for arbor, 88
    rot-resistant, 14
wood cranesbill, 137
wood ferns, 42
wood vamp, 100
woodbine honeysuckle, 154
working drawing, 18, *21*
    features to include on, 20
wrought iron, for deck furniture, 115, 119–120

Y

yarrows, 38, 52, 111, 134
yellow archangel, 139
yellow columbine, 135
yews, *40,* 44, 148
Young's epimedium, 137
Yucca filamentosa, 38, 143
Yucca spp., 52

Z

Zinnia spp., 38, 48, 50
zone map, 156
zucchini, 46

Other Storey Titles You Will Enjoy

Garden Stone, by Barbara Pleasant. Full-color photographs and clear instructions provide readers with visual inspiration and creative ways to use stone in the garden. 240 pages. Hardcover. ISBN 1-58017-406-X.

Grasses, by Nancy Ondra. Whether on their own or as backdrops for colorful flowers, ornamental grasses provide color, movement, and texture to any garden setting. Learn how to use them for dramatic effect, care for them, and combine them with other plants. 144 pages. Paperback with French flaps. ISBN 1-58017-423-X.

Herbalist's Garden, by Shatoiya and Richard de la Tour. Come inside the garden gates of North America's most enchanting herb gardens and hear about their owners' gardening joys and challenges and favorite plants. 240 pages. Hardcover with jacket. ISBN 1-58017-410-8.

Lawn and Garden Owner's Manual, by Lewis and Nancy Hill. This homeowner's ultimate landscape care and maintenance manual allows the reader to diagnose and cure lawn and garden problems, rejuvenate neglected landscaping, and maintain beautiful and healthy grounds. 192 pages. Paperback. ISBN 1-58017-214-8.

Outdoor Woodwork, by Alan and Gill Bridgewater. Furnish your deck and garden with these sixteen attractive projects, including fences, gates, benches, chairs, decking, arbors, pergolas, trellises, planters, and more. 128 pages. Paperback. ISBN 1-58017-437-X.

The Practical Guide to Container Gardening, by Susan Berry and Steve Bradley. This inspiring and beautiful book is a comprehensive reference for choosing the best containers for specific plants, planning seasonal planting schemes, and using simple planting techniques and proper plant maintenance. 160 pages. Paperback. ISBN 1-58017-329-2.

Quick and Easy Container Water Gardens, by Philip Swindells. Lavishly illustrated with 150 color photographs, this highly visual guide teaches readers how to create exciting water gardens in containers. 128 pages. Hardcover. ISBN 1-58017-080-3.

Quick and Easy Topiary and Green sculpture, by Jenny Hendy. In this fully illustrated handy guide, readers will find everything they need to know to create instant plant designs using a wide range of topiary frames and a full range of plants. 128 pages. Paperback. ISBN 0-88266-920-6.

Simple Fountains for Indoors and Outdoors, by Dorcas Adkins. Fountain designer and manufacturer Dorcas Adkins reveals her trade secrets for making 20 creative fountains—from a small, tabletop fountain to a full-sized waterfall. 160 pages. Hardcover. ISBN 1-58017-190-7.

The Vegetable Gardener's Bible, by Edward C. Smith. Discover the last W-O-R-D in vegetable gardening with Ed Smith's amazing system — Wide rows, Organic methods, Raised beds, and Deep soil. 320 pages. Hardcover. ISBN 1-58017-213-X. Paperback. ISBN 1-58017-212-1.

These books and other Storey Books are available at your bookstore, farm store, garden center, or directly from Storey Books, 210 MASS MoCA Way, North Adams, MA 01247 or by calling 1-800-441-5700. Or visit our Web site at www.storey.com